CW00801939

THE GREATEST
PUNJABI STORIES EVER TOLD

In the same series

The Greatest Bengali Stories Ever Told (ed.) Arunava Sinha

The Greatest Urdu Stories Ever Told (ed.) Muhammad Umar Memon

The Greatest Odia Stories Ever Told (ed.) Leelawati Mohapatra,
Paul St-Pierre, and K. K. Mohapatra

The Greatest Hindi Stories Ever Told (ed.) Poonam Saxena

The Greatest Tamil Stories Ever Told (ed.)
Sujatha Vijayaraghavan and Mini Krishnan

The Greatest Assamese Stories Ever Told (ed.) Mitra Phukan

The Greatest Gujarati Stories Ever Told (ed.) Rita Kothari

The Greatest Kashmiri Stories Ever Told (ed.) Neerja Mattoo

The Greatest Telugu Stories Ever Told (ed.)
Dasu Krishnamoorty and Tamraparni Dasu

The Greatest Goan Stories Ever Told (ed.) Manohar Shetty

The Greatest Marathi Stories Ever Told (ed.) Ashutosh Potdar

The
GREATEST
PUNJABI
STORIES
EVER TOLD

Selected and edited by
RENUKA SINGH AND
BALBIR MADHOPURI

ALEPH

ALEPH BOOK COMPANY
An independent publishing firm
promoted by *Rupa Publications India*

First published in India in 2023
by Aleph Book Company
7/16 Ansari Road, Daryaganj
New Delhi 110 002

This edition copyright © Aleph Book Company 2023
Copyright for individual stories and translations vests
with respective authors/proprietors.

Introduction copyright © Renuka Singh
The Acknowledgements on pp. 309–12 constitute an
extension of the copyright page.

All rights reserved.

This is a work of fiction. Names, characters, places,
and incidents are either the product of the authors'
imagination or are used fictitiously and any resemblance
to any actual persons, living or dead, events, or locales is
entirely coincidental.

No part of this publication may be reproduced,
transmitted, or stored in a retrieval system, in any form
or by any means, without permission in writing from
Aleph Book Company.

ISBN: 978-93-93852-84-7

1 3 5 7 9 10 8 6 4 2

Printed in India

This book is sold subject to the condition that it shall
not, by way of trade or otherwise, be lent, resold, hired
out, or otherwise circulated without the publisher's prior
consent in any form of binding or cover other than that
in which it is published.

CONTENTS

INTRODUCTION

RENUKA SINGH

There is a cultural curiosity in contemporary times to explore and enjoy our regional literature, even if the new space created for its flourishing is interlinked with business interests, promotions, and prizes. The sole intention of this work, however, is to connect with the reader.

My father, Pritam Singh, migrated to Delhi from Preet Nagar, near the Wagah border, after the partition of India. His friend, Dr M. S. Randhawa—then the deputy commissioner of Delhi—helped him acquire office premises in Chandni Chowk, where he established his firm, Navyug Publishers. This became a literary hub for Punjabi writers. Most of the writers included in this collection frequented his office (as he was their publisher and editor of the prestigious literary magazine *Arsee*). I often went to his office after school hours and keenly listened in on the writers' conversations. They spoke about the travails of their love lives, monetary miseries, and current projects. I was drawn to Papaji's adda as I was smitten with books and the office provided a stimulating atmosphere for my emotional development. The writers infused their words with power and, at times, impetuous actions, transmuting lived experiences into fiction. Little did I realize then that one day I would have to string together the stories written by these writers into a book.

Balbir Madhopuri (my co-editor) and I have undertaken the daunting task of weaving this volume together based on writers' recommendations, aesthetic experience, and selective memory. Four generations of Punjabi writers have been covered in this collection. The exclusion of other popular and celebrated writers is by no means due to an underestimation of their capacity to reveal the hidden realities of human lives or of their contribution to the corpus of this genre. Rather, we hope that uninitiated readers will be able to sense the essence of the Punjabi literary imagination and Punjabiyat in the rural–urban continuum/divide presented in these stories. We invite you to this act of 'communion'. While Balbir and I may have different opinions about certain issues, methodologies, and literary agendas, this selection is all the more richer for it. Nevertheless, the biggest danger here is the loss of melody, meaning, energy, and spirit of language—a limitation we humbly accept. Needless to say, the churning of this collection has resulted from the availability of limited time and space.

The capital of India was shifted from Calcutta to Delhi in 1911. Delhi, a union territory now, was carved out from the former Punjab. Pakistan and India partitioned the remaining area of Punjab. Today, a sizeable section of Punjabi-speaking people still resides in Delhi, Haryana, and Himachal Pradesh. Punjabi is spoken by about 152 million native speakers around the world, of which almost 40 million reside in India and 111 million reside in Pakistan.[*] It is the fourth most widely spoken language in the UK[†] as well as in Canada where it registered a 49 per cent growth between 2016 and 2021.[‡]

The modern literary perspective in Punjabi was pioneered by Bhai Vir Singh (1872–1957) although earlier writings of Sheikh Farid (1173–1266) are currently available in print and are an integral part of the Shri Guru Granth Sahib. Vir Singh's couplets contain references to God, morality, and spirituality. Moreover, the

---

[*] From worlddata.info/languages/punjabi.php. Accessed 23 June 2023.

[†] I. P. Singh, 'Punjabi UK's 4th main language, Sikhs 4th largest religious group', *Times of India*, 1 December 2022.

[‡] I. P. Singh, 'Punjabi 4th most spoken language in Canada; sees 49% jump in 5 years', *Times of India*, 19 August 2022.

Sikh Gurus structured their poetic works on the basis of metre, rhyme, ragas, and alliteration. Guru Nanak, a poet, used analogies from nature, verdure, as well as pastoral aesthetics and activities to propound his philosophy. The Muslim fakirs (Sufis) and poets of romantic tales (kissa poets) combined the divine with worldliness in their works. Shah Hussain, Sultan Bahu, Bulleh Shah, and others are some of the most famous lyrical poets.

Most of the twentieth century modern Punjabi writers included in this collection were influenced by the Progressive Movement in Punjabi literature. The Progressive Movement, secular in nature, aimed to resist imperialism, feudalism, theism, caste and untouchability, communalism, and oppression of women. In Punjab, the major centres of progressive literary activity in the 1930s were in Lahore and Amritsar. Gurbaksh Singh, an engineer who returned from the US after receiving his educational degree (and the first contributor in this volume), and later became a full-time writer, established Preet Nagar in Amritsar in 1935 (inspired by Tagore's vision of Shantiniketan) with an eclectic community that was inspired by his idealism and utopian vision. The Progressive Writers' Movement drew well-known Punjabi writers into its fold, both as cosmopolitan members and ideologues of modernism. Besides the Marxist and Freudian interpretation of personal, social, economic, and political realities, literary movements like surrealism, expressionism, existentialism, structuralism, and post-modernism left a mark on Punjab's literary output, and yet it retained its cultural complexion. Humanism, nevertheless, remains a powerful thread in the Punjabi narrative tradition.

The Punjabi short story, merely a century old, is an important part of Punjabi modern literature. In the Punjabi sociocultural context, many aspects of human issues and concerns form its constituent elements and, symbolically, Punjabi philosophical thought and life-world emerges vividly through descriptive accounts. One must confess though that through translation these stories have acquired a new and different flavour. Relishing them in the original is certainly more delicious.

The sheer volume of recent literature written in Punjabi cannot be contested. Many of the writers have benefitted from internal migration, the expansion of the education system in Punjab, and the publishing industry in Punjab and Delhi, in addition to the numerous literary magazines like *Preet Lari*, *Arsee*, *Nagmani*, *Sirjana*, *Samdarshi*, *Samkali Sahit*, *Wagha*, *Hun*, *Kahani Punjab*, *Akhar*, *Sahitak Ekam*, *Shabd*, *Lakir*, *Kaav Shastra*, *Nazaria*, *Samvaad*, etc. We are also well aware of the fact that prolific Punjabi writers are publishing their stories (written in both Gurmukhi and Shahmukhi scripts) in the hundreds all over the world, especially in India, Pakistan, United Kingdom, Europe, North America, New Zealand, and Australia. In this collection, we have restricted ourselves to a selection from India. To understand the history of the Punjabi story one may refer to the works of Baldev Singh Dhaliwal (*History of Punjabi Story*, 2019), who classifies it into mini, short, and long, characterized by four major phases of realism: idealistic, progressive, objective, and post-modern.

Being a self-enclosed cosmos, these stories interface between the individual, community, and the wider world, whereas a few are avenues of cultural, societal, and political protest. Besides gendered violence and family crises, commonplace themes, beliefs, desires, tensions, and values have been addressed in exceptional ways as well as disputed. Tradition is both reinforced and subverted in order to open up new spaces. Hence, these texts establish a value within the contexts of writers' intentions, motivations, society, culture, and their corpus of writing. Some of these stories are illuminating, their sarcasm biting and satire piercing.

The themes covered in these stories are not exhaustive. They pertain to family relationships, and alienation; rurality, urbanity, and development; partition; patriotism, martyrdom, and state repression; and human connections, place, people, and sexuality. Under the first theme, Amrita Pritam's story 'The Stench of Kerosene' is about the agonies of a man and a woman in their marriage and the psychosomatic consequences of their loss. Ajeet Cour's 'Green Sparrows' symbolically points to the alienation in a family, and the hope and healing that can be found in nature—human beings die in parts whereas the sparrows sing forever. Ram Sarup Ankhi's 'That Woman!' deals with the bitter existence of a mother of five sons, and how she waits for her departure from this world after gifting her land to them. Jatinder Hans's 'All Else Is an Illusion' is a story about generational gaps and the preciousness of life told through the lens of an eternally loving father and an emotionally ambivalent and sometimes aggressive son.

The second theme is reflected in the following eleven stories. Kartar Singh Duggal's 'Majha Is Not Dead' relates to the dialogical relationship of a widower with his horse as he plies his tonga in New Delhi to earn his living. Jaswant Singh Kanwal's 'The Great Mother' is about an inter-religious, inter-caste cultural ethos of forgiveness versus revenge in a rural setting, through the life of a young girl on the verge of dying by suicide. Sukhbir's 'In Between the Books', cosmopolitan in nature, brings a man and woman together in a library and shows how books act as a catalyst to materialize their nebulous attraction. Gurdial Singh's 'Dog and Man' deals with the kinship between a neglected husband and his pet. Navtej Singh's 'The Charity Coat' depicts the socio-economic reality of the lower middle-class through the touching tale of a teacher who is punished for accepting a gift. Sukhwant Kaur Mann's 'The Survivors' unfolds the pauperization process of villagers in the wake of urbanization, all the while depicting that their life goes on. In Gulzar Singh Sandhu's 'Hopes Shattered', Bebe, the dethroned queen of a village feels betrayed after her paralytic attack, always feeling as though people are playing tricks on her. In Waryam Sandhu's 'To Everyone, His Share', three sons of a deceased mother quibble over the expenses of her last rites yet claim their full share of the property. Ajmer Sidhu's 'The Colour of Betrayal' reveals the gap between the ideal and the real within a corrupt educational system. Gurmeet Karyalavi's 'Death of the

Lute' presents the value, and makes a case for, the preservation of the Dalits' traditional music and entertainment in this age of science and technology. In Sarghi's 'The Rod' one comes across the impact that modern media has, through graphic images of crimes against young girls, on the psyche of a working mother as she remains entombed in her fears and anxieties.

Mohinder Singh Sarna's 'Savage Harvest', Sujaan Singh's 'Sunrise at Last', Sant Singh Sekhon's 'Dance of the Devil', and Gurdev Singh Rupana's 'The Wind' deal with different aspects of Partition—the ensuing tragedy, destruction, inhuman torture, horrifying images of starvation, and the wounded and traumatized psyches. Nevertheless, there is also a flicker of hope, generosity, and warmth in the kindness shown by people from both sides of the border that strengthen human bonds.

In Gurmukh Singh Musafir's 'Daughter of the Rebel', a twelve-year-old ailing girl fights for the freedom of the country in her own way. Kulwant Singh Virk's 'The Proverbial Bullock' shows how martyrdom is always around the corner for our forbearing soldiers. Kesra Ram's 'Whither My Native Land' highlights the inexorable tensions of and trouble encountered by migrant labourers during the Covid-19 pandemic, as well as, ironically, both the brutality and humanity of police officers.

The last theme related to the formation of human connections is clearly depicted in the remainder of the stories. Gurbaksh Singh's 'Bhabhi Myna' portrays the plight of a widow and a sublime attraction between her and an adolescent boy. Nanak Singh's 'Bowl of Milk' is a humorous tale expressing the love, affection, and hospitality of an aunt for her nephew in a rural setting. Gurbachan Singh Bhullar's 'I Am Not Ghaznavi' is about emotional reluctance and the remembrance of lost opportunities in love. Mohan Bhandari's 'Doe's Eye' brings to the fore the sense of guilt and remorse a man feels for not taking a decision that could have saved the life of a stupefied woman during the 1984 Delhi riots. Bachint Kaur's 'Eradicator of Suffering' speaks to how suffering can bring out the beggar in anyone, whether the person be rich or poor. Devendra Satyarthi's 'Kung Posh' is about an encounter with a beautiful Kashmiri girl in the saffron fields and presents a vivid picture of the region in autumn. Balwant Gargi in 'The Moscow Girl' describes flawlessly the interpenetration of place and person in Moscow. Finally, Sukirat's 'Home' revolves around accepting emotional sensitivities and being comfortable with one's identity and sexual orientation.

We hope that this melange of stories will not be merely enchanting but, at least partially, mirror the bones, blood, guts, and dreams of the inner and outer cultural imagination and sensibilities of the people of Punjab, and unite the web of history and lives lingering in one's psyche that will bind the invisible and intangible ties. Let this collection be a discovery of a new range of feelings that are not judgmental but work to expand our moral consciousness.

BHABHI MYNA

GURBAKSH SINGH

There was hardly a gap of three-and-a-half yards between the two houses. The first floor windows also faced each other. Through one of these could be seen the opposite wall of a mostly empty room with a big rectangular mirror fixed on it. The room's contents included a cot, a low woven stool, a few books, a comb, oil, one or two pictures adorning the walls, and some clothes.

A lone woman lived in that small room. Sometimes she could be seen doing embroidery, reading a book, or lying prostrate on her bed. At other times, she would stand before the mirror and comb her hair. She combed her hair several times a day; her family thought she had become obsessed with it.

She had long shiny hair that cascaded down to her ankles. Had someone seen her hair under a bright light, they would notice how it shimmered.

She was a tall woman with beautiful features. The colour of her eyes was not visible from the front window but one could tell they were sweet, though filled with a kind of melancholy.

While she stood at the window, she would keep shedding tears. Nobody had ever seen her peek out of the window to look outside, but those who lived on the street were aware of her presence. If someone called out to her while going past the window, she would respond sweetly, leaning towards the window but never poking her head through.

When she was not in the room, the window remained closed. During winter, this window was opened at twilight while in

1

summer it was opened at about twelve o'clock. She could be seen sitting beside the open window, occasionally looking out onto the part of the street visible from her vantage point.

At a certain time each day, Kaka, an adolescent boy, would return home from school, a bag slung over his shoulder. As he would turn into the street, she would abandon whatever work she was doing and stare in his direction from the window. The boy too would sometimes casually look up and then disappear into his house.

She could hear the sound of his footsteps and though she had never gone to his house, she was well aware of the number of steps leading up to his drawing room. She knew someone had entered the room on the first floor once she heard the door open. Yet, she never actually saw him enter.

Keeping his school bag aside, Kaka would open his window and look out at the facing window. But the woman never looked in his direction. She remained focused on the arrival of that boy. If he was ever late on his way back from school, she felt the need ask the other boys about him, though she never did.

After a short while, the boy would leave the room, closing the door behind him, and climb up to the roof of his house.

Days and weeks passed like this. Now Kaka was almost thirteen. The sight of the window excited him. He asked his mother one day, 'Ma, all the neighbours come to our house now and then. Why does no one come from the opposite house?'

'Kaka, they are Jains...they are the only Jain family in the locality. They are very strict vegetarians. That is why they don't have any social interaction with Sikhs.'

'But, Ma, we are also vegetarians.'

'But they treat all the Sikhs alike.'

'But do Jains never go out of their house either?'

'They do go out, Kaka, but this particular family.... Death has devastated them in a big way. They were left with only one son. He was happily married but he too passed away. A child was born after his death. The baby too could not survive. Now the house is inhabited by three widows who have to live with their agony.'

'To which of these widows did the child belong?'

'To Myna; you must have seen her sitting at the window.'

'But why does she keep sitting there all the time?'

'These people keep a very strict watch on their young widowed daughters-in-law. And the poor things don't have much to do at home.'

'Why do they guard them like this?'

'So that they don't share any family news with others.'

'Ma, so many women who live on the street come to our house. You ask me to address someone as chachi, some others as masi, and still others as bua. What should I call her if I happen to meet her some day?'

'Who? Myna?'

'Yes, the same person who's always sitting at the window.'

'She is your bhabhi. Her husband was like a brother to you.'

'But what kind of name is this—Myna?'

'Don't you like it?'

'No, no, it's a beautiful name. But I have never heard it before. Myna, if I am not wrong, is the bird which Mamaji keeps in a cage in his home. It speaks very sweetly. A parrot is no match for it in speech.'

'Yes, you are right. The same.'

'Would you get one for me?'

'Kaka, ask your mamaji for this favour.'

A few days later, there appeared a cage with a myna in Kaka's room. When he went to the roof he would take the cage along with him.

He taught his myna to say, 'Bhabhi Myna is sitting at the window.' The window Myna, who had never spoken to him, still liked this gesture.

In the winter, Bhabhi Myna would sleep in her room. Kaka's exams were round the corner and since he had to stay up late studying long after dusk, he started sleeping in his drawing room. Bhabhi Myna could sometimes hear the sleeping boy's breathing. Getting up from her bed, she would listen to this sound.

She was nearly twenty-five now while Kaka had not yet turned thirteen. She longed for the freedom to talk to this boy but had to be content to merely watch him coming back from school by looking out towards the street from behind her window. She wished to at least be able to go to his house to enquire about his well-being when he was ill. How could that hurt anyone?

Then she would persuade herself that no one was going to allow her this kind of liberty. She would grow old in this very room and Kaka would get married in due course of time. Then this window would not remain open any longer. 'For whom will I wait then to spend the long days of summer and equally long nights of winter?' she thought.

Thinking thus, she felt a tug at her heart. Getting up from the bed she went to the window. It was a moonlit night and a slender beam of light was falling through the window onto Kaka's face. The boy was fast asleep and the sound of his breath was clearly audible. Her heart surged. She estimated the gap between the two houses; it didn't look that large. She would build a bridge between the buildings and somehow reach Kaka. But she would not awaken him, and instead come back to her room after kissing him from afar.

However, neither was the distance slight nor did she have the courage. So, she lay back down on her cot. After some time, she heard a voice from Kaka's room: 'Bhabhi Myna....' Startled, she got up. But it was the caged myna's voice. Kaka was still peacefully asleep.

Meanwhile, Myna's mother-in-law had woken up to answer the call of nature. She heard some noise coming from Myna's room and thought she had heard the words 'Bhabhi Myna'. She called out to Myna who responded. It confirmed her suspicion that her daughter-in-law was awake.

'You aren't sleeping, Myna? It is half past midnight now.'

'Oh! My sleep was disturbed for nothing,' Myna answered.

The mother-in-law came into Myna's room. It looked to her like a man was sleeping outside the front window.

'Were you talking to someone?'

'No, who's there to talk to?'

The mother-in-law again looked towards the front window.

'That's Kaka from the Sikh household. He is fast asleep,' Myna said.

The mother-in-law left but kept thinking about what she had witnessed. Kaka, though yet a child and at an innocent age, was a man after all. Why should a widow even look at male children? All Myna did was watch him as he returned from school. Kaka also kept his window open. And he had seemingly grown up since last year. These signs could not be ignored. Sometimes, the smallest clouds in the sky cast the largest shadows.

The next day when Kaka returned from school, Myna's window was closed. It remained closed through the night as well.

This window had become a big part of Kaka's life. He felt almost unwell while playing with his friends. It was no use asking his mother anything since there was no routine interaction between the two houses. They crossed each other's thresholds only on special occasions like weddings to exchange sweets.

It was a moonless night and a scratching sound could be heard coming from inside Myna's window, like someone was trying a bunch of keys to open a lock.

Then the window opened and Myna looked out. Kaka was asleep but she could hear him breathing. It was pitch dark but Myna's longing eyes were able to trace an outline around Kaka's limbs.

'Kaka…. Kaka…. Kaka….'

He was still asleep. She called to him, her voice scarcely audible:

'Kaka….it is your Bhabhi Myna. Please wake up for a moment…just one word…and then…it's all over….'

Kaka woke up with a start.

Myna felt very ashamed. Now she realized that she had been speaking out loud this whole time and had woken Kaka up. He came and sat at the window, from where he could sense Bhabhi's presence. He had craved several times to hug Bhabhi Myna. He had been very sad to see her window closed.

'Bhabhi Myna…. Bhabhi Myna….'

'Yes…Kaka…my pretty Kaka…but please speak softly, I will hear you even at the lowest volume.'

'I can also hear you very clearly…. You speak very softly.'

'Yes…Kaka…my darling Kaka.'

'Where were you for so many days?'

'My room has been converted into a police lock-up. This window too has been closed.'

'But why?'

'The other day your myna called out. I woke up. I thought you were awake. My mother-in-law was also up at that time. She thought I was talking to you.'

'Then what happened? Mother said you are my bhabhi.'

'Kaka, so much has transpired. All doors have been closed to me. Therefore, I must leave here now. This is my last night in this house. I wanted to see you before going. I hope you won't tell anyone.'

'I won't disclose this, Bhabhi, but why are you going? Please don't go. When I grow up, I will get married…. I will send my wife to your house…. She will call you and you may come to see her…. Then nobody will object…. So please don't go.'

'But Kaka you are still so young…. Your marriage is a far-off dream. How shall I spend so many years in this prison when I am not allowed even to look at you?'

'Where will you go? I will definitely come to see you there.'

'No, Kaka, I am going where no man is allowed to talk to me.'

'Don't go there.'

'I'm left with no other way out. I have decided to become a Jain nun.'

'What is that?'

'The Jain sadhu women with tonsured heads, covered mouths, and bare feet.'

'No Bhabhi Myna, please don't embrace this path. Those women scare me...they look so strange.'

'Kaka, I am left with no other option,' she said as she threw a small item through the window. 'Please keep this as a memento from me. You can pick it up in the morning. Doing so right now might wake someone up.'

With that, Myna closed her window. Kaka heard the sound of a key turning in the lock. He could not go back to sleep.

The next day when he came back from school his mother told him what had transpired. Myna had been very upset. Her mother-in-law had picked fights with her every day and thrown jibes at her. Fed up, she abandoned the house, leaving behind a written message: I am going to become a Jain nun.

'But, Ma, couldn't she become a nun here?'

'No. The one who chooses this path has to leave her city for an upashray in another city. The novice is interviewed there. If convinced, the postulant is taken care of, fed well, and dressed in finery. She is allowed to fulfil her heart's desires for a few days. Then the new aspirant's head is tonsured and she is given entry into the Jain fold. Thereafter, she can neither eat nor dress well, nor talk to men.

'So where could Bhabhi Myna have gone?'

'We'll find out soon.'

'If it's some nearby city, will you take me there?'

'They have a very important upashray in Pindi. Your masi is also there. You can go there for a couple of days. If she is there you will be able to see her. When someone joins the Jain monastery, there is a great celebration in the city.'

Kaka wrote to his masi asking her to let him know if any such event was to take place.

Within a week or so everybody in the locality came to know about Myna; she became the talk of the town. People praised her for never violating the norms of widowhood. She had very beautiful black hair which she cherished. Now she would lose this valuable asset and have to pluck her hair out one by one.

Kaka reached his masi's house. His masi had seen Myna that day. She was dressed gorgeously and was wearing jewellery. The jewellery had been lent to her by the people of the town. A musical programme was also being held. Kaka's masi was also drawn to Myna. She attended each and every ritual and told Kaka about how beautiful she looked.

'Tomorrow, they will seat her in a palanquin and take her around the city. People will shower her with flower petals and sprinkle rose water on her,' she told him.

Kaka was impatient to see this spectacle. So far, he had only seen her wearing white but she looked beautiful in that too. How beautiful she would look in jewellery and bright clothes! He had never seen her laugh before. Masi had mentioned her captivating smile.

He had the handkerchief, the memento she had given him, in his pocket. He had not told anybody about it so far but would lovingly gaze at it every day. He had learnt the Devanagari script since she had embroidered these words on the handkerchief: Bade pyare Kaka ke liye, uski bhabhi ki oar se (For very dear Kaka, from his bhabhi).

The next afternoon, Kaka's masi told him that Myna's palanquin would be taken out in a procession.

Kaka plucked a handful of flowers from his masi's garden and tied them in a handkerchief. When the palanquin went past their home, he deliberately separated from his masi's family, who stayed behind. He did not want to just take a look at the pageant and return. He wanted to stay with the palanquin the whole way.

The uniformed musicians played their respective instruments. The Jain devotees were showering money on the palanquin that carried his lavishly dressed bhabhi. Although her face seemed to have undergone a makeover it still retained a lot of its earlier wistful look. Kaka loved her pensive eyes far more than this cheerful mien. People remarked that the nun was exceptionally beautiful but Kaka missed the simple dignity of her looks in this entirely made-up appearance.

He decided he would throw the flower petals at her only when he felt she had seen him. She folded her hands but this respect was meant for the crowd. 'How could she spot a small boy in the crowd?' Kaka thought.

At a turn, the palanquin happened to be quite close to him. He was about to throw his flower petals when Myna noticed him. Her half-closed eyes opened wide. She looked intently at him. Then she gathered the courage to ask for the palanquin to stop, saying, 'That boy is from our street. He wants to shower flowers on me but they won't reach me. Bring him to me for a minute.'

This behaviour was inappropriate but the wish of a nun in the making could not be ignored.

'Come, Kaka, give me the flowers. You have come from so far.'

Kaka was delighted at having been noticed by Myna Bhabhi and her acceptance of his floral devotion. He was happy that along with the flowers she had accepted the handkerchief as well. Bhabhi will keep it as a souvenir of love from me, he thought.

The procession reached the upashray and the people dispersed. Accompanied by some women, Myna climbed the stairs. As she was about to put her foot on the first step, Myna saw Kaka sitting on a bench in front of the building.

Myna was asked to sit before the senior monk.

'Have you finally made up your mind now?' the monk asked.

'Yes, of course, Maharaj.'

'You will have to say goodbye to jewellery for life.'

'I know, Maharaj. I have no desire for them.'

'You will eat and drink also according to the rules of this institution.'

'Agreed, Maharaj. I don't need any rich food.'

'What to speak of touching, even thinking about men is prohibited in our faith.'

Myna took a deep breath at hearing this. It felt as if Kaka's handkerchief was unfolding in her pocket. And the ends of the kerchief were turning into small arms and clasping her around the waist. Containing herself, she said, 'Yes, Maharaj. This is also acceptable to me.'

'Now go to that room, change your clothes, and wear the ones you are given. And, you will have to get your hair cut. Your honourable 'mother' will tell you how each and every hair can be plucked out.'

The mention of cutting and plucking the hair made her sigh deeply again. But then she found the courage to say, 'Maharaj, can I be exempted from getting my hair cut?'

'How is this possible?' the startled senior monk retorted.

'I know this is a strange demand on my part,' Myna felt as if she had acquired some inner strength, 'But if you accede to my request, I will not provide you any chance of complaint. I will serve you in such a way that the whole fraternity will be amazed. Please…. Please don't make me cut my hair.'

'But it's not possible at all,' said the senior monk. 'Didn't you know all this?'

'I did. I knew it and was ready for this but now that the time has come I feel as if there is life throbbing in my hair. My hair has been the product of my life. Whenever I combed it or it touched my legs, I felt there was life in it. For years I have talked only to my hair. It was my only companion. (With folded hands). O Maharaj! Kindly try that which has so far been unprecedented. I assure you, you will not regret your decision.'

The hoary monk mellowed in his heart but kept a stern face.

It was unthinkable. What would people say at the sight of a nun's hair?

'No, Beti, this is not at all acceptable.'

'Then, Maharaj! Kindly leave me alone for five minutes and let me talk to myself,' Myna said with a steely resolve.

'Okay, go. Sit at the window and introspect.'

Myna rose slowly but walked to the window with a firm step. Below she could see the market on both sides of the road.

She stood up after a while.

'She really is a unique woman. I have performed the initiation ceremony for so many women but she is thought-provoking, indeed! Once she comes into our fold, she will earn a great name,' the senior monk said.

'But—see—why is she standing on the window ledge?' another monk asked, flabbergasted.

The senior monk looked over to see her standing precariously on the ledge. She undid her bun and her shiny black hair cascaded down her back, below her waist. Suddenly the ends of her hair fluttered and waved in the air....

'Ah! So long....'

'What...!' Together, the monks rushed towards the stairs. There was no one on the ledge.

What a scene! What a hue and cry in the marketplace. A teenaged boy sat before a mangled Myna. He had straightened the parting of her hair by moving the dishevelled hair from her forehead. Blood shone in her black hair like vermilion. Tears flowed incessantly from the boy's eyes and he looked into the eyes of the fallen woman. They were wide open. Kaka had never before seen the colour of these eyes. They were as dark as the last moonless night when she had woken him. Those eyes had in their depth a sun that had ignited in him a quest for her. Myna's eyes were as dark and luminous as they had always been but the sun was now missing.

Translated by Parvesh Sharma

BOWL OF MILK

NANAK SINGH

More than ten years had passed since I had last met my bua. Of my elders, she was the only one left who was worth mentioning. I vaguely remember that when I was a child she would lovingly let me hold her finger when she walked me to school. During the half-day recess, she would bring me a bowl of creamy milk.

That was almost thirty years back. All those who had the right to call me a lad or son have since died. But my aunt survives like a tree on the river bank. This time when I went to attend the marriage ceremony of a friend's son, I could not resist my desire to see her. It did not matter that I had to cover ten miles, five to go and as many to return, to meet her.

It was summer and the marriage ceremony was of the rural sort. If an urban person has to eat food at such marriages, he will definitely not be able to survive without taking some digestive aid.

I thanked my lucky stars that the two nights passed peacefully. Bidding farewell to members of the marriage party on the third day, I left for my aunt's village. I remembered how fondly she used to feed me delicate rotis baked upon a fire.

No arrangement could be made for a vehicle to take me to her village. Leaving at noon, I had to trudge on foot all the way, sometimes walking through fields of crops, at other times going on the road. I felt greatly relieved on reaching her village late in the evening. The moment I arrived, I had to touch her feet with reverence. Out of modesty, I could hardly say a word to my sister-in-law. Telling my aunt anything was in vain. I earnestly told my aunt that I could not manage to eat even one bite for I had overeaten at the wedding. Without listening to what I said, she kept repeating her pleas: 'Kaka, they are very light rotis. Eat, dear. Eat!'

Looking at the dishes laden on my tray, I exclaimed, 'How can one eat so much, Bua!' I repeated my words but she cajoled me affectionately, saying that they were only to sweeten my tongue. In this village, no good food was available in the bazaar, unlike in towns and cities where all things were available. So true was the saying: 'In cities dwell angels while in villages ghosts roam.' Only dal and leafy vegetables were readily available. Then she rambled on: 'When your uncle was alive, we happened to go to Amritsar. Blessed is that pious city. It so happened we had a glimpse of the Almighty! How odd is it to leave behind the wrangles of the household! That happened only because the last remains of my elder sister-in-law had to be consigned to the Ganga. So, he said to me, "Shankar's mother, going ever so often is not possible. It is so difficult to fulfil our daily needs. So, you also come along now." Thus, I went with him. My ardent wish is to go again for a glimpse of Ganga Ma. Several times had I beseeched him for a chance to perform this good deed, as well as a hundred others, and earn credit but he hardly listened.'

Just as I thought my difficulties were over, she herself began to feed me. I had hardly eaten a couple of mouthfuls when my sister-in-law poured a bowl of ghee on the vermicelli, which began to look like a tiny island in the sea. I tried my best to dissuade her but it was of no avail.

I couldn't see how to get rid of self-invited trouble. I somehow managed to swallow the two rotis dripping with ghee, but felt incapable of consuming the vermicelli. It struck me, that blind as my aunt was, I could throw away fistfuls of the dish without her noticing. This could lighten my burden a bit. But how would I manage my sister-in-law, endowed with good eyesight? She had, after pouring ghee from the bowl, seated herself beside us very comfortably.

Putting some vermicelli in my mouth, I munched each small mouthful like a sparrow. Suddenly, my sister-in-law got up and went inside. I hastily looked around me to see where I could throw some of the vermicelli. The wall at the back had a furnace at one end. I thought it would be best to throw the vermicelli there for now. I would find a chance at night and cover it with the ash.

Very decisively, I picked up all the vermicelli I could hold in my palm. I had just lifted my hand from the tray when my sister-in-law arrived to put another paratha in the pan. Putting the vermicelli back in the bowl, I felt utterly defeated—it was all over.

After I had somehow eaten half the dish, I got rid of that death-like bowl. However, I barely had the strength to move to the cot. My stomach was about to burst and it was hard to breathe. Somehow this adventure was over. Time and again I reprimanded myself, thinking that if I had to breathe my last it was better to do so at home. It was hard even to breathe and I kept on tossing but received no relief. My stomach was bloated and hurting. I was sweating profusely and the bedding was turning moist. A hand fan lay close by but I did not have the strength to use it to fan myself.

For half an hour or so, I writhed like a fish out of water but the pain was unbearable. I got up and began to wonder if someone could be called to bring parsley seeds. To my utter shock and horror I saw my sister-in-law coming, with a long veil covering her face. Just as I thought I had escaped, she approached me, with the final nail in my coffin: a bowl of milk full to the brim.

Had my wife been there in her place, I might have thrown the burning hot milk in her face. But I was utterly helpless, for she was, after all, a sister-in-law, my aunt's daughter-in-law, with whom no exchange of words was possible. In spite of my thrice-repeated refusal, she uttered not a word but kept on standing there holding the bowl of milk in her hand.

Greatly troubled, I struck upon a plan when nothing seemed to work. I took the bowl of milk and told her that I drank only cold milk.

Perhaps she did not want her older brother-in-law to worry about it. Or maybe she thought I wanted to drink the milk right away.... She ran and brought an empty vessel and began to cool the milk by pouring it from one vessel to the other. Once again, the bowl was in my hand. I hoped she would go away but her mother-in-law had demanded that she bring back only an empty bowl. Had someone given me poison instead, I would have thought better of him. Valiantly I sipped the milk little by little, but could not empty the wide, pond-like bowl.

Damning my restraint and ready to die, I remarked that what I had drunk was enough and I offered the bowl to her. Instead of taking the bowl, she drew back as if its touch would pollute her. Abashed, I withdrew my hand, for anger and pain was making me mad. 'Okay, I'll have it after some time,' I said and deliberately put the bowl on the back frame of the bed. It was not wide enough; the bowl fell over and the milk spilt all over the floor. Uttering an apologetic 'Oh!' I picked it up from the floor and my sister-in-law grabbed it from my hands at once.

'What has happened?' Bua asked as she walked towards me, leaning on her walking stick.

'Nothing, the milk spilt,' the daughter-in-law replied in an abashed tone.

'So, what? There's no dearth of milk here.' Saying this Bua came to me and began to exchange formal information. 'I wanted to talk to you about a few things. But I didn't want to trouble you and thought I'd let you rest for an hour or so.'

In my heart of hearts, I felt that this would be cathartic for her. Just then her daughter-in-law whispered something in her ear and she replied angrily, 'What? You have added culture to the whole milk! Oh God, how wretched I am! What was the need to do this? What will my son drink now? He has been hungry since the morning. All he has eaten are the two pieces of bread. He won't come to this house again. Bring a bowl of milk from Rama's house.'

I implored her, 'Dear Bua, don't send her to bring milk.'

'Why? Is it so strange?' Bua retorted affectionately. 'You've been hungry since morning. No shame in asking for milk! It is not the house of a complete stranger. I had prayed so much for you to be born. You are the only male descendant in the three families. We took so many steps for you to be born. Your father had two brothers. Many were the vows we undertook so that the eldest one got married. The ceremonies were hardly over when he became a widower. He shut himself indoors and never opened up. Next was Daulat Singh, your father's elder brother. He was tall, strong, youthful, and very handsome. Cursed death snatched him away...like plucking a fully bloomed flower.' The dimples in her cheeks were filling up with the tears flowing from her eyes. She went on speaking in this vein.

The daughter-in-law had gone away but Bua kept on speaking: 'Not even a year had passed and the acacia flowers had not dried when death devoured him. His young widow was left helpless. Your father was the youngest. It had been eight years since he got married but was yet childless. My son! No sacred place remained unvisited, no pir or fakir was left uncontacted, and all vigils were performed to placate Hanuman, virgins were fed to placate Bhairon. Pirs were offered sweets and thick rotis were given to Baba Kamliwala. Every method was employed to placate the divine. Wherever hope had scope, there we went. Finally, from nowhere came the reward. Last of all we prayed at Dina Shah's shrine and our prayer was accepted. My son, such gifts are rarely found.' Saying this, she began to kiss my face.

My ears were tuned to Bua's talk but my attention was riveted upon the door. My sister-in-law came in and I heaved a sigh of relief. She had an empty bowl and said despairingly, 'The little buffalo has drunk all the milk.' On hearing this, Bua said in a helpless tone, 'The whole village be damned. The milk that even dogs don't like has become so rare. Famine is around and our son will think that he has come to such a miserly home. Not a drop of milk is available here.'

Filled with shame and pity, she patted me on my back and said, 'Kaka, will you go to sleep hungry? My son, how terrible this is!' I looked at the milk spilt on the ground and gave thanks in my heart. At last, my life is free from torture.

My luck has turned!

Translated by Tejwant Singh Gill

DAUGHTER OF THE REBEL

GURMUKH SINGH MUSAFIR

1

When he saw the police arrive, Kishan Singh announced promptly, 'The Khalsa is ready and waiting.' But he could not quite hide his inner turmoil.

'If you are late, you will have to spend the night in the lock-up. I expect you understand the difference between a prison and a lock-up.' The police inspector asked him. Kishan Singh said, 'Both are the same to me; I have already spent many nights in the lock-up of police stations.'

'No. What I mean to say is...' the police inspector interrupted him.

'You mean to say I should hurry up? Let us leave then, I am ready.' Kishan Singh uttered these words confidently, but he was actually thinking of something else. It seemed as though he was missing something. If he could take care of that he would be able to leave for the prison with greater peace of mind.

'Sharan?' Kishan Singh called out. His sister Veeran Wali responded from inside the house, 'Brother, sister-in-law has gone to attend a meeting.'

The inspector became alert. Kishan Singh continued, 'Veeran, bring the chart with details of Laj's fever.' Veeran came out to hand the chart to Kishan Singh, saying, 'Bhabhi told me that if the fever went beyond 102 degrees, ice-cold bandages have to be placed on her forehead.'

It was not the first time Kishan Singh was going to prison.

The inspector was well aware of his courage and determination. He had come to understand the reason for Kishan Singh's unease. The word 'meeting' had pierced the inspector's ear like a splinter of glass, spurring him to action. He jumped onto his bicycle, called the two constables to him, and whispered some orders. Then he said, 'Sardarji, take your time to get ready. I'll come back in a little while.'

The inspector pedalled through the big gate of the factory on the other side of the road. One of the constables sitting there remarked, 'Perhaps inspector sahib has gone in there to make a telephone call.'

At this point, Veeranwali was on the verge of tears. But Kishan Singh's angry glare made her move quietly to the other side of Laj's bed where she sat down on a stool. Kishan Singh lovingly smoothed Laj's hair and said, 'Child, now you are much better. Your fever has lessened, by tomorrow it might be gone completely. If you were not suffering from a fever, I would have already gone to prison by now. All my companions have already surrendered.'

His beloved daughter Laj said feebly, 'Father, I have been weak and have hampered your good work.'

'No, my dear daughter Laj, it is not your fault. You have no control over illness. I have never had to leave you before this. The day our leaders were arrested in Bombay, I spoke for barely five minutes on the resolution and congratulated them. Then I was busy getting your medicines. I had no time to go anywhere. Usually they arrest the leaders first, we workers are arrested later. But we have no problem. They can arrest us now.' Kishan Singh had hardly finished uttering the last sentence when Laj muttered: 'Let them.'

As Kishan Singh talked to his only darling daughter, he began to feel less burdened. Now he was impatient, waiting for his wife Sharan Kaur. He kept an eye on the veranda as well to assure himself that the inspector had not returned.

Veeranwali, who was sitting silently nearby, had not said a

word for fear that her tears would spill over and she would start crying. But now she plucked up the courage to speak: 'Laj, if your father is arrested who will bring medicine for you? Won't you feel sad?'

'Buaji, you, my aunt, are here to take care of me. And Mother is here. As far as missing him is concerned, when I recover fully, I'll also go to prison to be with Father this time.' Hearing this, Veeranwali couldn't suppress a laugh.

Laj said, 'No, Buaji, this is no laughing matter. There is no harm in going to prison for your country. This time I am going to accompany him.'

'Laj, you are not even twelve years old,' Veeranwali protested. Laj turned to her father, 'Daddy, listen to what Buaji is saying! Has Buaji never gone to the gurdwara and heard the discourses? Daddy, tell her how old the sahibzadas were. Even at that young age they chose martyrdom. Can I not even go to prison?' What to say of Veeranwali, now even Kishan Singh could not control his tears. But his were tears of happiness and contentment.

Kishan Singh pulled out the house keys from under Laj's pillow. He went to the storeroom, changed his clothes, and came back to Laj. She asked him, 'Daddy why have you changed your clothes now? Are you going somewhere?' This question made Kishan Singh's task much easier. Until now Kishan Singh had been worried about how he would break the news of his arrest to his sick daughter. Veeranwali's anxiety had already revealed the situation to a large extent. Kishan Singh brought out a dictionary, the Gutka Sahib, the book of everyday prayers, and the annotated holy texts from the almirah in Laj's room and put them in his small box. When he heard the sound of boots in the veranda, Kishan Singh kissed his feverish child's warm forehead and caressed her. 'My Laj' were the words that he uttered. The solidified pearls of tears melted and began to flow freely. The young girl, Laj, comforted him as though she was the mature wise person, 'Daddy, don't worry about me.' Just then, a young man entered the house from the street entrance to avoid the police, and whispered something in Kishan Singh's ear and disappeared. Once again, the expression on Kishan Singh's face became very grim. He gave some instructions to Veeranwali about Laj's well-being and went out to join the policemen in the tonga.

2

The telephone rang in the police station; the police party was ordered to be ready immediately but it was allowed to leave only after an hour. Just as the police surrounded the old haveli near the market called Chote Bazaar, a woman wearing a coarse home-spun khaddar dress came running into the side street from a room at the left end of the haveli. She had the national flag in her hand and she carried the traditional kirpan with the cross strap which Sikhs wear. She was instantly followed by many other women wearing khaddar saris and holding the Nishan Sahib. Another wave of women spilled out into the street shouting nationalist slogans. The constable guarding the gate was helpless and simply watched them go out into the bazaar. The slogan, 'Bharat mata ki jai' echoed through the air. Within minutes such a large crowd was gathered there that the path through the market was blocked. The woman carrying the national flag raised it high and shouted 'May our national flag…' and the crowd answered, '…always fly high.' One police constable came forward and tried to snatch the flag from her. The woman with the flag in her hand marched ahead undeterred. The policeman's hand brushed against the kirpan the woman was wearing. In the ensuing struggle, the kirpan was unsheathed and the policeman's hand was scratched such that a little blood oozed out. The police party began attacking the crowd with their wooden lathis, dispersing most of the people who had collected there. But the woman with the flag held it firmly in both hands and sat in protest on the wooden platform in front of a shop. Other women too joined the demonstration and sat down on the ground. After most of the crowd had melted away, the police officer in-charge tried to take the flag away, first authoritatively, and then gently, persuasively. But neither worked because of the woman's firm conviction. She told him firmly, 'You will not take this flag as long as we live.' Finally, all the women were arrested and put into tongas and carted away. At the gate of the prison the dispute about the flag was revived. The women insisted that they would take the flag into the prison and install it above their barracks. They were still arguing when the police party escorting Kishan Singh reached there. Kishan Singh was not at all surprised to find none other than his wife, Sharan Kaur, sitting at the head of the group, the flag held in her hand. It appeared as if Kishan Singh already knew about this situation. Kishan Singh advised the women, 'You have expressed your faith in the national flag very well. You have saved it from being dishonoured as long you were outside. Now you are in prison. Even if you put the flag on your barracks, the prison employees will lock you in and tear down the flag. This is not going to help in any way.' Finally it was decided that the national flag should be sent to the Congress office with all due respect. As she entered the prison, Sharan Kaur asked her husband about their daughter's health, but the gate of the women's ward closed before he could answer.

3

The desire Laj had to go to prison for the service of the country did not diminish despite the pain and suffering she endured because of the fever and the news of the imprisonment of both her parents. Within a few days she recovered and was able to walk. Veeranwali, her aunt, had spared no effort in looking after her. After her parents' arrest, Veeranwali took her to her home. Veeranwali's husband, Hushnak Singh, a jamadar in the army, got the news of his brother-in-law and wife's arrest from an acquaintance while he was on a train home on his annual leave; there was no newspaper available in the cantonment. No one knew he was coming home. When Hushnak Singh's tonga reached his home, he saw Laj standing at the door. She ran in to break the news of her uncle's arrival to her aunt. Coming back outside, she hugged her uncle as he was alighting from the tonga. Veeranwali came out and greeted her husband respectfully with, 'Sat Sri Akal', and then hurriedly went in to tidy up. Standing in front of the mirror, she combed her hair, changed her dupatta, came out and excitedly busied herself in taking care of his luggage. Laj also began helping her bua in her work. Neighbours and friends came to greet Hushnak Singh. Veeranwali put the kettle on the fire to make tea for the visitors. It was only after the visitors had left that Veeranwali got a chance to talk to her husband as she offered him a cup of tea. Mixing sugar into his cup, she asked him, 'How are you? Is everything alright?'

'It has been fine till now, but it seems you will not let it stay that way.' Veeranwali had anticipated such a response from her husband judging by the expression on his face. She had clearly understood that he was in a sour mood but she had not been able to guess the reason for his irritation. She decided to drop the matter there. Her husband reluctantly took the cup of tea. Veeranwali didn't give him an opportunity to raise any issue till dinner time. Fuming with anger, Hushnak Singh somehow managed to eat two rotis that night. Veeranwali wasn't hungry at all and ate nothing. Then, changing into his night clothes, Hushnak Singh lay on his cot. Veeranwali gave Laj her meal, finished her chores in the kitchen, and went to sit next to her husband on the pretext of massaging his legs. Neither of them spoke for ten or fifteen minutes. Hushnak Singh turned on his side and yawned as if he had been asleep and had only now realized that Veeranwali was sitting there. Veeranwali said, 'Ji, look at me. You don't even know how to stay awake. I have grown tired of waiting for you and you won't even talk to me! How long is your leave?' Hushnak Singh turned in his bed again and, covering his eyes with his arm, said, 'Consider this a long vacation. You don't know how to live in comfort. Now it is the time for my promotion, but you won't let me achieve anything!'

'What's the problem?' she asked, puzzled.

'What should I tell you? Don't you know this is war time? The government does not want any army man to have any kind of contact with the rebels. Firstly, the government should not even know that we have any connection with any rebel. And if the government comes to know, we can easily say that we have no control. But you! You have deliberately got me into trouble. Do you understand what a serious crime it is to give shelter to a rebel's daughter?'

Hearing her husband's words, a shiver ran down Veeranwali's spine. She had never realized that bringing Laj to their home in these circumstances could be so harmful to her husband. She broke out in a sweat and began to tremble. Grinding his teeth, her husband lashed out, 'Why did you bring this girl to my home?'

Veeranwali narrated the whole sequence of events to him in a voice heavy with emotion, like a devotee praying to a goddess in the hopes of a cherished boon. But she soon felt that her husband was no better than an unmoving stone statue. What dreams she had harboured for when her husband came home on leave! Now she saw all those dreams shatter in a moment. She had no idea what it would mean for her husband to shelter Laj. Lying where she was, she passed the night somehow. She begged with her precious pearl-like tears but the stone statue showed no sign of softening. Her husband's stubborn obstinacy hurt her deeply and Veeranwali began to believe that she was the guilty party in all this.

A panic-stricken person tries to hide the cause of his panic in such a way that his panic becomes even more apparent. Friends and acquaintances came to know about it. Wise elders reasoned with him and explained that he was in no way responsible for the actions of his brother-in-law, but their words cut no ice with Hushnak Singh. He was convinced that keeping Laj in his home would mean the end of all his hopes and aspirations. He had been sure that he would at least be promoted to subedar major during the war. Laj overheard some of the things that were being said about her. When his leave came to an end and it was time for him to return to the cantonment, Hushnak Singh called a tonga to his door. Holding Veeranwali by her arm, he forced her into the tonga, then locked the front door of his house and put the keys into his pocket. Laj was playing with some other girls in the street and saw her helpless aunt, sitting in the tonga, staring at her with tear-filled eyes. She watched as the tonga drove away and could no longer be seen in the distance.

4

'Brother, how is Laj?'

'Veeran, we had left her in your care.'

Veeranwali was visiting her brother in Central Jail, Multan, a year or so after he had been taken to jail. She had asked only one question and her brother, Kishan Singh, had said only this. These were the only words that they spoke to each other during an hour-long meeting. After that both of them sat silently and occasionally looked at each other with teary eyes. Only an expert in the art of speechless communication can tell what else was said during that meeting. The officer supervising the meeting rang the bell signalling the end of the allotted time. Brother and sister looked at each other without a word and then Veeranwali left. Kishan Singh knew it was the last time he would meet his sister.

Prisoners are continuously shifted around from one jail to another during the period of their incarceration. Kishan Singh had found out that Laj had been admitted to the tuberculosis hospital in Lahore. But no one had informed him that Veeranwali was suffering a much worse imprisonment. No one told him, yet somehow he knew. Even a bird could not enter the cantonment without permission. No one could have told Veeranwali anything about her rebel brother, sister-in-law, or the daughter of the rebel. And no one knew how Veeranwali managed to reach the prison for that meeting. She endangered her own life and succeeded in keeping her meeting with her brother secret from Hushnak Singh. But she could not bear the guilt of not having been able to keep her niece safe. Hushnak Singh didn't pay any attention to the real ailment plaguing his wife and all traditional medicines proved ineffective in the face of her sorrow. In the meantime, Sharan Kaur's prison term came to an end. Before Veeranwali could present herself before her sister-in-law and admit her guilt of betraying their faith in her, admit that she had failed to protect their daughter, she passed away, achieving eternal freedom. Sharan Kaur, on being released, went straight to the hospital in Lahore. The main gate was closed. The gatekeeper told her, 'It is time for the patients to rest.' To the left of the gate was a house where the sweepers lived. Seeing this strange woman in a coarse khadi dress, a sweeper woman came up to her. She asked, 'Who do you wish to see?' Sharan Kaur was glad to be able to elicit some information. She replied, 'My daughter, Laj, is under treatment here.' The sweeper woman asked her about the ward and room number and declared, 'I have not heard about any patient with this name. Every day I go to every ward to clean it.'

Sharan Kaur persisted, 'I don't know about the ward, nor do I know about the room number. But I have heard that my Laj is admitted here in this hospital.'

'You have heard?' the sweeper woman asked surprised. 'Were you not the one who got her admitted here?'

'No, we were in prison. She fell ill later.'

'She must be the daughter of the rebel!' said the sweeper woman on hearing the word prison. 'No one here knows her name is Laj. She is a slim, fair-complexioned girl, twelve or thirteen years old. She is so sweet to talk to. Listening to her, sometimes one feels like laughing, sometimes one cries. She was with her bua?' Sharan Kaur nodded in agreement.

'Then she is the same girl. When she came here for the first time, she asked someone, 'Who is a rebel?' Then she said that her uncle scolded her bua, saying, 'Why have you brought the daughter of a rebel to my home?' From that day, everyone started calling her the Daughter of the Rebel. Whenever a doctor visits the ward, she asks him to take her to her parents in prison. The doctors laugh it off.' Sharan Kaur stood there like a statue listening to the sweeper woman.

The sweeper woman asked, 'Sardarji is not here?'

'He still has to complete his jail term. He got three years imprisonment, half of it remains.' On hearing this, the sweeper woman sighed and said, 'The girl is very sensible. She says, "My uncle took my aunt away and I fell asleep outside on the doorstep. I caught fever because of the cold. Then a friend of my father's took me to his home. When my condition worsened, he admitted me here. I protested a lot and said take me to prison but they didn't."' After saying all this, the sweeper woman remarked, 'Now she is just waiting for you.'

Sharan Kaur understood the implication of the sweeper woman's last sentence. Her tears had stopped flowing by the time she reached Laj's room. On seeing her mother, Laj opened her eyes wide and her head fell sideways. It was the last glimpse of the morning light she would see.

Translated by Paramjit Singh Ramana

KUNG POSH: KASHMIRI SAFFRON

DEVENDRA SATYARTHI

1

Most flowers blossom in spring but kesar, saffron, blooms in autumn. Ababeel, the swallow that has just spread its wings and flown away from that hillock over there, was perhaps waiting to take a good look at the saffron flowers. Would this land ever become so barren that saffron would stop growing here?

What cheer, what hustle and bustle can be seen here! Are these girls or brightly coloured fairies? They are picking saffron flowers. When I see their beauty, I cannot help but admire that Sculptor who has sculpted their fine features and moulded their bodies so perfectly.

My heart, which was calm and colourless like the Jhelum River flowing under the Amira Kadal bridge, is now dancing with joy in the presence of these waves of colour. Are all the women of Kashmir equally attractive? No, neither are all of them equally delicate, nor supple or vigorous. Their complexion is unique, their features too are unique.

The contractor shouts, 'Hurry up, hurry!'

The girls are enthusiastically harvesting the flowers. The contractor's harsh yelling startles them for a brief moment, then the animated conversation resumes. It is as if all the beauty of the past, present, and future has come together in this field—their fair, pretty necks, shining black eyes like dark black clouds brightened by lightning, lips, full and fine, like fresh drops of honey. When they talk, the corners of their lips move, enthralling my heart.

Some old women too are collecting flowers. They have spent their youth doing this—picking saffron flowers year after year. Even when they came here as young brides, saffron grew in these fields.

A young woman wearing a bright red dress is perhaps pregnant. As she picks those flowers, she looks tired, like the branch of a tree bending under the weight of rain.

My gaze turns to a young cheerful maiden who is wearing a green woollen gown. Her lovely eyes reveal an element of bashfulness, some hesitation tinged with timidity. The naughty, childish glow on her face is slowly fading and she takes the first steps towards the sobriety of an adult. It is not that she hasn't noticed me. There is nothing wrong in looking at someone. I wish to ask her if it is not unfair to slyly look at some stranger and then turn your gaze away. Should I observe the smooth shape of her arms or the contours of her slender fingers?

The contractor yells again, admonishing them, disturbing them. His face red with anger, he shouts, 'Quick, quick, hurry up!' All their faces fall, even that of the old ladies.

The petals of the flowers are purple. Every flower has six projections: three orange stigmas, three yellow stamens. After picking the flowers, they are spread out in the sun to dry. And then the orange stigmas, which are to be used as saffron, are separated. The yellow stamens should be thrown away but often they are either carelessly or deliberately mixed with the saffron to increase its weight.

Last week when I came here with my wife and daughter to see the saffron flowers on a moonlit night, these flowers shone like gold. I kept shifting my gaze between the stars in the sky and the saffron flowers in the fields.

A very beautiful picture has stayed in my mind. The young lively girl in the green dress looked in my direction again. I came to Kashmir seven years ago. The picture that was etched in my mind from that visit is still there. There were no saffron fields in that! Now I can imagine them.

As the maidens go about picking saffron, they sing a song that even the old contractor knows and feels like singing: *'My lover has gone to Pampore and the saffron flowers there have caught hold of him. Oh! He is there and I am here. O God, answer my prayers!'* A song of longing.

Perhaps when that coy girl in the green dress grows older, she will sing this song to try to refresh and enliven the fading colours in her life.

This land here is contoured and uneven. Some of it lies next to the banks of the Jhelum and the rest is inland. I can see many small mounds rising here and there. I ask the contractor, 'What do you call these mounds in Kashmiri?'

He says: 'vooder' or 'karewa'.

The deeply wrinkled face of the contractor turns solemn, as if he is a very important person and the only one who is capable of answering such a question.

He invites me to sit next to him on the cot and tells me that these vooder or karewa are very fertile pieces of land entirely dependent on rain for irrigation.

'Does saffron grow on all these mounds?'

'No, no. Saffron grows on the vooders of Pampore only. This twelve-thousand-acre bit of land is a special boon from God.... Saffron can grow only in this soil.'

He also informed me that all that land was the personal property of the king. Whoever takes this land on lease must distribute half the saffron yield among the tillers working under him. The other half he keeps; the lease amount is paid from his share.

'To get half a chhatak, around twenty-five grams, of saffron we need 4,312 flowers,' he tells me proudly, as if his elders and ancestors were always contractors of saffron-producing lands. His experienced eyes shine with pride and self-appreciation. They glow as if he has inspired me to become a contractor for saffron by informing me about that great secret.

2

I have fallen in love with saffron. I want to see it growing everywhere. I wish to spread saffron everywhere on the map of India.

'Blessed is that land to which kesar belongs.' Saying so, the shopkeeper weighed five rupees worth of saffron for me. Taking the money out of my pocket, I thought: who knows, Kesar could be the name of the wife of this trader in Srinagar. And reaching home at night, he may again say in her presence, 'Blessed is that land to which Kesar belongs!' That lady will believe her beauty is being praised not knowing that her husband had sold a little saffron to a wandering writer and earned a little money.

My imagination runs riot and revolves only around saffron. My wife wears a saffron sari. Imitating her, my daughter has also chosen a saffron frock to wear. And I feel happy.

I wish that coy girl in the saffron fields had also worn a saffron-coloured gown. Then her fair complexion would have taken on a golden hue. She would have appeared even prettier to me. And I would have thought of her as the daughter of that saffron field. Perhaps as the goddess of saffron.

When I look at the saffron smile of the first rays of the day, I feel the 'morning' has understood my message. But this colour has always been a favourite of the morning. Every morning brings a new shade of saffron and all those colourful images that have always bathed poets and writers in their tantalizing shades.

Looking at the saffron-coloured early morning glow, did it ever occur to that shy, lively girl that she should also wear a saffron-coloured gown like the morning? Or does she wake up late, after daybreak? If not the early morning hues, she must at least see the saffron streaks in the flowers when she picks them in the fields. Looking at them, she must surely become lost in thought. In this situation, she can easily think about the saffron gown. But who is to tell her that the cream white gown that she has so fondly got, or is going to get, should be dyed in saffron?

Pampore is not very far from Srinagar. Tongas are available. But tonga travel will never be as much fun as travelling on foot. Many a time I have gone to Pampore, but more than the saffron flowers, it is that coy, lively girl that attracts me.

Every time she is in the same gown, the same green one. Does she have only one gown? Such poverty! I feel I should not buy a new sari for my wife till all her old saris are worn out. Does that lively girl not have the same desires? Is her heart made of some different matter?

I try my best to push that girl out of my thoughts but she is deeply entrenched in my mind. Many a time I have dreamt about her. Why does she not leave me alone? Why does she stare at me? Why does she burst out laughing? Did I know that feelings can run so high? What if she protests: why should there be such hatred for her green gown? Grass is also green. In fact, she wants me to wear green as well. Trees are covered in green…. 'But since you won't agree to wear green, I will agree…I will wear the saffron gown…. Did you think that I don't have a saffron gown? Great! What ideas you have! Last year I got a saffron gown stitched. But I did not know that a wanderer would come and ask me to wear it…. Okay, see here, look at me…I am wearing the saffron gown now. Am I the daughter of the saffron fields or am I a goddess of saffron?'

Yesterday, all day long, I kept trying to prevent that girl from occupying my mind. When I sat down to write an essay, I felt as if that goddess of saffron was asking me, 'What will you write about? About that saffron field where you saw me for the first time? Or about that contractor who did you the honour of allowing you to sit next to him on his cot?'

When I went to have a bath, I heard the voice of the goddess of saffron coming from some deep recess of my mind, 'Is the water very cold? I know you don't like to bathe in cold water. Why didn't you tell me? I would have immediately lit a fire and heated the water...I wouldn't have refused. Do you have some soap? Okay, good! Have your bath. I'll go now.'

When I came out of the bathroom after a bath, I looked gloomy. My wife asked, 'What's the problem? You look rather lost.' I simply smiled and shook my head. What could I say to her? I was feeling a little embarrassed and regretful; why did I go to that saffron field? When I went for my walk along the banks of the dull-looking Jhelum, I felt as if I was being followed by that goddess of saffron. The colour of saffron has wings: it comes flying. The colour took its place and spoke, 'What is my fault in this? If you were going to jilt me like this, you should not have called me...you should not have aroused my dormant emotions. What rules of conduct are you following? Why did you stand near the edge of the field and stare at me without blinking? You didn't talk to me but your eyes said so much. Why didn't you restrain them? Not once or twice but seven times you walked up to the fields in Pampore. When I knew this, I fell in love with you.'

I was confused. Couldn't say a word. What could I say? I was guilty after all. I didn't take offence at what she said. But I was in no position to welcome her into my life. I wanted her to leave me alone, to forgive me. When I saw tears in her eyes, I froze like a startled deer. Initially I thought of telling her straightaway: what love are you talking about? Which pleasure? But I could not say that to her in so many words. Rather, I said to her: 'Don't cry, you goddess of saffron. What is the use of crying? Look at the world around you. Look at the length and breadth of the world. At least look at Pampore. Tear-filled eyes try to see but through a hazy layer of water. There should be no tears blocking your vision; that way the colours lose their brightness...then your life is like that swallow ready to fly away. And won't your tears make your wings heavier? Your lover will find you one day. But leave me alone, forgive me.' She didn't agree, but continued to cry uninterrupted. Had I not gone into that saffron field, I wouldn't have had to face this problem.

I turned and entered the market. I was nervous still. There, I felt I was alone, which was better. I felt easy walking around. The market is nobody's personal property. I was free there.

Then, casually, I happened to look up. I felt a sliver of colour from my mind fly out and get stuck in the window in front of me. I stood fixed to that spot. What a smooth face! Cherry red cheekbones on a rosy face like two lamps burning bright...and the eyes! Two dark nights where one has to watch his every step!

3

I try my best but can't restrain my heart. I am always feeling lost and confused, disordered like my long dishevelled hair. I am afraid to go out. First it was that goddess of Pampore: saffron idea of my mind. Now this woman who sits in that window as if she were a picture fixed in a frame. Why is she looking at me? I feel a little ache in my heart as if some innocent child has torn away a part of a colourful painting. Was she guilty? No, she was innocent. Then who was guilty? Was I the culprit?

Yesterday again I saw her from a distance; she kept looking at me innocently. When I turned back towards home, I felt two dark mesmerizing eyes following me. Two dark nights were attempting to fuse with the brightness of my life. I sought out my wife and got shelter from her. My heart was racing.

But I can't control my heart. I don't understand what lies buried in it: '*The heart is deeper than the ocean; who can fathom its mysteries? ...In there is the boat, the oar, and the boatman,*' so the Sufi poet sings. In this ocean of the heart everything drowns: the boat, the oar, the boatman! Was that farmer from Punjab also caught in such a quagmire like me?

Now when I look in that window, I feel that the goddess of Pampore has transformed herself into this form. But her gown was green and this woman likes light blue. Why does she not wear a saffron gown? But every flower likes its own colour, just as every bird likes its own song.

I remember, as a child, I had got a light blue coat stitched. It didn't look bad. Mother used to say every colour gives a new kind of joy. If she came to know about this situation, she would say at once, 'Don't you like this blue gown? Have you forgotten the time when you used to go to school wearing that light blue coat? You didn't even know if the light blue suits girls more or boys.'

She has such bashful eyes. If she were not shy, she would have looked rather vulgar. But to be too shy to open one's heart to anyone is also not good. Why do I look at her? Why is my heart beating faster?

How did she become the queen of that window? Who fixed her up in that bright frame? Who will answer me? Who will tell me her story? Who prompted her to revolve around this axis? Whosoever else may be at fault, she is innocent. I look at her from a distance. There is no harm in looking at her. Anyway, it is not as though I hate her.

Sometimes happiness also appears on the face of that dark-eyed woman just as lightning brightens up a dark cloud-covered night with innumerable streaks of whiteness. I feel a little anguished thinking that when she cries, kohl streaks her face.

Does she not remember the muslin-like carpet of fresh green grass that lay under her feet? Surely she has not forgotten—the soft lovely scent of the grass that, in addition to the aroma of flowers, must have fascinated her a thousand times. She must have been born in a poor farmer's house. She does not appear to have a very old connection with that faded house. She is in no way a daughter of a prostitute; this I can easily vouchsafe. Otherwise, she would not look so naive. She likely comes from a well-to-do background.

But why doesn't she sing? Surely, she knows how to sing. It is not necessary that someone should be there to blow into a flute...the wind itself can play some notes. Musical notes are never too hard to bring alive...they are easily roused. Sometime or the other, she must have hummed some song, who knows, maybe out of fear. So not only my eyes, my ears too keep taking rounds around her attic. Now I realize my ears are more restive than my eyes. How I wish to hear her animated singing even from far away! I keep thinking, my ears always attentive in her direction. A fascinating vibrant vision spreads out in front of my eyes. Longfellow has written: 'And the night shall be filled with music / And the cares, that infest the day, / Shall fold their tents, like the Arabs / And as silently steal away.' Perhaps, he too had to wait anxiously like me. The folk songs of her village must have come to her lips unconsciously, at one time or the other.

Who can I share my secrets with? I am worried society may steal from me all my cherished dreams that I have nurtured with all my passion. But this worry will always remain. Very often I think all my worries and fears are pointless: the fear of religion, fear of God, fear of society. But I just cannot get rid of them.

What is the meaning of those morals, that virtuousness that is solely based on fear? A virtuousness that teaches hatred, teaches enmity? No, I am not going to be afraid any more.

Last night, mustering up all my courage, I went to her home. I looked at her wide-eyed. She eagerly stood up to welcome me. With a lot of respect and honour she asked me to sit on a black Kashmiri blanket.

'Goddess of Pampore.' I addressed her so in my mind. But I asked: 'What is your name?'

'Kung Posh.' She replied in a very sweet voice.

I saw a saffron hue appear on her cheeks, signifying her coyness.

'Kung Posh?' I asked. 'What does Kung Posh mean?'

'Kung Posh means saffron flower.'

Having found her at such a place, it immediately occurred to me: all the other flowers blossom in spring but the saffron, kesar, blooms in autumn.

The words of the song I had heard in the fields of Pampore rang in my ears: '*My lover has gone towards Pampore and saffron flowers there have caught hold of him. Oh! He is there and I am here. O God, answer my prayers!*'

I began to think that similar thoughts were perhaps passing through the mind of my wife: *My lover has gone towards Pampore and saffron flowers there have caught hold of him. Oh! He is there and I am here. O God answer my prayers!*

Kung Posh appeared to be very happy. Her face was radiant and exuded great joy. I was the first person to visit her home that night. She must have expected that I would not just give her money but also give her a green chinar leaf, signifying my commitment to her.

Then Kung Posh brought a few almonds and cardamom pods placed on a handsome chinar-leaf shaped tray carved from walnut wood. I picked up one almond nut.

'Thanks.'

'Won't you taste the cardamom?'

'I have already had one.'

The coal in the kangri was burning hot, like her cheeks. Kung Posh pushed the kangri towards me.

Kung Posh was not naive in any way but she was bashful. In the light of the electric bulb, her light blue gown looked beautiful on her.

The conversation in the women's quarters is restricted to certain kinds of formal speech. I was not aware of that. How could I notice or understand the meaning of fast-changing expressions of protest, thankfulness, or gratefulness in Kung Posh's eyes? My heart was beating fast. Could I laugh aloud freely—an easy effortless laughter that sounds like the music of a fountain in the mountains?

Kung Posh once again offered me almond and cardamom by extending the chinar leaf shaped tray made of walnut wood towards me. Without saying anything I picked up a cardamom and put it in my mouth. She looked at me. She really was as lovely as a saffron flower. I smiled and she smiled back. I was perhaps Nag Rai and she Himal, characters from a famous Kashmiri folk tale. And that love story was going to be repeated. But I controlled myself and said: 'I collect songs.'

'Songs? What songs?'

'Folk songs, songs of the villages.'

'Song...song.'

She could not say anything more. I looked at her. I felt as if the flashy bridal dress of a newly-wed woman had been soiled in front of my eyes.

With an effort she raised her tired hand and, with a trembling finger, pointed to the room above on the other side of the road where music was playing under flashy bright lights: 'Go, go there. Songs are sold there and....'

Her voice had the musical flavour of the fields and I got up to go towards those fields in whose fertile soil saffron grows.

All the other flowers blossom in spring but kesar, saffron, blooms in autumn.

Will this land ever become so infertile that saffron stops growing here?

Translated by Paramjit Singh Ramana

DANCE OF THE DEVIL

SANT SINGH SEKHON

All the Muslims of the village, including the women and children, were forcibly moved to a dharamshala at the far end of the village. Four armed men stood guard to prevent them from escaping. Although the captives numbered more than fifty, they were not able to offer any resistance. Three of the guards carried swords and the fourth had a gun.

Around midnight, a young man among the captives tried to escape by climbing over the wall. His aged mother was also among the people being held in the dharamshala. As the man was trying to get up after jumping over the wall, the guard with the gun shouted, 'Stop! Stand straight or I will shoot you!'

The man who had jumped over the wall froze. The armed guard rushed towards him and said in a threatening voice, 'So you were trying to escape! I will not let you get away so easily, you filthy Muslim.'

'No, Sardarji, I came out to relieve myself,' said the man in a pleading tone. He did not recognize the guard. The guard was not from his village but an outsider. The man who had jumped the wall thought to himself that if the guard had been from his village, he would have made a concession for a fellow villager and allowed him to escape.

'So you came out to relieve yourself?' said the guard. 'Go and do whatever you need to do.'

'May I do so far away or close by?' the Muslim youth asked in fright.

'Go ahead a few steps. If you try to run, I shall shoot you dead.'

He had hardly taken ten steps when, from behind came the order, 'Sit down, no further.'

The Muslim youth stepped back, and five minutes passed. 'Have you not shat yet?' the guard roared. The Muslim youth did not reply.

After a couple of minutes, the guard said, 'Are you not done yet? Now get up.'

'Sir, I have failed to go,' the Muslim man replied. The guard came closer and asked, 'Where have you gone?'

'Sir, nothing came out,' replied the captive, very peevishly.

'How come you had the urge to defecate?' he asked.

The Muslim youth had no answer; he could not come up with anything. 'You bloody swine! You intended to flee. If you had not eaten anything since morning, how could you then have the urge to relieve yourself?'

'Must have felt the urge out of habit. I swear I haven't eaten anything since the morning,' replied the young man.

'Why haven't you eaten anything?' the guard questioned sternly.

'Sir, my aged mother was very distressed and could not cook anything.'

'You could have cooked something,' the guard countered.

'I was also not well and there is nobody else in our family,' replied the man.

The guard smiled and said, 'All right, jump back across the wall and get in.'

As the man climbed over the wall, the guard hit him hard on his buttocks with his rifle. The man was in extreme pain for the rest of the night. He couldn't gather the courage to try and escape again.

'If anyone feels the urge to defecate, do what you must inside. Anyone trying to come out will be gunned down,' the man standing on guard announced for all the prisoners to hear.

After some time, the guards were changed, and a new group of four took over. 'The rascals try to escape by faking the urge to relieve themselves. Be cautious,' the departing guard cautioned the one who had come to replace him.

The new group of guards did not encounter anyone trying to escape by pretending to need to defecate. They could hear the men snoring and women sobbing throughout the night.

At daybreak a group of around fifty men, armed with spears and guns, arrived. The leader of the group called the guard on duty and said, 'Now we will take them to the ravines in groups of ten. From there they will be dispatched directly to Pakistan.' The ravines were a mile away from the dharamshala.

The guard responded with the promptness of an army man, 'Right, sir.'

'Now we are going to the ravines,' the leader of the group addressed a team of around eight. 'You get these swines there in groups of ten.'

The larger group left for the ravines and the team of eight separated from them as per their plan. Four of them entered the dharamshala and shouted at the captives, 'Ten of you come with us.' A chill went down the spine of the captives.

'Are you all sleeping?' the guards nudged one of the captives. One of the guards shouted, 'You scoundrels have gone and voted for the Muslim League in droves. Now face the consequence.'

An old man who had woken up said in a feeble voice, 'Sardarji, we do not even have the right to vote. There are only two or three Muslims in this village who have studied till class five and thus can vote.'

'But you people did go to vote in large numbers,' retorted the guard.

'Those must have been youngsters going for some fun. I did not even go,' replied the old man. Another guard came in and rudely woke up another man. 'Come on, let's go now.'

Nudging them with spears and swords, the guards brought

ten captives out of the dharamshala. The women and children started wailing on seeing the men leave.

'Sardarji, please don't kill me with the spear, don't make me suffer,' the old man requested. 'Finish it with one stroke of the sword.'

'But you are a Muslim. You should be given death by "halal",' shouted one of the butchers with a crooked smile on his face.

'We are not sure if we are going to kill you. We may decide to drop you to the camp at Ludhiana. There are two trucks waiting and should be able to accommodate all of you,' said one of the guards to give some hope to their victims. With these words, four men with swords led the ten captives towards the ravines.

As the armed men returned to the dharamshala, another group of ten men was ready to be taken away. This group consisted of younger men, some of them barely eighteen.

'Sardarji, please listen to my request,' said one of the boys among the captives. 'Why don't you let us become Sikhs. We were anyways your servants as Muslims. We will continue to serve you as Sikhs. Even otherwise we do not have much to look forward to,' he pleaded.

'But you have scored a huge victory by creating Pakistan. We haven't got anything,' retorted one of the guards. 'Your brothers in Pakistan have pushed our people out. Now we are at the mercy of Brahmins and Banias,' an intellectual among the guards spoke.

'The creation of Pakistan has no meaning for us. Very soon our graves will be seen here,' the young man pleaded. 'If you show mercy on us, we will live our lives in your service.'

'Now don't waste our time with all this talk,' shouted another Sikh guard and nudged the captives with the tip of his sword.

In this manner, forty captives, including women and children were taken to the ravines. The last group of ten women and a few children was brought to the door of the dharamshala. Among the women in the group was a young woman of about twenty-five. Her four-year-old son was holding her hand and she was carrying her one-year-old son. She was exceptionally beautiful. Even in the difficult circumstances she was facing, she looked ethereal.

'Please don't send her to the ravines,' one of the Sikh guards pleaded. 'Give her to me.'

'Don't let your amorous desires interfere with your religious duties,' warned another guard.

'It's not about lust. I will have her adopt the Sikh religion and take her as my wife. What will she do even if she reaches Pakistan?' he requested in an earnest voice.

As if the woman saw a glimmer of hope in this conversation, she stepped away from the group. The Sikh guards were talking among themselves. The four-year-old child saw something on the ground and leapt to pick it up.

'Look at this, Mother!' the child showed her a picture from a page torn from a book. The woman briefly looked at the picture and then turned her face towards her captors.

'Leave her here and take the rest,' ordered the seniormost among the guards. The guards nudged the captives towards the ravines and the woman and her two children were left behind.

'So, Bibi, are you willing to become a Sikh?' asked the elderly guard.

'What will I do by becoming a Sikh? Please kill me as well. I would rather reunite with the father of my children in death,' replied the woman.

'We will make you this person's wife. He has land and a house. The community will adopt you as our own,' argued the elderly Sikh guard.

'Let him keep his land. It's of no use to us poor people,' the woman started sobbing. Her four-year-old son was fiddling with the sword of the Sikh guard.

'She doesn't seem interested,' the elderly guard told the guard who was hoping to find a wife.

'All right then, she can also be dispatched like the others,' said another Sikh guard who was standing nearby.

The woman realized that her death was now a certainty. She started wailing in despair. Her four-year-old son also started crying.

'If you don't want to die, consider becoming Sikh,' the guard tried again.

'You can kill me if you like, but please spare my children. They can live as your servants,' the woman requested.

'Your kids will also go with you. They are of no use to us.' Hearing this, the woman began wailing again. Her children also started crying loudly.

'Don't waste your time. If somebody from outside comes here, we won't be able to keep you,' said the guard looking for a wife.

'But he must already have a wife,' the woman protested.

'Even his father did not have a wife,' joked one of the younger Sikh guards.

The woman and her children stopped crying.

'He has nobody he can call family. His wife died and he does not have any children. He owns twenty acres of land,' reasoned the elderly Sikh guard.

'There is no dearth of matches for him; I wonder why he has his heart set on you,' said another guard in jest.

'He is a prize catch,' another guard continued the banter.

'You should agree to the proposal,' the elderly Sikh guard advised the lady. She burst out crying.

'So, you don't seem to like the proposal,' the bride-seeking-guard came closer and asked. He seemed to be enamoured by her beauty. 'I am a well-respected man in the community,' he argued in his favour.

'We are decent people; that's why we are asking for your opinion. Nobody could stop us from having our way with you if we wanted,' another guard added.

These words shook the lady to her core. The dreadful images buried deep in her psyche were brought to the fore by the threat.

'What will happen to my children?' she asked.

'I will raise them as my own. Now, in the name of God, let

me take the boy,' the guard seeking a wife took the boy from her lap with mild force.

'Now you take her to the village' instructed the elderly guard. 'It will become complicated if more people arrive here.'

'Come with me, fortunate lady,' said the guard eagerly.

'I will agree to anything for the sake of my innocent children,' the woman sighed as she walked with the guard, holding her four-year-old son.

'You also come with me, brother,' the would-be groom requested a middle-aged guard. 'With you around nobody will trouble us.'

'Tomorrow morning, we will have the marriage ceremony for the two of you. Stay away from her until then,' cautioned the elderly guard.

Translated by Amaninder Singh Dhindsa

SUNRISE AT LAST

SUJAAN SINGH

Naseem was the beloved daughter of advocate Nazar Muhammad from Amritsar. She was married to the only son of the numberdar Muhammed Yaseen of Kathania. Her husband, Waris Muhammed, was serving as a captain in the army. After their wedding, the newly-weds went to Kashmir for a month and a half. Most of their time was spent on a beautiful houseboat on Dal Lake.

After spending some time at her parents' house, Naseem joined her husband at the Meerut Cantonment. Apart from learning the etiquette required of an army officer's wife, she also learnt to drive. Even though her family and her in-laws were conservative Muslims, they allowed their girls the freedom to come out of the veil and to learn to sing and dance. These practices were otherwise considered anti-Islamic.

When her village was attacked by a Sikh jatha from Kathu Nangal, she was in the tall fodder crop in the fields adjacent to the village. The intense fighting between the villagers and the jatha lasted for more than two hours. Naseem, who usually never stepped out of her house, hid in the crop for safety. She was sweating from the heat and fear. It seemed as if her blood had turned to water and was flowing in the form of sweat.

Finally, the village was overrun. The jatha entered from the south and started attacking whoever came their way. Fear made Naseem react cleverly. The Muslims were losing hope and had started moving westwards as the jatha closed in on them. Naseem drifted towards the east instead.

On the way she tripped and fell into water puddles and was bitten by insects. She crawled like an insect at night and reached a well near the village. In the distance, she could see a big mansion on fire. She guessed it was her in-laws' house. She realized that nobody in the village would have survived the pogrom.

In the middle of all the fear and grief, she felt relieved that her husband was safe as he was not in the village. For a second, she thought that there was a possibility that tomorrow he would come looking for her in a Pakistan Army truck. At the same time, she realized that tomorrow was still a long time away and a lot of horrible things could happen to her in the meantime. This thought was even scarier than the thought of death. 'Bloody kafirs,' she mumbled under her breath to overcome the frightening thoughts.

She realized that her old father-in-law and mother-in-law must be dead. There was no way anybody could have survived the storm of that fire. Although she had escaped once, she did not know how long she would be able to survive. Scared for her life, she started moving towards Mohanpura, a village inhabited by Hindus and Sikhs.

There had been some rain showers the day before. The intense summer sun generated unbearable humidity after the rains. Even the most hardened farmers were unable to survive such terrible weather. The humidity was further intensified by the water in the paddy fields that Naseem was passing by. Suddenly, she heard footsteps coming her way. She also heard the sounds of people brushing against the tall crop along the edges of the field embankments. She was too far from the taller crops now and the next field of fodder crop was some distance ahead.

Scared that she may become part of the loot of the mob coming her way, she lay down in the paddy field. The dark night gave Naseem an effective cover even though the paddy crop was not dense. A long chain of marauders passed that way as Naseem lay still. The bubbles generated by the weight of her body travelled some distance before bursting.

Being a delicate girl, Naseem was losing consciousness due to the heat and humidity. More than death, the fear of being kidnapped and brutally raped forced her to remain in her senses. Finally, the stream of marauders ebbed.

Even in the darkness, Naseem could see girls and young women from her village being led away by men carrying spears and swords. She moved further away to hide. Her silk salwar got entangled in the thorns of the wild growth and was badly torn. Finally, she reached a platform with an abandoned well next to it. She had never been there earlier but had heard that it was on the outskirts of the village.

There was a rumour that the area was inhabited by poisonous wild snakes. As a result, the gang of looters stayed away from there. She felt safe in the territory of the poisonous snakes. She lay down peacefully in a field of cattle fodder. Her wet and soiled clothes were sticking to her body.

With her arm under her head, she stared at the stars above. The stars were briefly covered by passing clouds but would reappear to shine even brighter after the clouds passed. She felt temporary clouds of pain and suffering had covered the stars of her destiny. She thought of the venomous snakes several times but instead of scaring her, it strengthened her resolve to stay where she was. Even the noise of the crickets appeared like the hissing of a snake to her at times. The grasshoppers came and sat on her delicate face, and she gently removed them with her soft knuckles. It appeared to her that the cruelty of wild insects was nowhere close to the barbarism displayed by human beings. She was reminded of the lines of the Duke from Shakespeare's play *As You Like It*:

'Blow, blow, thou winter wind,

Thou art not so unkind....'

And she added on her own:

'As a religious fanatic.'

Today she was thinking beyond the hard-line policy of the Muslim League. She dozed off in the middle of all these thoughts.

It is said that a person can fall asleep even while being taken to the gallows. Her extraordinary effort to save herself had tired her so greatly that she fell fast asleep lying on the stubble of harvested crops. She slept till well after daybreak. She woke up startled and shouting, 'Please have mercy, I am pregnant.'

She noticed that the sun was up and had even dried up the dew drops on her face. Her clothes were still wet and clinging to her body. She tried getting up but could not. It appeared as if a venomous snake had sucked the life out of her. Little did she know that she was entangled in the creepers growing on the field embankments. The feeling of being in danger forced her to gather all her strength and get up. She went and hid in the tall fodder crop close by. She saw passers-by carrying their looted items in broad daylight. The looters included both Hindus and Sikhs. Some of them who had lost their way passed very close to the field where she was hiding.

She could hear one of them saying, 'Let's target the fields owned by these bloody Muslims. We will take away the fodder crop tonight.'

'We have got enough loot already. There are several villages still left where Muslims need to be killed. We haven't been able to lay our hands on any woman till now,' replied another.

A third one added, 'Some of these Muslim women are like fairies.'

The first one responded, 'You are up to no good, Majha Singh. We are not going to spare even their crop of cattle fodder and are going to let our animals into the fields to have a free run. God has given us an opportunity to avenge the murder of the children of our Guru.'

Naseem realized that the cattle fodder fields, the abode of venomous snakes, were not safe for her. She thought, 'Who knows? They might start cutting the fodder crop even during the day.' She looked around and noticed that there was a hut near the well. When nobody was around, she ran and hid there. She had made a huge mistake but she had no other choice.

Throughout the day, she could see people carrying away the loot from the village. She could not come out of the hut. The humidity and the lack of ventilation inside had turned it into a furnace. She felt as if her body were made of wax and was melting. But she had no choice other than seeing her worst nightmares playing out in real life.

The unthinkable had happened. A line had been drawn dividing the land into two parts. On one side of the line was written 'Pakistan' and on the other was written 'Hindustan'. She was in 'Hindustan'. On the Pakistan side, the Sikh and Hindu women were being traded like sheep. The traders were poking them to assess their price. On the Hindustan side, Muslim girls were being paraded naked. On both sides there were people who were enjoying the barbarism.

In Pakistan, the Hindu and Sikh train travellers were not getting water to drink. In Hindustan, Muslim mothers were forced to give urine to their kids to save them from dying from thirst. In Pakistan, Hindu and Sikh children were pierced with spears and their mothers were made to walk behind them in a procession. In Hindustan, Muslim mothers were being raped in front of their children and Hindu–Sikh women were rejoicing at the sight.

Naseem was a fan of dark movies like *Cowboy* and *Dacoit*. The visuals in her nightmare were so horrific that these movies paled in comparison. She had never imagined that her nightmares would play out in real life. But the present situation was much worse than anything she had ever imagined. It appeared as if Hindustan and Pakistan were competing to surpass each other in terms of barbarism and cruelty. People on both sides seemed to have been overtaken by the Devil. Naseem dreamt that an old man with fiery eyes was poking her with red hot iron rods as she helplessly pleaded, 'Babaji, please don't do this to me. I am going to become a mother in five months.'

She was relieved that she woke up at this moment and the

chain of nightmares was broken. At the same time, she realized that there were unfortunate girls who had to live through these nightmares on both sides of the line drawn by a cruel foreigner. Muslims in Pakistan and Hindus–Sikhs in Hindustan had all lost humanity.

Naseem was no longer in her senses. Her throat had dried up due to the intense heat. She wanted to stick her tongue out like a dog. She wanted to escape from the heat of the hut near the well, but it was even more dangerous to step out.

Life is beautiful when you have hope. She finally stepped out despite her fears. She realized that it was late in the evening and that there was nobody around. Maybe the crowds would have moved to destroy another settlement. The pots used for drawing water from the well had dried up. She was desperately looking for water to drink. The Persian wheel used for drawing water from the well was too heavy for her to operate. Even if she had the strength to turn the Persian wheel, she could not do so as the noise would have attracted the attention of the looters. She drank some muddy water from a ditch close to the wheel and it seemed to her like the elixir of life. Little did she know that dogs usually drank water from that ditch. Even if she had known, it would not have mattered at that point of time.

Suddenly she heard somebody shout from the field next to where she was standing: 'Who is that? Please come and help me lift this fodder.'

Naseem stood still and thought for half a minute.

The person in the field shouted again, 'Why are you not coming? Who are you?'

Naseem started running blindly in the direction that she had come from the previous night. The person in the field pulled a sickle from the fodder that he had cut and ran around the standing crop. In her panicked state, Naseem could not understand what he was doing. She kept looking back to make sure that he was not following her. She was about to enter the next field when he came around and caught her.

'Who are you?' he asked again but did not get a response. Based on her looks and attire he guessed, 'Muslim?' Naseem did not respond to that question either. The Sikh pulled her by the arm. But she refused to get up. He again tried to pull her up with all his strength. She screamed and tried to fight him off, but the fear of the shining sickle in his hand forced her to sit down.

'You come with me or I will...' the Jat Sikh pointed the sickle at her chest and threatened. Naseem was not scared. She adjusted her clothes and attacked the Jat with all her might. He threw away the sickle and tried to control her using both his hands. However, Naseem proved to be tougher than he expected. The Jat had to struggle for more than five minutes before he managed to catch her right hand and twist it behind her back. But by then Naseem had already scratched his face several times and the thick hair from his beard was caught under her nails.

'So this fox is not easy to subdue,' the Jat said to himself loudly and hit Naseem hard in the waist with his right knee. Naseem fell to the ground but showed no signs of pain. As she lay helpless on the ground, the Jat ran to her and tied her hands with his turban. He then pointed his sickle at her and ordered her to get up. 'Please kill me, devil. I will be grateful to you, and it will be considered a mercy in the eyes of the Almighty,' Naseem cried lying on the ground.

'I will not harm you if you come with me. Otherwise, I will hit you so badly that you will remember the pain for the rest of your life,' he told Naseem sternly.

His intention was to keep the prize, the beautiful Naseem, all to himself. Naseem stayed where she was with her face buried in the ground. He pulled her by her hair and forced her to stand up. Her nose was bleeding.

'You better come with me,' he said, gruffly. At the same time, it appeared that he did not want anybody around to hear what was going on.

The sun had already set. Naseem had lost faith in humanity. She did not want to cry for help but instinctively she shrieked, 'Somebody please save me from this devil! For God's sake, please help!'

Her shrill voice finally reached the right ears. The demon threatened her: 'Beware! One more squeak out of you and I will pull out your intestines with this sickle.'

He did not know that Naseem was no longer scared of death. The only thing keeping her alive was the hope of being reunited with her husband. She did not move. Another blow from his knee landed on her back, and she almost fell. She regained her balance and stood straight again. The Jat hit her between the shoulder blades with the handle of his sickle. She did not move. The enraged devil held her by left arm and put his hand under her knees and lifted her. She was shouting and crying all this while.

Suddenly a stern voice came from the dark 'Don't you dare move.' There was a sardar standing in a corner of the field with a cloth tied around his face to hold his beard in place. However, he was not armed.

'Who are you to stop me?' demanded the kidnapper.

'That does not matter. You let her go,' replied the Sardar.

'So you can take her?' the kidnapper challenged. To gain his support and to make him a partner in his evil designs, the kidnapper mentioned, 'She is Muslim.'

The Sardar charged towards them. The kidnapper lowered the girl off his back and took the sickle in his hand to fight the Sardar.

'Look, Atma, one more step and I will send a bullet through you,' warned the Sardar. The kidnapper froze with fear. The Sardar held a pistol under his shirt and was ready to shoot.

'Mehar Singh, you are not doing the right thing. Don't forget that you are going to live here only. You will not be spared. You are not a true disciple of the Guru. You are protecting these bloody Muslims. Aren't you afraid of God? Oh! But you people don't believe in God,' replied the first Sikh, running scared like a dog with his tail between its legs but still barking and baring its teeth.

Naseem had realized that her saviour was an atheist. The words of her kidnapper assured her that this man would not harm her. She moved towards the Sardar. He untied Naseem's hands, and they started walking in the direction opposite to which the kidnapper had gone. The Sardar turned back and shouted at Atma, 'Pick up your turban. Don't be in such a hurry to run off.'

After walking some distance, Mehar Singh told Naseem, 'Bibi, we will have to take cover behind the crop in the fields and walk in the same direction that you came from. The Muslim camp is around five miles from here and now the marauders will chase us on horseback. These days every household has firearms, and we will have to be smart to escape from here. They will not be able to spot our footsteps in the dark. I hope you are not scared, my daughter.'

The respectful words like 'Bibi' and 'my daughter' used by Mehar Singh to address Naseem calmed her frayed nerves. She felt lighter as she walked along. She felt like a small girl again and imagined saying to Mehar Singh, 'Brother, I am not scared as long as you are with me.'

They walked in the opposite direction and went around the village towards the north. Late at night they reached another village. Mehar Singh knocked at the door of a mud house on the outskirts of the village. He had to knock several times before the door opened. An old Hindu gentleman stepped out. Even though it was pitch dark, looking at Naseem, he asked, 'Is she a Muslim Bibi?'

Mehar Singh confirmed and the old man told Naseem, 'Daughter, there is a cot in the next room. Please go and rest. I will send some milk for you to drink.'

Naseem drank milk to her heart's content and fell fast asleep. She did not want to wake up in the morning. She was probably dreaming of a life in heaven. She was given a cotton suit to wear and a sheet to cover herself. She was asked to wear a kada, an iron bracelet, usually worn by Sikh women. Mehar Singh and Naseem stepped out of the house at dawn. They walked through fields until they reached the main road. They stood on the road for some time as if they were expecting a lorry to arrive. Finally, Naseem, covered in the sheet, was asked to sit down. Mehar Singh had changed his appearance to look like a Jat farmer who had been ploughing his fields.

At last, they saw an army truck coming their way. Mehar Singh signalled with a torch light for the truck to stop. The truck had Muslim villagers and some Pakistan Army soldiers inside.

'Sister,' Mehar Singh told Naseem, 'come, they will take you to your destination.'

He looked at the army soldiers and said, 'She is the wife of Captain Waris Muhammed.'

Naseem was helped aboard the truck. A person on the truck shouted, 'Mehar Singh, you are surely going to be killed by your brethren.'

'That's all right, Zahoor, I don't fear getting killed for a noble cause.'

Zahoordin was considered a kafir and atheist among the Muslims of the area. Naseem had already heard about him.

The truck started moving.

'Brother, we will meet again,' Naseem shouted as she waved to Mehar Singh.

And the whole way she was thinking to herself: what kind of kafirs were these?

Finally, there was the sunrise.

Translated by Amaninder Singh Dhindsa

THE MOSCOW GIRL

BALWANT GARGI

'Just show me a glimpse of the Moscow night,' I said to the stout, well-built Russian interpreter who spoke fluent English.

'What do you mean by glimpse of the night?' She asked.

'I mean the taverns here where people drink and dance all night.'

'Why do you want to meet the alkies in particular?'

'This is what we call life,' I replied. 'It is denser and more intense at the bottom. On the surface it's all froth.'

'Well, you want to see Russians stumbling and falling!'

'Yes, I have always seen them in high spirits so far. Let me see how they fall also.'

'You can't make a fair assessment of our country like this.'

'My assessment of this country can be complete only this way.'

I did not go to the theatre that evening. My interpreter went home early and I walked out into the streets for a stroll.

The sun had plunged in the west. Kremlin fort dominated the copper-tinged sky. The Red Star glowed on its minaret. It was the month of September. The scent of walnut trees and the fresh aroma of apricots and apples laced the air. Some women were selling flowers at a corner of Hotel Moskva. Young college girls, their hair in braids, were sucking on ice lollies. People sitting in the small coffee houses along the way were enjoying their coffee.

I wandered about here and there, walking past well-bedecked shop windows and attempting to read signboards written in Russian. The aroma of spices wafted out of a cafe. My nostrils flared a little; it was the aroma of Asian kebabs. It was Baku

Restaurant. I went in and handed my overcoat to an old man in charge of the cloakroom. This scarlet mouthed man, with a handlebar moustache twirled into points at the ends, led me to the basement of the cafe. The stairs were sticky and the air looked murky yellow and smelt spicy. The clinking of spoons and cups, and the mild, tinkling laughter of women and boisterous guffaws of men could be heard outside. Black-eyed and black-haired young girls attired in long robes served as waiters there. I sat at a table that was already occupied by three other men. The tablecloth was stained with liquor and gravy. The fragrance of fried fish and gusts of hot air escaped from the kitchen. I ordered a rice plate, two lula kebabs, and a glass of wine. I ate with a relaxed mood, drank my wine, lit a cigarette, and stepped out of the cafe.

Smoking my cigarette, I started walking on the broad pedestrian path under the trees. The faces of people looked purple in the blue electric glow of the street lights. Laughing merrily, various couples promenaded arm in arm on the pathway.

A hefty man with a salt and pepper stubble came up to me and tapped on my shoulder hard. He mumbled something in Russian. I stepped back, saying, 'No no, twarash!' He left. Walking a little ahead he did the same to a bulky woman. She stood at an ice cream stall, arms akimbo. She brushed his hand off her shoulder and the man staggered away. Two women walked past, scowling at me. They held hands with fingers clasped. Who were they? I was surprised—maybe they are some collegians returning from the theatre. A pink-faced girl wearing a green skirt and a wide-bordered straw hat approached me. She said something hastily. I replied to her only with, 'Thanks.'

She came closer to me, gave me a little peck on my cheek, and went away, shrugging her shoulders.

I kept strolling, thinking about life in Moscow, looking at the people and enjoying their laughter. I stopped under a tree to light another cigarette. A man alone finds companionship with a cigarette, otherwise he feels like a lamb separated from the herd. A light breeze was blowing.

Two young women came towards me. One of them was wearing a floral bracelet while the other had big earrings in her ears. They stopped near me. The one with the bracelet nudged the other lightly, said something in Russian and laughed heartily. The one with the big earrings said something that I didn't understand. When I looked at her blankly, she guffawed and asked, 'You don't know Russian?'

'No,' I shook my head.

The bracelet woman smiled and looked at me intently as she began to walk away. I strung together some Russian words in order to speak to her.

'From Italy?'

'No, from India.'

'India? Wow!' She cheered up at the very mention of India.

I offered her a cigarette. She looked carefully at the cigarette packet, smelt it, took one, and lit it with my cigarette. She puffed a few times and said, 'Spasiba (Thanks).'

She entwined her arm with mine and started walking with me. Four young men passed by. They gave me a disdainful look. I withdrew my arm from hers. She raised her face and murmured, 'Ya lyu blyu vas (I love you).'

I got a whiff of alcohol from her mouth or maybe it was the smell of raw apples. In the blue light her red lips looked maroon. Her curly hair had a whitish tinge. She was a plump and buxom woman. Her top button was undone. Her neck, shoulders, and tanned cleavage were clearly visible. She was a strange woman. What interaction could I have with her without knowing even the alphabet of her language? Desire oozed from her eyes, mouth, and cleavage. It oozed from each and every limb of her body. She pressed my hand every now and then and said, 'I love you.'

A constable looked at me with a piercing look. But we kept walking.

Once we reached the corner of a park near Bolshoi Theatre I felt very embarrassed. I was the focus of so many eyes. How strange must a foreigner look walking arm in arm with a Russian woman! Her big earrings—the type gypsy women wear—particularly irritated me. I've seen French prostitutes—well-dressed and their hair held back in a ponytail. They can be seen roaming the streets wearing open-necked chequered coats and tight trousers, their feet in golden slippers. I had also seen sex workers in London. They would stand under the lamp post in Hyde Park wearing bright lipstick and rouge on their cheeks. Their sharp eyes glow with the fire of mischief and desire. They are very good at their profession and direct enough to ask, 'Do you want to enjoy, mister?'

Then they will strike a bargain with you in a very matter-of-fact-way. They will make clear their terms and conditions with the adroitness of a salesperson. But this Moscow girl seemed different. She did not have the glamour of the English or French sex workers. Nor did she appear to be as dexterous in this art as they are. She was essentially Asian—hot, sizzling, and hard. She drew me to her and then began moving leftwards. Her lips were shining and a tiny speck of saliva gleamed at one corner of her lips like a ray of moonlight.

'Where are you taking me?' I asked.

Signalling towards the street corner she said, 'There, towards Moskva River.'

Should I go with her to the Moskva River bank for a stroll in the dark? This very thought bewildered me. Why was that constable looking at me with suspicion? Why had an old woman carrying a bagful of turnips turned to look at me with her piercing eyes?

'Come with me. You are a very nice guy. Come, why are you thinking so much?' she insisted.

I pulled my hand away from hers and said, 'No, thanks. I can't go with you.'

Saying this, I ran away from her. Crossing the road, I started walking on the boulevard where there were a large number of people.

There I met three of my French comrades also staying at Moskva Hotel. They called out to me affectionately and we started talking about the pleasant weather and beautiful theatres of Moscow.

'The air in Moscow is as crisp as the French biscuits. I feel like taking a bite out of it,' said one of them.

'This evening in Moscow, wow! But these blue lights are very irritating. The ice cream in Moscow is really very yummy. Red Square looks very big in pictures but in reality, it is not. Life is very colourful here.' We laughed and chatted like this....

Suddenly I felt a tap on my shoulder. I turned back to find that it was that girl. She had noticed me crossing to the other side of the road. Having looked for me here and there, she had finally found me.

All three French friends of mine laughed at this. One of them knew a little bit of Russian. He started talking to her. But she did not respond at all. She just screwed up her nose and, punching me on the shoulder said, 'Come.'

The tall young Frenchman winked at me and said, 'Go, bro, she has developed a liking for you!' And he laughed, exposing his horse-like teeth.

They left. The woman and I started walking along a hedge near the park. I took out a pack of cigarettes from my pocket and offered one to her. She looked irritated, then snatched the pack from my hand and thrust it into her pocket. She gave me one cigarette.

'How greedy!' I thought.

After some time, she asked where I was staying.

'Hotel Moskva,' I said.

She held my arm tight as we walked slowly. Time and again she would close her eyes and rub her cheek on my shoulder. I touched her earrings and asked whether they were real or artificial. Perhaps they were artificial like her. Hmm…. It means prostitutes are roaming about in Moscow also. I started wondering what had forced her to resort to this means of livelihood. It could be greed rather than need. The need to get rich quickly is a human weakness after all. Just see how she grabbed my cigarette pack.

She stopped near a lamppost and draped her arms around me. I could not put up with this in full public view. So, I shook her arms off at once. But she kept standing there. I thought she was not going to leave me without earning some money. After all, I was a state guest of Soviet Russia, and a foreigner. So, I did not want to be caught in a mess. Being unfamiliar with the language of this country, I could not understand anything. I rummaged in my pockets and gave her a fifty-rouble note that had Lenin's photograph on it saying,

'Take this and leave now.'

She shook her arm violently and said in exasperation, 'Nyet nyet. (No, no.)'

I looked at her in embarrassment. What was she saying? Did she want more money? Perhaps she did not think fifty roubles was sufficient. She could not buy even a pair of shoes with that. Then I offered her a hundred-rouble note but she crumpled the note and thrust it into my pocket. Her face was strained. She was annoyed. I kept walking with her silently.

A couple came around the corner. They sat on a bench. I stopped near them. The woman had tied her hair with a red handkerchief while the man wore a loose yellow necktie. I told them that I wanted to go to Moskva Hotel.

The man looked up. He knew a little bit of English.

'What do you want?' this was what he meant in his broken English. The girl accompanying me said something to him and they started talking to each other. I could understand only some Russian words like 'krasiva' (beautiful), 'Indiski' (Indian), and 'da… da…da…' (ha…ha…ha…).

The man looked at me and said, 'Your friend likes you very much.'

'But what does she want from me?' I asked.

They both continued talking in Russian.

Again I caught only some words like Indiski, Nehru, spasiba, Raj Kapoor, krasiva, and a few others.

The man told me, 'She works in a bakery. When Pandit Nehru had come to Russia, she had prepared a special cake for him. She has seen Raj Kapoor only in films. She has seen India also through films. She loves India. You have come from India— the land of Nehru and Raj Kapoor. So, she wants to walk with you on the riverbank so that she can proudly tell her colleagues in the bakery that she had a stroll with an Indian. She simply wants to kiss an Indian. For her it would be as good as kissing Nehru or Raj Kapoor.'

I looked at her. Her face radiated in the pale bluish light of the distant lamps. I embraced her lovingly and kissed her.

She took out my cigarette packet from her pocket and gave it back to me, saying something that clearly meant that smoking is injurious to health. That is why I snatched it from you, she seemed to say.

I took my cigarette pack from her, and walking slowly, I reached my hotel.

The next day, as I came down from my room in the twilight hour to leave for the theatre, an old employee of the hotel said, 'Comrade, a woman has left this cake for you.'

It was a very big round cake with the words 'For my darling India' piped on top with frosting.

Translated by Parvesh Sharma

MAJHA IS NOT DEAD

KARTAR SINGH DUGGAL

Majha is engaged in a monologue with his horse.

'Come, puttar! Your harness is ready. Let me fasten your belly band. Why is your harness becoming looser day by day? Are you becoming weak? No, my friend, don't leave me in the lurch. You know that last year Karmi, my wife, left for her heavenly abode. But somehow I adjusted to that loss. I don't care about anybody else so long as you stand by me. Anyhow, she had a habit of going to visit our son and daughter-in-law very often. Is this how a sensible wife behaves? Come, puttar, I have to worry about your food also. God willing, I will definitely give you masala* today. I had promised it to you yesterday…and the day before also but couldn't keep my word. But don't worry, God willing, I will today. This normal fodder doesn't have any nutritional value at all. Although, even the masala we get these days is not as good as it used to be.

'In those days, I mean in your mother's time…what to say of that! Sometimes, while feeding masala to your mother I also used to savour some of it myself. While it was being eaten by your mother, its aroma would whet my own appetite. The pungent odour of the masala would emanate all day from your mother's body. While rubbing her down in the evening I would put my nose to her body so as to smell it properly. O my Neelam Pari—my Sapphire Fairy! It was I who had given her this name. Perhaps I have told you earlier also that Neelam was so clean that she

---

*A special dietary additive for horses with ingredients like rock salt and thyme.

would not let a single fly sit on her...and now these flies are a constant menace to you.

'Come, puttar, start walking in the name of Allah. I have heard that a large number of firangis are in the city today. Look, I have adorned the seats with new covers; see how the tonga is shining today. You heard what Bhalwan was saying? He said, "Majha, your tonga is in perfect condition. Most of the tongas look worn down but yours still has the same sturdy and strong feel."

'Just see, puttar, how its bell resounds. Just one peal is enough to startle anyone when they first hear it.

'Look! See how that sardar has stopped and is looking at your tonga; he is surprised that a bell like ours can still be heard today. And, what a beautiful rubber-tyre Peshawari tonga! See how it glides, whispering to the wind. I have never let any rickshaw overtake me. The rickshaw pullers tire out their legs while I can even leave behind good scooters. I defy anyone to come and race with me on King's Way, the imperial avenue.

'Stop a little, puttar, we have a red signal ahead. This red light is a new problem created by the government. It gets switched on even though there is no vehicle in sight. What is the rationale here? So, hold on. Don't be hasty. The red signal will be followed by yellow and then green. Only then shall we move. We shall pass by Bangla Sahib and then after paying obeisance there we shall bow our heads at the masjid of the pir. Then we shall go to Curzon Road. These firangis, particularly their wives, the madams, are very fond of travelling by tonga. Today, I will erase all your complaints. Who else have I to look after? It is only the two of us—you and I. You eat as much masala as you like today, I won't stop you.

'Now the yellow signal is on. So, push forward, otherwise the motorists will not let you pass. You keep moving, let them blow their horns. This is not a tonga; this is a Rolls-Royce. Lo! We have crossed. Had you been lazy and not moved in time we would have got stuck there. It has happened several times earlier. Often the line of vehicles has not crossed by the time the red signal appears again. This often happens in Connaught Place. That is why I normally don't come here. I don't want to deal with traffic lights.

'Salute Bangla Sahib. Yes, like this—bow your head! It is always rewarding. Nobody returns empty handed from here. In the evening, don't you see how many big cars are parked here! Rich ladies decked in gold come here in big luxurious cars to pay homage at the shrine. They go back fully blessed. Now bow your head at the masjid also. Well done! Some say Bangla Sahib has great power while others say the same about the masjid of the pir. We have been to both places. So, puttar, now gallop to the destination. Madam with bare legs is waiting for you.

'Puttar, you know, once…I think I didn't share this with you. It was a long time ago. Those were the days of war and curfew. You had not yet been born! I was returning home one evening. It was a pitch-black winter night. You couldn't even see your own hand. At this very crossing—the meeting point of Jai Singh Road and Ashoka Road—a young woman hailed my tonga. She was drunk. She was dressed in a mini skirt and smoking heavily, taking long drags from her cigarette. She asked me for a lift, but I declined; I was going to my house, tired and exhausted. But she jumped into the tonga—sat in the front seat next to me. She took your mother's reins from me and drove the tonga with the dexterity of a professional tonga-driver, as though she had done that all her life! Your mother rose to the occasion and did herself proud. The woman drove the tonga behind the Birla temple and up to the top of the hill. O God! What a woman she was! And when I dropped her off and reached home, my wife pounced on me and began interrogating me. Why were my clothes reeking of the perfume of a woman? I deem myself very talkative but that day I was fumbling for the right words. She kept hitting me with her chappal and I put up with it meekly.

'Come, puttar, this lady is not going to be our passenger. She is just looking at us. This is how these people are. They can wait for a whole hour for the bus but will never sit in a tonga. With this kind of miserliness, they save a little bit of money and then they fritter it away in Chandni Chowk on cosmetics, lipstick, and face powder. Or, they prefer an autorickshaw, which is more fashionable. Those are very bumpy vehicles and thus very uncomfortable. They shake up your insides. Once I took an auto but got off after a short ride. It is far better to walk than ride in an autorickshaw.

'Cycle rickshaws are also in vogue in old Delhi. I think it is just like carrying a man on your shoulders. The rickshaw puller, poor man, is drenched in perspiration while the passenger sits in the back comfortably. I would never ride in one. Much better to walk. It really is torture for the rickshaw puller. You see what man has to do to make a living. I have heard that most of the rickshaw pullers suffer from piles. What else can be the result of such a physically demanding job?

'On the other hand, the tonga is a royal vehicle. During your mother's time, a beautiful courtesan named Balo sat in my tonga. People nearly fainted on seeing her captivating beauty. You see for yourself, puttar, is this ever possible in a taxi or an autorickshaw? As she got down in the evening after her outing, she said to me, "Majha, I don't feel like getting down from your tonga," and thrust a ten-rupee note in my hand as she left.

'Lo, puttar! While talking we have already reached our destination. If I don't share my feelings with you, I start feeling uneasy. I used to talk to your mother too. She would understand what I meant even before I completed my sentence. She understood every sign I made. She was very sympathetic. She would become sad in my sadness and happy in my happiness. Once I fell ill and she gave up eating her fodder for a few days. On my part, I also treated her well. I massage your coat also but the way I massaged hers was something unique. My wife used to be jealous and thought of her as a rival. She and your mother did not get on with each other.

'See, the passenger is coming to us. Didn't I say that I would keep my word today? While the firangis are in the city for just ten days we might be able to earn enough for the whole year!

'Oh, he has signalled the cab. These cabmen are another nuisance for us. Anyway, I have nothing against them. Taxi is a gentlemanly mode of travel. No doubt they fleece the passengers. Okay. So let those who want to be looted like this hire the taxi.

'Puttar! Let us wait under this neem tree. Relax here until some policeman comes to shoo us away. Even the sentry won't be a problem. A little bit of grease in his palm will shut his mouth also. Majha has come across many such officials. Everybody can be bought. Pay the price and then walk away even after committing daylight robbery if you wish. Just look! Think of the devil and the policeman appears. Let him come. Majha doesn't bother about such constables. But, puttar, why are you standing with your hoof twisted? Your shoe is troubling you, I think. Oh, it's not there at all. Maybe it has fallen somewhere. First of all, let me get it for you otherwise your hoof will get hurt. Come, puttar, let's get it done first.'

'Why, Majha? Why have you turned your back at the very sight of me?'

'No no, havaldar sahib, nothing of the sort. My horse has lost its shoe somewhere. I noticed it well in time otherwise it would have damaged his hoof in a big way.'

'You have never been of any use to me. I wanted you to drop me off at Parliament Street Police Station.'

'I have just come from there, havaldar sahib. I would never have said no to you sir. But now I am going to the farrier for shoeing my horse. This expenditure has suddenly emerged early in the morning today.'

'I know you have to get it done in Paharganj, I am going halfway there.'

'You are welcome on my tonga then. We will be going a little slow. My horse has become very delicate and ease-loving these days. Let today's bohni, my first income of the day, come from you.'

'Majha, you won't stop annoying me. I could also have my bohni by challaning your tonga for having parked under the neem tree.'

'O sir, I was just kidding. I can't banter like this with the autorickshaw people who drive so rashly through the city.'

'I have always set everybody straight this way.'

'Havaldar sahib, just tell me if these taxi men also fall into your net sometimes.'

'Whether cabman or tonga driver, whosoever lands in the police net has to pay the price.'

'The drivers have become degenerate these days.'

'Thousands of men are coming for a conference. That is why this new building has been constructed on Curzon Road and one thousand more licenses have been authorized for taxis in Delhi city. My duty is on Curzon Road.'

'Then it's a golden opportunity for you to feast your eyes on the naked legs of the madams and fleece the cabmen at the same time.'

'For us there is no difference between taxi and tonga. Well, Majha, drop me here. I will walk up to the police station.'

'As you wish, sir.'

'But, Majha, what is wrong with you? You have not even offered me a bidi today.'

'O sorry, havaldar sahib. I have lost my wits today. Here, please take it. I only keep bidis for guests like you.'

'Okay, Majha. Keep up the cheerful spirit! But avoid parking on the road. Inspectors are always on the prowl these days like rabid dogs.'

'Now you see, puttar. The bastard got a free lift, smoked one of my bidis, and then showed that he had the upper hand! "Don't park the tonga under the neem tree," he says. Should I park it between his mother's legs then? There are taxi stands for cabmen. Telephone facility is also provided to them. But nobody cares for the tonga drivers just because a tonga ride has gone out of vogue these days. People think it wastes too much time. Puttar, I wonder what people do with the time they save with all this hectic running around. They keep standing for hours together in the queues of cinema houses, post offices, or milk booths. On the one hand, they save time and on the other, they waste it like this. They are rushing about throughout the day and then waste their time in hotels and clubs in the evening. Oh, why have I indulged in thinking about such useless things? What is it to me? Puttar, here, we have reached Bhalwan's shop. Let us first get your shoe fitted.'

'Salaam, Bhalwan ji.'

'Walekum, Majha, you see now that my word came true?'

'Bhalwan ji, it was bound to be true. We have always treated you as an ustad and you were right.'

'I had asked you to replace all the shoes if even one is lost.'

'Agreed, Bhalwan ji.'

'Man too has a fixed age. Obviously, if one shoe is lost, the others too must be due for replacement.'

'One was lost last week and today the second one is gone.'

'Now, get the other two also replaced.'

'I wonder how the shoes wear out when we don't get enough passengers.'

'God takes care of our daily bread also.'

'But why does Majha always have to suffer?'

'O Majha, why do you worry about anything when this son of yours is with you.'

'He says I need not worry as long as you are with me,' Majha is talking to his horse again, 'why, puttar, shouldn't I have any worries? Bhalwan has taken his own time, it's well past noon. But he does a very good job. It is a joy to watch him! Come, puttar, let us go past the bus stand. So many people are waiting for the bus. Maybe someone will get fed up and actually take our tonga…and we can at least offset the expenditure on the shoes. No, they won't move. The ladies these days may dry up in the heat waiting for the bus but will never even look at the tonga. I can't shout out to call them. However, I have rung the bell. If no one has responded to your bell, nobody will come. So just keep moving. Sometimes, one or two passengers step in from Gol Market. This is the time of day when the wives of officers return home after making miscellaneous purchases. Most of them are Bengali women holding jars of rasgullas in their hands. Their speech is as sweet as the dish. I had met such a Bengali lady one day under that tree. O my God! She was huge! Must have been about one quintal in weight at least. She said, rather insisted, that she would pay only eight annas to go to Ashoka Road. That is the usual fare. I assessed whether the tonga could bear such a load. Then I whispered to her, "Okay, sit in the back but don't look at my horse." As soon as she put her foot in the tonga it lifted from the front due to her weight! So I had to sit on the wooden frame of my vehicle to balance it. Perched in this hazardous manner, I travelled up to Ashoka Road. Sometimes you have to risk a lot for the sake of passengers.

'Lo, autorickshaws are parked here under every tree. They carry a lot of luggage along with passengers. For money, they serve as pick-up vehicles also. No, puttar, we have no chance here. You see how a passenger has silently entered the autorickshaw. He is reading the meter. They are also right. Just read the kilometres covered from the meter and pay what it adds up to. They don't have to waste energy haggling.

'Come, puttar, let's go to our own stand. Look, a gentleman is signalling a rickshaw driver. For these people, sitting in a tonga is demeaning. To hell with them! Nobody can deprive us of our morsel of bread.

'Well, I was talking of bargaining. This too is not everybody's cup of tea. Most of them do it in a very aggressive manner. For example: "I will pay one-and-a-half rupees only. If that's acceptable to you, then fine, otherwise go your way." During those days the one who wished to pay one-and-half rupees would start with one rupee. We also knew he would stop at one-and-half-rupees. So we began with two rupees and ultimately the deal was struck at one-and-half rupees. To arrive at this amount we would talk of market prices, the current news in the papers, weather conditions, Hindu–Muslim amity, etc. Everybody has his or her own way of bargaining. Some passengers start bargaining from where they stand while some others come close and start talking by holding onto the hood. Some others will get into the tonga and then start…. There are those who will bargain after the tonga has already started moving. There is also a category of passenger which does it after reaching their destination. Such passengers shell out the fare as they see fit but then keep adding to it, taking coins of different denominations out of their pocket. The tonga driver is always out to charge a little extra while the passenger feels content if they save a little.

'Puttar, do you want water? Are you thirsty? You must drink a little even if you are not thirsty. It is not easy to find pastures these days. You have to walk a mile before coming to one. Earlier, there was something by the side of every road or street corner. During the British regime there used to be residential quarters for tonga drivers. The accommodation was not sufficient for all but at least they cared about us. Now nobody cares for tonga drivers. These scooterists have created a lot of trouble for us. If they are in a good mood, the Bhapas of Rawalpindi take the passenger free of charge also. On the way, they may take pleasure in talking sweetly to the lady passengers. Or else they pilfer something from the passenger's belongings while offloading their luggage.

'By Allah! Majha has never done such a thing in his life. Once a passenger's full purse slipped out of his pocket onto the tonga seat. It gave me a sleepless night. The first thing I did the next morning was return the purse to the owner. The man was fast asleep. He had fainted at the very thought of having lost the purse. I could hardly restrain my laughter at the sight! Another time a maulana left a wooden casket with jewellery in my tonga. His daughter's wedding was in progress at home. He had offloaded everything including the bundle of clothes, sacks of flour, dal, and utensils. But on reaching home he realized that the casket was nowhere to be found. The maulana was terrified. A cloud of grief swept over the house because of the loss of the jewellery. That night I went back to their house and handed over the casket to its owners. One time a woman, seemingly of loose morals, with a brood of young children like a litter of puppies, came to sit in my tonga. Settling her toddler to sleep on the front seat, she sat with her kids in the back of the vehicle. When she got off in the falling twilight, she took all her children with her but overlooked the youngest lying asleep on the front seat. Getting off the tonga I collected the fare from her and went to a kiosk to buy bidis and paan. As I returned to the tonga, I found to my astonishment that the child was still comfortably asleep on the front seat.

'See, puttar, we have reached our destination while engaged in conversation. There must be a passenger around here. In the meantime, you eat something, have some fodder. I remember I have to give you masala by this evening. This is my promise. Have some hay now, you must be hungry. It is going to be dark soon. Let me smoke a bidi.

'Oh…no passenger so far? Perhaps I dozed off. It's because of this weather. When winter is about to leave and summer is round the corner, I feel very sleepy. Maybe some passenger came and found me asleep. There is very little chance that no passenger came in all this time.

'Doesn't matter. If a passenger did come by in the last few minutes, others will definitely come as well. Nobody can snatch the bread that's destined for us. Look, some people have come out

of the courts. They look like tonga passengers. Looks like they will
hire the tonga for a long journey. They look like the passengers of
Shahdara or Mehrauli. Even a single round will make us enough to
buy rotis for the whole day. Oh! They have turned towards the bus
stand. The bus is also visible…see, they have boarded the bus. It is
already overstuffed but still people prefer taking the bus. Had they
given me as much fare as they are giving to the bus conductor, I
would have taken them to their destination comfortably. The bus
takes the passengers from the bus stop and drops them at a bus
stop. On the other hand, the tonga can enter the narrow lanes
and drop passengers right at their doorstep.

'You are feeling uneasy, puttar? You are right to feel like this.
The shadows are disappearing and no passenger came even today.
Our people don't sit in the tonga these days. A white-skinned
man will come and make up the day-long loss.

'Do you see how much smoke these buses belch out? It
looks like a jet of smoke is being released. Puttar, your mother
never defecated on tarred roads. How can these dunces know the
value of tongas? I won't take any Indian passenger in the future.

'The shadows are waning.

'Why do I feel so tired today, puttar? You too look very sad
to me, puttar. I know your legs ache. You don't feel as tired while
running or standing as you do when you wait all day. Puttar,
you must be thinking that I am addicted to smoking bidis. But
unlike other tonga drivers, I don't smoke sulfa and ganja. You
know all about the drugs tonga drivers are addicted to. I have
never even touched ganja or tasted liquor. I hate opium. What
I am addicted to is the cheapest thing in the market, the bidi.
Bhalwan said horse shit is stuffed in my brand of bidi. If that is
true, so be it. Who will smoke horse shit if not a tonga driver?
The cabmen drink liquor which is said to have the blood of
male goats. Let me not lie, by Allah. I had a drink only once.
It was when your mother was alive. I had wet your mother's
nostrils also with a cotton swab. Intoxicated, she had closed her

eyes. She was happy in my happiness. My wife would disagree with me over some things, but not your mother. She respected the will of her master.

'Lo, the shadows have waned now and immediately night descends. I should worry about the lights. I had them filled with oil only yesterday. If you start putting oil in the lamp while the passenger is there it wastes time. No one can tell when death or a passenger will come! It can happen at any time.

'See, a passenger is coming.

'No, the taxi driver has usurped him.

'That madam will come. No, she has been picked up by that gentleman who came from behind in his car.

'Hordes of people are coming out of that gate. Everybody is turning towards the taxi stand or their own vehicles are waiting for them.

'They will come. The mother and child are by themselves, and they are coming this way.

'No! They have hailed an auto. The whites too seem to be impoverished these days. They take an auto. Going by auto is a sign of poverty, puttar.

'Let me turn away from that side. I have observed that if you keep waiting for the passenger with your eyes wide open, nobody will come.

'Puttar, you look very sad and irritable today. I will definitely feed you masala today. This is my promise. Masala definitely today....

'Lo, passengers have come and sat down in the tonga. Didn't I tell you they would come when I stopped looking for them? Come, puttar!'

'Well, Connaught Place, sahib?'

'No, we want to go to Lodhi Garden.'

'Come puttar, speed up. Fly to his destination....'

'We are not in a hurry. You can move at ease, tonga man.'

The passenger was not familiar with their language. The Indian girl accompanying him was directing Majha.

The tonga must have gone a few yards on the road when Majha turned to look back at the passengers. He had never done this before. He thought that the girl looked familiar, that maybe he had seen her before.

'No no, all girls with short hair look alike these days,' he thought. They wear the same lipstick, same rouge on the cheeks, their hair is shoulder length and the locks partly cover the forehead and ears. The horse was galloping. After all, these were his first passengers since morning that day. Darkness was no obstacle for the steed. The tonga was running majestically with its metal bell ringing all the way.

'Hey, tonga man, don't be in such a hurry. We have all night....'

Once again the voice sounded familiar to him and Majha looked questioningly at her. She was in the arms of her white friend. Her kohl-lined eyes were beautiful under her slanting eyebrows and the locks of hair curled on her forehead. He was certain he knew this voice.

Then he recalled, in astonishment, 'If I am not wrong, isn't she Roy Sahib's daughter?' Meanwhile she spoke again: 'Tonga man, keep going at a slow pace. We want to keep you for the whole night. You can demand any fare you want.'

Yes, it was her. For a moment the reins of the horse fell from his hands as he recognized her. Majha began to sweat. At last he said, 'Beti, you belong to Delhi, I think...?'

'Yeah, of course...'

'You live on Hailey Road?'

'Yeah!'

'You are the daughter of Roy Sahib Kishori Lal....'

'Yeah, I'm the daughter of Roy Sahib.'

In a drunken state, the girl took the cigarette from her white friend and took a deep drag.

Majha pulled the reins of the horse at once and stopped the tonga.

'Get off my tonga.'

'But why?'

'Propriety demands that you get down immediately.' Majha's eyes were red with rage.

'Here? On this desolate road?'

'Yes. I tell you I will not take you in my tonga.'

Before an irate Majha could say anything else, the girl mumbled something to her companion in English, and they got down from the tonga. Arm in arm they headed towards the taxi stand which was quite a distance from there. Within a few minutes, they faded into the darkness.

Majha kept looking in their direction as if turned to stone. Then he shook the reins of the tonga and turned towards his house. He began talking to the horse again.

'Puttar, you know who this girl was? But how can you know? Had it been your mother she would have recognized her immediately. She is Police Superintendent Roy Sahib Kishori Lal's daughter. When she was younger, I used to take her to school in the morning and then in the evening bring her back in this very tonga. She used my tonga from her first class to the tenth. Her school was not nearby; she studied in Birla Mandir School. A tender young creature! She would sit stone-faced in the tonga without looking this way or that. I recall that when she grew up, her father asked me to put curtains on both sides of the tonga. I said no one can even dare to cast an evil eye at Majha's passenger. O God! Was this the same Lily! Livleen? What has gone wrong with the world? The world is on fire...truly....'

Thus, grumbling and complaining about the ways of the world he returned to his dera, home, empty-handed and hungry.

'Puttar, even today I couldn't keep my promise. I remain a liar.' As he unhitched the horse and removed the bit from his mouth, the horse started gently licking the hand of its master.

Translated by Parvesh Sharma

STENCH OF KEROSENE

AMRITA PRITAM

Outside, a mare neighed. Guleri recognized the neighing and ran out of the house. The mare was from her parents' village. She put her head against its neck as if it were the door of her father's house.

Guleri's parents lived in Chamba. A few miles from her husband's village, which was on high ground, the road curved and descended steeply downhill. From this point one could see Chamba lying a long way away at one's feet. Whenever Guleri was homesick, she would take her husband Manak and go up to this point. She would see the homes of Chamba twinkling in the sunlight and would come back with her heart aglow with pride.

Once every year, after the harvest had been gathered in, Guleri was allowed to spend a few days with her parents. They sent a man to Lakarmandi to bring her back to Chamba. Two of her friends, who were also married to boys outside Chamba, came home at the same time of the year. The girls looked forward to this annual meeting when they spent many hours every day talking about their experiences, their joys and sorrows. They went about the streets together. Then there was the harvest festival. The girls would have new dresses made for the occasion. They would have their dupattas dyed, starched, and sprinkled with mica. They would buy glass bangles and silver earrings.

Guleri always counted the days to the harvest. When autumn breezes cleared the skies of the monsoon clouds she thought of little besides her home in Chamba. She went about her daily chores—fed the cattle, cooked food for her husband's parents, and then sat back to work out how long it would be before someone would come for her from her parents' village.

And now, once again, it was time for her annual visit. She caressed the mare joyfully, greeted her father's servant, Natu, and made ready to leave the next day.

Guleri did not have to put her excitement into words: the expression on her face was enough. Her husband, Manak, pulled at his chillum and closed his eyes. It seemed either as if he did not like the tobacco, or that he could not bear to face his wife.

'You will come to the fair at Chamba, won't you? Come even if it is only for the day,' she pleaded.

Manak put aside his chillum but did not reply.

'Why don't you answer me?' asked Guleri in a temper. 'Shall I tell you something?'

'I know what you are going to say: "I only go to my parents once in the year!" Well, you have never been stopped before.'

'Then why do you want to stop me this time?' she demanded.

'Just this time,' pleaded Manak.

'Your mother has not said anything. Why do you stand in my way?' Guleri was childishly stubborn.

'My mother....' Manak did not finish his sentence.

On the long-awaited morning, Guleri was ready long before dawn. She had no children and, therefore, no problem of either having to leave them with her husband's parents or taking them with her. Natu saddled the mare as she took leave of Manak's parents. They patted her head and blessed her.

'I will come with you for a part of the way,' said Manak.

Guleri was happy as they set out. Under her dupatta she hid Manak's flute.

After the village of Khajiar, the road descended steeply to Chamba. There Guleri took out the flute from beneath her dupatta and gave it to Manak. She took Manak's hand in hers and said, 'Come now, play your flute!' But Manak, lost in his thoughts, paid no heed. 'Why don't you play your flute?' asked Guleri coaxingly. Manak looked at her sadly. Then, putting the flute to his lips, he blew a strange anguished wail of sound.

'Guleri, do not go away,' he begged her. 'I ask you again, do not go this time.' He handed her back the flute, unable to continue.

'But why?' she asked. 'You come over on the day of the fair and we will return together. I promise you, I will not stay behind.'

Manak did not ask again.

They stopped by the roadside. Natu took the mare a few paces ahead to leave the couple alone. It crossed Manak's mind that it was at this time of year, seven years ago, that he and his friends had come on this very road to go to the harvest festival in Chamba. And it was at this fair that Manak had first seen Guleri and they had bartered their hearts to each other. Later, managing to meet alone, Manak remembered taking her hand and telling her, 'You are like unripe corn—full of milk.'

'Cattle go for unripe corn,' Guleri had replied, freeing her hand with a jerk. 'Human beings like it better roasted. If you want me, go and ask for my hand from my father.'

Amongst Manak's kinsmen it was customary to settle the bride price before the wedding. Manak was nervous because he did not know the price Guleri's father would demand from him. But Guleri's father was prosperous and had lived in cities. He had sworn that he would not take money for his daughter, but would give her to a worthy young man of a good family. Manak, he had decided, answered these requirements and very soon after, Guleri and Manak were married. Deep in memories, Manak was roused by Guleri's hand on his shoulder.

'What are you dreaming of?' she teased him.

Manak did not answer. The mare neighed impatiently and Guleri, thinking of the journey ahead of her, rose to leave. 'Do you know the bluebell wood a couple of miles from here?' she asked. 'It is said that anyone who goes through it becomes deaf.'

'Yes.'

'It seems to me that you have passed through the bluebell

wood; you do not hear anything that I say.'

'You are right, Guleri. I cannot hear anything that you are saying to me,' replied Manak with a deep sigh.

Both of them looked at each other. Neither understood the other's thoughts.

'I will go now. You had better return home. You have come a long way,' said Guleri gently.

'You have walked all this distance. Better get on the mare,' replied Manak.

'Here, take your flute.'

'You take it with you.'

'Will you come and play it on the day of the fair?' asked Guleri with a smile. The sun shone in her eyes. Manak turned his face away. Guleri, perplexed, shrugged her shoulders and took the road to Chamba. Manak returned to his home.

Entering the house, he slumped listless on his charpai. 'You have been away a long time,' exclaimed his mother. 'Did you go all the way to Chamba?'

'Not all the way; only to the top of the hill,' Manak's voice was heavy.

'Why do you croak like an old woman?' asked his mother severely. 'Be a man.'

Manak wanted to retort, 'You are a woman; why don't you cry like one for a change!' But he remained silent.

Manak and Guleri had been married seven years, but she had not borne a child and Manak's mother had made a secret resolve: 'I will not let it go beyond the eighth year.'

This year, true to her decision, she had paid 500 rupees to get him a second wife and now, she had waited, as Manak knew, for the time when Guleri went to her parents' to bring in the new bride.

Obedient to his mother, and to custom, Manak's body responded to the new woman. But his heart was dead within him.

In the early hours of one morning, he was smoking his chillum when an old friend happened to pass by. 'Ho Bhavani, where are you going so early in the morning?'

Bhavani stopped. He had a small bundle on his shoulder: 'Nowhere in particular,' he replied evasively.

'You must be on your way to some place or the other,' exclaimed Manak. 'What about a smoke?'

Bhavani sat down on his haunches and took the chillum from Manak's hands. 'I am going to Chamba for the fair,' he replied at last.

Bhavani's words pierced through Manak's heart like a needle. 'Is the fair today?'

'It is the same day every year,' replied Bhavani drily.

'Don't you remember, we were in the same party seven years ago?' Bhavani did not say any more but Manak was conscious of the other man's rebuke and he felt uneasy. Bhavani put down the chillum and picked up his bundle. His flute was sticking out of the bundle. Bidding Manak farewell, he walked away. Manak's eyes remained on the flute till Bhavani disappeared from view.

Next afternoon, when Manak was in his fields he saw Bhavani coming back but deliberately he looked the other way. He did not want to talk to Bhavani or hear anything about the fair. But Bhavani came round the other side and sat down in front of Manak. His face was sad, lightless as a cinder.

'Guleri is dead,' said Bhavani in a flat voice.

'What?'

'When she heard of your second marriage, she soaked her clothes in kerosene and set fire to them.'

Manak, mute with pain, could only stare and feel his own life burning out.

The days went by, Manak resumed his work in the fields, and ate his meals when they were given to him. But he was like a man dead, his face quite blank, his eyes empty.

'I am not his spouse,' complained his second wife. 'I am just someone he happened to marry.'

But quite soon she was pregnant and Manak's mother was well pleased with her new daughter-in-law. She told Manak about his wife's condition, but he looked as if he did not understand, and his eyes were still empty.

His mother encouraged her daughter-in-law to bear with her husband's moods for a few days. As soon as the child was born and placed in his father's lap, she said, Manak would change.

A son was duly born to Manak's wife; and his mother, rejoicing, bathed the boy, dressed him in fine clothes, and put him in Manak's lap. Manak stared at the newborn baby in his lap. He stared a long time, uncomprehending, his face as usual, expressionless. Then suddenly the blank eyes filled with horror, and Manak began to scream. 'Take him away!' he shrieked hysterically. 'Take him away! He stinks of kerosene.'

Translated by Khushwant Singh

THE GREAT MOTHER
JASWANT SINGH KANWAL

Satya was going to turn thirty-seven soon. The ethereal beauty of her youth had turned out to be a curse. Like every young girl, she had dreamt of a life full of joy. Instead, she got a life of pain and suffering. Despite being badly broken, both physically and mentally, she had not lost hope. The help and support that she got from Maria gave her the strength to live on.

Maria was the principal of the Mission School and Satya passed her matriculation examination under her tutelage. The principal noticed the girl because of her performance in the school plays. The continuous appreciation and encouragement by Maria led to a bond of friendship between them.

Satya became a regular visitor to Maria's home. Maria's husband, a padre in the local church, was a saintly figure. The church and the school received financial assistance from foreign countries. The couple's children, a boy and a girl, were in the USA for higher studies. Satya visiting their home fulfilled their need for the affection of their children. They also loved and respected Satya.

Maria encouraged Satya to get admission in a college. But Satya did not want to add to the financial burden of her widowed mother. Her mother had a small shop in the poorer section of the city and earned just enough to make ends meet. Her father had passed away after a long struggle with tuberculosis. Their meagre savings, in the form of cash or gold, had all been spent in getting him treated. Satya was only ten years old when her father passed away and left the mother and daughter to fend for themselves.

Satya was only five years old when Pakistan was created. She still remembered her father sitting in his shop and incessantly smoking cigarettes. Having grown up in such difficult circumstances, she could not think of joining a college. However, she was given a full fee concession on Maria's recommendation. The books that she needed were also arranged. As a result of her dedication and effort, she reached the final year of her BA. But the cataclysmic events that happened that year turned her life upside down.

The villain, the cause of her trouble, was her classmate Ramdev. Ramdev was the son of a temple priest; he was always fashionably dressed, and sported a stylish Lenin-style beard. Satya's mother was a devotee of Vishnu. Every morning and evening, she would sit before the idol in the temple where Ramdev's father was the priest and bemoan her poverty. The priest would console her and assure her that her fortunes would also change one day. However, her wait for better times was never-ending. She was happy to see her young daughter growing up. At the same time, she was apprehensive about the safety of her daughter in a harsh world.

Ramdev would boldly come to their house, sometimes to hand over a book, sometimes to borrow a notebook. The mother tried her best to warn her daughter to stay away from the boy but Satya did not share her mother's concerns. Ramdev and Satya acted together in the play *Shakuntla*. Ramdev played the role of Dushyant. They won the zonal trophy and placed it on the principal's table.

Ramdev become a hero of the college. He in turn was captivated by Satya's beauty. Satya tried to restrain her emotions, but his flattering praise and sweet talk succeeded in eventually winning her over. The two of them stood before Vishnu's idol and took vows to spend the rest of their lives together. Ramdev was a man of progressive views and Satya had full faith in him. Her blind faith, however, destroyed her life. She soon discovered that she was two months pregnant.

At this point Satya pressed Ramdev to marry her. He went

to his father and asked for his approval. But he didn't reveal the real underlying issue. How could a priest of a temple, who was himself a defender of Hindu rituals and traditions, agree to the marriage of a Brahmin boy to a Khatri girl? He refused. The boy rebelled and the father turned him out of his home.

Disrespecting traditions would have meant the loss of all privileges and perks for the priest. Ramdev approached some quacks and hakims for a solution to the pregnancy but nothing worked. Finding the situation getting out of hand, the Brahmin boy chose to vanish from the scene like Vishwamitra.

Ramdev's disappearance meant that Satya was left groping in the dark. She couldn't think of any way out. She had not gone to college for a week. Her face had darkened over in a deep gloom. Finding no support anywhere else, she went and begged Maria for help and guidance. Maria's face turned sombre. She was frightened seeing the expression on Satya's face. She thought, if they don't find any way out, she would commit suicide for sure. She sighed.

'Come with me.' She hugged the girl with one arm. 'There is no point in blaming you. But why did you choose a coward? Why has he left you alone in the time of trouble to face this crisis all alone?' She was very upset with Ramdev. What is the use of a companion who deserts you in times of need?

Satya blamed herself: 'I had lost all sense; why did I fall into his trap?' She cursed herself. Maria helped her get up and took her to face Mother Mary's portrait.

'Do you see the Holy Mother?' the girl nodded her head. 'She faced all her struggles with courage and fortitude. Her pain turned out to be the great saviour for the suffering and the wretched of this world.' Satya had no option but to accept her situation. 'Look here, I'll stand by you in every way. But you have to promise me in the presence of the Holy Mother that you will not even think about suicide, not even in your dreams. God is with those who have no one of their own; Jesus himself comes to their aid. You should not take any wrong decision in desperation. In a desperate situation, one can think of any option, can take any step.'

'I agree with you. I won't take a wrong step. But how will I tell my mother? She'll die of shock.' The girl was frightened by this impending situation.

'Look, your mother has to be told. There is no other alternative. It would be better if Ramdev comes back and marries you.'

'He would not have disappeared if he was going to do that.' A darkness was consuming the girl.

'Have faith in God. Don't waver. I am with you.'

Maria did her best to calm and console Satya and sent her home. But Satya's travails were far from over. Her mother became hysterical and started wailing when Satya opened up to her.

'You wretched girl, your mother was already as good as dead; did you have to bring this shame on me to kill me with a ruined reputation?' For a long time, she kept muttering in anger and frustration. She could not hit a grown-up girl. She could not shout at her. Revealing the secret would have destroyed the family reputation. Finally, she went to the priest and implored him, touching his feet.

'Priest, we are ruined, I and my daughter. Only you can save us.'

'How can I save you?' The priest pretended ignorance.

'Your son has destroyed the life of my daughter. Find him and get them married. The reputation of both the families will be saved. Otherwise, my daughter and I will kill ourselves at your door. They have taken marriage vows in front of Vishnu Bhagwan.'

'My son could not have done this. Anyway, let me talk to him.' The priest thought it prudent to postpone the matter.

But Ramdev did not return and neither did the priest try to search for him. Satya's mother boiled copper coins and prepared concoctions for her daughter; she tried everything but there was no abortion. Now Satya was nearly three months pregnant. Whispers turned into open condemnation. Women from the neighbourhood taunted, 'Is this what you get from acting in plays?' Mother could not take it any longer. Finally, people found her dead in front of Vishnu at the temple. A clear bright day turned into a terrible night for Satya. She froze, unable to cry or shed a tear. She stared like someone who had lost her senses. She had no one to call her own.

As soon as Maria came to know about the death of Satya's mother, she immediately took the girl to her home. Understanding the pain and suffering the girl had gone through and her fragile mental state, Maria bestowed boundless affection and care on her. Satya felt guilty for her mother's death. Ramdev's betrayal had taken away her ability to think sensibly. One day, Maria found Ramdev and brought him with her. Satya was reluctant to see him but Maria managed to persuade her. Maria wanted Ramdev to agree to marry Satya so that all their problems could be solved. Ramdev was mortally afraid of being declared an outcast by the Brahmin community. His child appeared alien to him. His love affair was destroying his name and reputation. He agreed to marry Satya in front of Maria and the priest but did not turn up at court to get the marriage registered.

The news reached the police but Maria's husband, the padre, did not let the situation get out of hand. He told the police inspector the truth. The inspector wanted to call the Brahmin priest and his son to the police station and teach them a lesson. But the padre stopped him. Satya gave birth to a son and the padre got Ramdev's name registered as the father. When Ramdev came to know about this, he was very upset but kept his feelings to himself. He would visit Maria's home off and on. Maria wanted Satya and Ramdev to become close once again and start living life as husband and wife. Satya affectionately called her son 'Raju'. As a child, she used to play with a boy called Raju. She had not forgotten him.

The padre advised Ramdev to get married and go southwards with Satya. There he would be made in charge of a church property; a sufficient salary would be arranged for them. Ramdev agreed and sought one week before going. Everybody was happy. Maria had persuaded Satya to agree to this plan. On the third day, Raju was found lying dead in his cradle. Satya was devastated. She broke down crying.

After the burial of the child, Satya said that Ramdev had visited them just before the child died. Maria was mad with anger. She wanted a murder case to be registered against Ramdev and for him to be arrested. But the padre regarded forgiveness as the right course. Satya had found some peace and happiness in Maria's home after her troubles and suffering, even that had been taken away. The loss of her beloved son had left a deep scar on her heart. Now she was on verge of insanity, constantly thinking about her past suffering and the dangers that lurked in her future. She would often stand silently before the portrait of the Holy Mother. Tears would flow down her cheeks like milk from a mother's breasts.

One day Ramdev told her he was ready to go south. For a moment Satya looked at the murderer of her child. Boiling with anger, she took off her slipper. Grabbing hold of Ramdev's shirt she chased him, beating him mercilessly with her chappal. The padre saved Ramdev from her with great difficulty. After this, Ramdev did not even dare to look in the direction of the Mission.

'Father!' Satya shrieked. 'Let me die. No, give me shelter under the patronage of Jesus. I am a sinner!' crying bitterly she embraced him.

'Daughter, we are all sinners. Human beings are sinners from the very beginning. But the Holy Father adopted all the sinners. He came to this world to eradicate the pain of the suffering humanity. God pardons everyone. Don't cry, my daughter.'

'No, I can't bear it anymore. Bring me under the protection of Jesus,' she kissed his hand.

Satya converted to Christianity. Hindu priests and newspapers protested, creating a big controversy. Maria was irritated: 'Ask the poor girl what her religion gave her. Those who do not know how to give can only take away.'

The padre patted mother and daughter on the shoulder.

'Maria, now we have to find some assignment for her. Remaining idle destroys a person.'

Satya got admission in a nursing school and after a year she became a trained nurse, a midwife.

She regularly went to the hospital. She finished all her household responsibilities before going. Life had fallen into a pattern after all. Now she was in a sense a daughter of the family.

Satya had taken shelter in Maria's home but she had not become a burden to them. She would do all the work in the house. Now she had become economically independent as well. But she never for a moment forgot what Maria and her husband had done for her. She knew very well that if Principal Maria had not stood by her in her time of need, she might have died like her mother. Serving her foster parents gave her special satisfaction. But she still felt the agonizing pain of losing her son.

Every newborn in the hospital looked like Raju to her. For a long time she would be lost, looking at a baby's features. Raju's image came to dominate every part of her being. Maria advised her to get married. But standing under Mariam's painting she refused to entertain any such thought. Days passed, turning into months and years. Now she was thirty-seven.

One day a rich lady came in her car and requested Satya to come with her to check on a patient. Once they reached her bungalow, she respectfully offered Satya tea. Then the lady began to talk to her.

'Sister, I wish to share a secret with you. Promise me that this will remain a secret between you and me.'

Satya had guessed from her anxious, scared face that there was something unusual going on.

'I will keep your secret. Go ahead.' Satya assured her confidently.

'Sister, my daughter has made a big mistake.' The lady confided with humility. 'The boy she is engaged to marry has gone to the USA for his PhD. We came to know about this misfortune later on.' She summed up the situation.

'If the boy agrees...' Satya trailed off.

'There is no problem with the boy, but how can we face his family, her in-laws?' the lady sighed anxiously.

'Let me talk to the girl first.'

The lady took Satya to a room at the back of the bungalow. A sickly pale girl lay on the bed. It appeared she had been fed many concoctions and potions already.

'Please go out for a minute,' Satya requested the lady

Drawing the curtains closed behind her, the lady left. Satya remembered her own experience and she felt the girl's pain. She had found the lady's story odd. She affectionately placed her hand on the girl's forehead, as if to comfort the girl by sharing her pain. Questioning the girl about how all this happened would have meant making the girl revisit her pain again. She tightly held the girl's hand in both her hands and comforted her:

'Worrying about a situation does not solve any problem. Be calm.' The girl didn't hear what Satya said. She was staring at a cobweb in the corner of the ceiling. 'Courage helps....' Satya broke off when she saw the girl turn her gaze towards her. It was evident that the girl was tired of listening to these platitudes. 'You tell me, what I can do for you?'

'Will you?' the girl's glare tore her heart apart. 'No, you won't.' The girl looked lost and hopeless again.

'No, I'll try my best.' Satya tried to console her.

'Let me die, help me get rid of this life.' The girl clung tightly to the midwife's hand. 'I'll give you all the gold you ask for.'

'Dear girl, gold is not more precious than life. Even saints and seers have made mistakes. There is hardly any human being who hasn't gone through such moments. You stay strong; I'll protect you in every possible way.' She lovingly patted her pale cheek. 'How far along are you?'

'More than three months.' She breathed deep and the bulge became more prominent.

Satya began examining the girl with her hands.

'Did you take anything, any potion?'

'A lot, all that rubbish. But nothing worked.'

'Don't worry, it will be fine. If you worry, you'll suffer more.'

After trying her best to console and calm the girl, she came out. The lady was nervously waiting for her. She was anxious to find some solution. Satya told her. 'It is a bit too late.'

'You perform the abortion. I'll pay you whatever you ask for, any amount.'

'Look, madam, it will be a big mistake—the girl could die.'

Hearing about the possibility of death of her only daughter, the lady almost swooned.

'Oh my God! Where can we hide! You foolish girl, you have destroyed our reputation.' Cursing the girl, the lady collapsed into a chair, holding her head in her hands.

For a moment, Satya saw her mother standing before her. But she controlled herself, thinking, 'Why shouldn't I become Maria!'

'Madam, don't lose heart.' She held the lady by her arm and, trusting her instincts, said, 'There is one way out.'

'What is that?' the lady got a new lease of life.

'Okay, first you promise me, by swearing on Baba Nanak, that you won't refuse my proposal.' She bowed her head to the big portrait on the wall, 'I will save your daughter's life and protect the reputation of your family.'

'You find some way out...I promise and swear on Baba Nanak.' She grasped both of Satya's hands.

The midwife said something in the lady's ear. The lady suddenly looked relieved.

'Definitely!' said the lady 'I promise in the name of Baba

Nanak.' She put her hand on her heart to promise and assured Satya again. 'We'll be obliged to you forever.'

'God is there to solve problems of one and all.' Satya left, having won the affection and trust of both the mother and the daughter.

After this, the lady barred the entry of outsiders to her house and started attending to all her visitors in the veranda or the drawing room. It was Satya alone who came every five or seven days and visited the girl in her room. Once in a while she sat with the girl and played a game of cards with her. By and by, the friendship between Satya and the girl grew deeper.

As the day of delivery approached Satya started staying at the bungalow. The girl didn't face any difficulty during childbirth. At night, Satya wrapped the child in a shawl and brought him home with her.

Coming home, she lit the candles in front of Mariam's image. Kneeling there, she uncovered the face of the child. It was exactly another Raju that lay beaming there. The boy started crying, swinging his legs and arms.

'Blessed Mother, shower your blessings on this sinner. You have returned my Raju to me. I am thankful to you.' She made the sign of the cross over and over again. 'Bless him with a long life and strength; may he grow up to help the poor and the needy. Amen!'

Maria slipped in silently behind her and held her by her shoulders. On learning about the child, she embraced Satya.

'Satya! You are the great mother.' Tears of gratitude appeared in Maria's eyes.

Translated by Paramjit Singh Ramana

THE PROVERBIAL BULLOCK

KULWANT SINGH VIRK

The village of Thatthi Khara was quite close to Amritsar and on the main road. The mood in which Maan Singh was going there was exultant. Although dusk had descended and the clip-clop sound of the horse pulling the tonga too was slowing down, he was not worried.

Maan Singh was a soldier on leave and Thatthi Khara was the native village of his close friend Karam Singh. He was on his way to visit his friend's home. The intensity of friendship and the bonds formed between soldiers cannot be seen elsewhere. Earlier they had been together in their regimental centre and had fought together on the Burma front in the same battalion. By virtue of his seniority, Karam Singh had reached the rank of havaldar (sergeant) while Maan Singh was as yet only a naik (corporal).

The most outstanding feature of Karam Singh's character was his sweet demeanour. Whenever other young soldiers of the village returned on leave, their interaction with the village folk would never cross the limits of the customary greeting: 'Waheguru ji ki Fateh'. But when Karam Singh came home, people would throng him. Those who came for a bath to the common village well would hang around hoping to chat with him. Sitting around the bhatthi (furnace) till midnight in the winter, the people would listen with rapt attention as Karam Singh recounted his adventures. In his former regiment he was known for his marksmanship. His shot would hit the target so flawlessly in the centre it looked as though he had placed it there by hand. On the front he had shot dead many camouflaged Japanese soldiers. This was his way of avenging the death of his own platoon colleagues. A single shot from Karam Singh's rifle would succeed where machine-gun bursts failed. Although his age was beginning to show, the energy he exhibited while performing gymnastics on the high bar made onlookers believe that he possessed supernatural strength.

But this did not happen during war time. Lots of activities were no longer allowed. The parade of soldiers, meticulously dressed in smart uniforms, along with martial band music had been stopped. There was no bazaar nearby where one could go attired in mufti. Therefore, when Maan Singh's leave was approved, Karam Singh felt very upset. Had his leave also been approved they could have gone together. Perhaps they could have spent time with each other and even returned together. Chooharkana was not very far from Amritsar; the distance would not have been more than 50 kos.* The former was known as 'Majha' and the latter as 'bar' (forested area). The former had been settled centuries ago while the latter was a new settlement.

Getting leave had become difficult. It was as rare a happening as winning a gallantry award during war.

When Maan Singh was about to board the army truck that would take him out of the cantonment, Karam Singh said to him, 'Visit my home also. When my family knows that I have sent you, it will be as though they have half met me in you. And, then as you come back from them, I will also feel as though I have met my family to some extent through you and the news you bring.'

Then to whet his interest in his hometown Karam Singh asked, 'Have you ever been there?'

'No, I just pass through Amritsar and have never gone anywhere else.'

'The important gurdwaras of our area are in Tarn Taran, Khadoor Sahib, and Goindwal Sahib. Pay obeisance at all these shrines for me. And visit my home as well. I will write to them

---

*A unit of distance measuring 2.4 kilometres.

to let them know you are coming.'

And so it was that before the end of his leave Maan Singh was heading towards Karam Singh's village in a tonga.

'Bapuji, I am Maan Singh from Chooharkana,' he introduced himself with folded hands to the old man sitting in the veranda of Karam Singh's house.

'Welcome! Come in. Please be seated.'

Maan Singh stepped in and settled himself on the cot. He felt that the old man was a bit uneasy at his arrival. At first, the man looked here and there but then sat silently with downcast eyes.

Maan Singh was an impatient man, quick to take offence. He was struck by this cold reception of a visitor. Maybe he is a guest or stranger...he thought.

'You are Karam Singh's father, I presume...?' he asked, hoping to break the ice.

'Yes, this is his home...' was the cryptic reply.

'Didn't he write to you about my coming here?'

'Yes, he wrote to us about your arrival,' said the old man and moved to the courtyard where he busied himself. He untied a heifer from one peg and tied it to the other. Caressing it, he put his hand in front of its mouth, which the heifer licked. Then he went inside and informed the others about Maan Singh's arrival and told someone to bring a cup of tea for him. It was almost as if he was avoiding returning to the veranda. He went to the mare tethered in the courtyard. He freshened the chaff lying in the manger in front of the animal, added some more feed to it, and then finally came back to the veranda. Now the man seemed more composed. He looked at Maan Singh and around the room. Had something gone wrong? Karam Singh had been so enthusiastic about a visit to his home!

'Where is Jaswant?' Maan Singh knew that this was the name of Karam Singh's younger brother.

'He will be coming soon with the cart of green fodder.' Meanwhile, Karam Singh's mother brought the tea.

'Bebeji, Sat Sri Akal,' Maan Singh greeted the old woman respectfully and smiled at her.

The woman's lips quivered a bit as though she wanted to speak but she did not utter a word. Maan Singh took the vessel of tea from her hands and she left. He thought silently, 'This family from Majha is so odd!' This was unexpected for Maan Singh. He was feeling very uncomfortable and ignored. But having reached his friend's house he could not just turn around and leave.

Anyway, I will spend just one night and then go back, he decided.

When Jaswant came home at night, he felt the gloom lift a little as they talked.

He started, 'You know Karam's Singh's unfailing aim with the rifle has become famous these days at the Burma front! Here he just has to press the trigger, and lo, a Japanese soldier falls there! Walking alongside him, I don't know how he spots the enemy!

Maan Singh paused, expecting some interest on the part of the family from Majha so he could continue with Karam Singh's tales of gallantry. He was bursting to share these stories but no one was listening to him.

Then the old man said to Jaswant, 'When is it our turn to get water for irrigation?'

'At three in the morning, the day after tomorrow.'

On hearing this, Maan Singh picked up the cue again. He wanted to talk about his friend to his heart's content.

'Good thing that Karam Singh avoided having to wake up at this hour. He is too lazy to get up early in the morning. He loves to lie in and is always the last to get up.'

Even this did not evoke any response.

Then dinner was served. They had served it with a great spirit of hospitality. Jaswant fanned Maan Singh while he ate. He was reassured that at least he was not being ignored, or slighted.

While he was eating, Karam Singh's little son walked up to

him. He could talk about Karam Singh to him at least. Maan Singh lifted him into his arms.

'Oi! You want to go to your bapu? Come! You come with me. It's very wet and rainy there. You can have great fun in the rain.'

Maan Singh's words stung Karam Singh's father.

'Take the boy away. At least let the guest eat undisturbed,' the anguished old man said sharply. The boy's mother came quickly and swept him away in her arms.

Now, Maan Singh was perturbed. He began to feel suffocated. He had come so far to visit this family but now wanted to return as quickly as he could.

'How far is Tarn Taran from here?' He asked.

'It's only four kos.'

'Can I get a tonga early in the morning?'

'Don't worry about a tonga. Jaswant will go with you. You should go together and come back after the visiting the gurdwaras.'

Maan Singh was pleased and agreed. Jaswant didn't seem like an unpleasant fellow.

But the next day as they walked to Tarn Taran together, Jaswant said very little. He would hurriedly greet any acquaintances they came across along the way and keep walking without stopping to chat. Maan Singh wanted to stop and talk to people. It was not every day that he came here.

Maan Singh tried speaking to Jaswant: 'Karam Singh earned a great name for himself in the army. Why didn't you join the army too?'

Jaswant shrank into himself as if caught red-handed. After a long pause he said tersely, 'Isn't it enough that one member of a family is in the army…?'

'What a great crop of sorghum and sugar cane this area has!' Jaswant changed the topic as they passed a field of sorghum.

Maan Singh agreed disinterestedly. He only wanted to talk about his friend.

When they returned in the evening, Maan Singh started

thinking of going back to his own village. He would board the night train from Amritsar and reach his village the next morning. Although everybody in the family had tried to make him feel comfortable, he had not enjoyed the visit as much as he had expected. Tea was being prepared for him right then but he had been left all alone in the veranda.

Suddenly he caught sight of the postman coming towards the house, a bag slung over his shoulder. At first, it looked like he would barge into the living area of the house. But he sat down on the cot in the veranda.

'What have you brought, bhai?'

'What can I bring now? It's poor Karam Singh's pension.'

'Karam Singh's pension? Was he killed?'

'My dear sir, the entire village is immersed in sorrow and you—sitting in his home—are asking: was he killed? It's been fifteen days since the letter with this shocking news was delivered here.'

For a minute or two Maan Singh felt his breath catch. His chest felt tight with grief. Then his body relaxed as the tears began to flow. He thought of Karam Singh's home, his father, his small child—and began to cry bitterly.

Having seen the postman coming from afar, the father had realized that the secret could no longer be guarded. He knew that it was of no use to carry the burden any more. The tears gushed forth from his eyes as if a dam had burst. Sitting close together, they allowed themselves the relief of grief.

'Why didn't you disclose it to me at the very outset?' Maan Singh asked.

'So as to not spoil your holiday. Let the boy get to know from the platoon when he goes back, we thought. This homecoming leave period is very dear to a soldier, I know. I could see it from the cheerful spirit of Karam Singh during his leave. The comfort loving residents of the bar area make a mountain out of a molehill. But see, we the people of Majha too could not conceal this truth properly and made you uncomfortable.'

On his way back, Maan Singh passed through the villages of Majha i.e. the region where people like this old man are from. There were ramparts for defence here and there. The tombs preserved the memory of those who fought the invaders in times past. This was the prime reason, perhaps, of the old man's fortitude and forbearance. It had enabled him to bear the burden himself so that others did not have to carry it. Maan Singh had so far only heard of the legend of the white bullock that bears on his horns the weight of the whole earth. In that moment, he felt that the bullock was none other than Karam Singh's father, one who had the strength to take on the burden of others despite being under an immense weight himself.

Translated by Parvesh Sharma

SAVAGE HARVEST

MOHINDER SINGH SARNA

As he bent over the furnace stuffed with hard coal, Dina's iron-black body shone with the sheen of bronze; in fact, he seemed to be moulded in bronze, resembling a statue of a healthy labourer. The muscles of his well-exercised torso rippled as he swung the hammer around his head, and a great blow fell on the red-hot bits of iron.

The blows continued to fall and echo. Immersed in his work, Dina was lost to the world until the hot sun of late August, streaming in through the open window, began to lick at his very bones. With a start, he looked out. Already the sun was at its height and his work was not even half done. He shut the window to keep out the heat but then found it difficult to breathe. A clammy sweat broke out on his forehead. It had rained furiously all night, as if the skies had opened up, and then continued to drizzle all morning. But now the sun shone brightly and a suffocating humidity had built up. He threw the window open again and bent over the furnace. The sweat was flowing down his ears onto his body in little rivulets. He wiped it off his forehead with his forearm. Thick drops fell on the fire. There was a little hiss and, for a split second, a piece of coal found some relief.

He seemed to be on fire with the combined heat from the sun and the furnace. This fire had dissolved into his blood and was now roasting the marrow of his bones. The sharp, roaring flames made his eyes burn. Every hair on his body had become a wick and it seemed to him that one of these wicks would catch fire any moment and blow up his body like a huge firecracker.

Suddenly he dropped his tools and went to the window. The sky was lit up by the screaming sharp sunshine. His eyes could not adjust to the brightness and he winced. When he could see, he gazed at the fields that spread far before him, and at the sandy path that cut through them and went all the way to the horizon like a straight white line. On the right of the path stood the cotton crop, and the puddles of water in the fields occasionally flashed silver. On the left, the ploughed furrows awaited the seed. The scent of the earth, wet from the recent rain, made him nostalgic and he wanted to jump out of the window. He wanted to roll in the fields and let the pores of his burning body soak in the moisture from the wet earth.

He loved the fields. During the sowing and harvesting, his blood would tingle and a strange freedom would enliven his limbs. He was the village blacksmith, but there wasn't much work for him in the village and he would spend a lot of time helping out the peasants in the fields. There wasn't a man in seven villages that could match him during the harvest or lift a larger load than him. Suddenly his hands yearned for the feel of a sickle.

Sickles, harvests, the sugar cane swaying gently in the moonlight. The call of the golden earth and the lilt in the songs born of this earth…. He forgot, for a moment, that a hellish fire raged behind him and that for the last twenty days he had done nothing but mould metal into axes and spears. The season of sickles and scrapers had passed; this was the time of axes and spears. And it had been a strange harvest. Instead of the wheat, those who had planted it had been chopped up.

What kind of a mess had he gotten himself into? It was as if he was shouldering the entire responsibility of arming the warriors of the newly born Pakistan. Pakistan already existed, but to complete that reality it seemed necessary to kill all the Hindus and the Sikhs.

He did not understand this fully, but this was what everybody said, from the village heads to the imams of mosques. And this jihad would succeed only if his furnace kept raging and spitting out fierce instruments of death.

He turned again to the fire. The sharp bits of metal in the furnace were brighter than the coals. His head began to swim. A sharp, hot pain rose inside him and he gripped his side. Hunger! He hadn't taken even a drop of water since the morning. Now hunger was ravaging his insides and thirst had turned his lips to wood.

'Oh! Bashir's mother!' he shouted towards the house. 'Give me water, quick.' A woman of about forty-five brought water in a jug. She wore a nose ring and her silver earrings swayed as she walked. She stared at her husband. He was panting with thirst. She had offered him food and water three times already since the morning, but he hadn't responded and had continued to blow at his fire. What had made him think of food and water now? She looked at the torrid fire, at the bits of iron scattered all over the floor, and at the evil pile of axes and spears. Then she stared at her husband's face for a long time, as if she didn't recognize him. Dina drained the jug at a go. 'More,' he panted. She brought more water and watched him as he drank. 'That's all,' he said.

The taut veins of his body and forehead relaxed. His breathing eased. And then a shadow of discomfort crossed his face. 'Why are you staring at me like that? Why don't you talk to me? And why do you stand away from me, as if I have the plague?' She didn't reply. Instead she went into the house and brought him food. 'I'm talking to you,' Dina shouted, shaking her by the shoulders. 'Why don't you speak to me? Have you put rice to boil in your mouth that you can't speak?'

The woman remained silent. Dina tore at a roti and tried to swallow a few large mouthfuls. But the food wouldn't go down his throat. He took a few bitter gulps of water and pushed away the basket of rotis. 'Not talking to me, just staring as if I've been possessed by demons.'

'Allah forbid,' she said, 'but it does appear so to me.' Dina's mouth fell open in surprise. He had lost all hope that Bashir's mother would ever speak, that she would break the stubborn silence of so many days.

When he recovered somewhat from his surprise, he said, 'I know what's on your mind, but what can I do? Your sons won't let me be. Now Bashir wants fifty axes ready by tomorrow night. He'll be at my neck if they aren't ready. I know you think otherwise but if I don't obey them they'll cut me into pieces.'

'Are they your sons or someone else's?' she asked, a little ashamed of her own question.

'Mine,' he replied, somewhat foolishly.

'Then should they fear you, or should you fear them?'

'You talk as if you don't know your own sons, what savages they are. Can I say anything to them? As if they wouldn't skin me alive....' said Dina.

'They are my sons, too.' His wife's tone was softer now. 'You know they shout at me and curse me. But I don't go making axes for them.'

'I only make the axes,' he replied. 'I don't kill people with them.'

'It's worse than killing,' she said. 'The killer kills one or two or at most, a handful of people. Each axe made by your hands kills dozens.'

A tremor passed through Dina's spine. Then this trembling touched every pore of his body. For a long time he was silent. And then, 'You are blaming me! Why don't you talk to your sons, the great warriors who burn two villages every night!'

'Nobody listens to me.' Her tone had grown even softer now. 'How can I tell anyone what to do? Everyone will have to answer for their own sins; why should I say anything to anyone?'

For some time, both of them stared at the floor, silently. Suddenly the woman said, 'And why don't you eat your food? Do you want to starve?' She slid the basket in front of him.

A soft knock on the front door shook Dina. He stood up in fright. It must be Bashir or his companions. They had come to threaten him. He hesitated with his hand on the latch and looked around. The fire in the furnace was raging; everything was in place. He opened the door. Rusted with the season's rain, it screeched on its hinges.

He jumped back several steps in fear, just missing the furnace. His wife's face drained of blood and a scream escaped her lips. At the door stood the old wife of the Brahmin of the thakurdwar, a net of wrinkles spread across the turmeric powdered on her face. Her head of snow-white hair shook uncontrollably. Their eyes filled with fear, Dina and his wife stared at the old woman. She seemed to be alive, even though she was most certainly a ghost.

At long last, Dina's wife took courage and said, 'Aunt, you are still alive?' The old woman did not reply. Dina's wife recalled that she had been hard of hearing. Perhaps the affliction had pursued her in death too. She went closer to the old woman and, loudly, repeated her question.

Understanding flashed in the old woman's eyes and she said, 'Can't you see that I am alive? Seven days was I racked with fever. There was no one to give me even a sip of water there. Tulsi has been away for many days. I could've died in his absence.... One can go anytime.... My fever went down today. I hardly had the strength to get up but somehow I have pushed myself till here. Why are the two of you staring at me so?'

The old woman was drenched in sweat from the effort of speaking and her breath came in uneven bursts. Holding her temples she sat down on the floor on her haunches. The light seemed to be fading in her pupils and every breath came as if it were her last.

Dina and his wife exchanged looks of immense relief. She really was the Brahmin's wife and not a ghost. The fever had saved her from the fate of the rest of the village. Her deafness had prevented her from hearing of the great sorrow that had befallen the village on Thursday night. She hadn't realized that her village was now in Pakistan. She did not know that Pakistan was now in her village. That not one Hindu or Sikh was alive except for a few girls in the hands of the rioters.

Suddenly, the old woman asked, 'Dina, have you seen my goat anywhere?'

Goat, thought Dina, her goat! In these days, when the rioters had cooked and eaten even the looted cattle, this old woman was bothered about a goat?

'I don't know where she has run off to,' the old woman continued, 'and she's due. I can't even look after myself now. I can't go looking for her, and how can I catch her anyway? If you see her anywhere, tie her up, God bless you. You know she's due. I hope she doesn't give birth somewhere outside.'

Dina said, 'Old woman, your goat is not there. She has been eaten up and has been digested by now.' But the old woman heard nothing. He was about to repeat himself loudly but a glance from his wife silenced him.

'And look at this,' the old woman said, 'I found this chain near the door of the thakurdwar. I don't know how this goat managed to loosen the chain. This link, where the lock goes, has been eaten through and through. I thought I'd ask you to fix it for me.'

For some time, Dina's wife had been staring at the old woman in a strange manner. She seemed to be wrestling with something.

And then, as if everything had suddenly become clear, she said, 'Aunt, why don't you stay here? You will be alone in the thakurdwar. And your fever has just abated. Cook your food here, and bring your own utensils, since you are a Hindu. Let Tulsi return, then you can go back.'

The old woman seemed to have grown even more deaf. Maybe it was the effect of the fever. She only caught Tulsi's name.

'I'm telling you, he's gone out of the village. He's gone with Ram Shah's daughter's betrothal party to Nawachak. On the first of next month, Preeto is to be married. I told Shah to gift me a cow. It's not every day that there are celebrations in the houses of the rich. And you know, Tulsi needs the milk and the curd for his health.'

Ignoring the old woman's talk, Dina's wife was trying to catch her husband's eye. She wanted to say something but before she could, Dina was already speaking.

'I know what's on your mind, but we can't do it. I have no objection, but where will we hide her? Soon your sons will be here, their nostrils sniffing out human flesh, and we won't be able to conceal her. They will figure it out instantly, and what will they do to us then?'

'She's old,' beseeched Dina's wife, 'the last of our village's Hindus. A God-fearing old woman. It's only a matter of a few days. Let her son return and then we will send her to some other village.'

'Which village will you send her to?' Dina was almost screaming now. 'Is there a village left where she will be safe? And her son: he'll never return. This time he has been sent to a place from where there is no return. All the Hindus of Nawachak have been killed. Not one of them is left.'

His wife's face fell. She put a trembling finger to her lips, begging him to lower his tone. 'Can't you speak softly? Or won't you be satisfied until she knows that her son has been murdered?'

Except for Dina's outburst, they'd been talking in whispers. But it was unnecessary, for even their loudest tones would not have reached the old woman through her deafness. She stared at them with her fevered eyes.

'What are you two whispering away about? And, Dina, why won't you look at me? Just repair this cursed chain. It's not that I'm asking for much.'

'Come tomorrow,' Dina shouted into the old woman's ear. 'I don't have any time today. And go home now.'

'All right,' the old woman croaked, putting her hands on her knees to steady herself as she rose. 'I'll go. If you say tomorrow, then let it be so, but keep an eye out for my goat. I've told you, just tie her up if you see her. Wretched thing. God knows where she has run away to.' And, before Dina's wife could stop her, the old woman had lurched out into the lane.

How much time this old woman had wasted, Dina fumed. He could have made five axes in that much time. And Bashir was not going to listen to any excuses; he would want his fifty.

But he could not put his heart into the work. Something began to gnaw at his heart. He could not dismiss the vision of fever-ridden eyes and snow-white hair. Those eyes were burning holes in his head like two red-hot embers. Most of all, it was her ignorance that bothered him. She knew nothing. That Tulsi was never to return, that Preeto was never to get married, that Bashir had already taken Preeto, along with her rich father's estate.

It was a rotten thing that Bashir had done. Defending the honour of the women of the village was a common burden. Everyone's daughters were just like your own. The loss of any woman's honour was a catastrophe for all.

A horrible scene appeared before his eyes—Preeto, wailing and clutching at her father's corpse; Bashir pulling her away by her hair. Imploring him, wailing and screaming, she had been dragged away. And then she had gone silent, just like a lamb in the moment before its slaughter.

And he, Bashir's father, had watched this evil sight unfold from the threshold. He had not stopped Bashir, or pulled him away by the scruff of his neck and thrown him on the ground. He had done nothing to save the honour of this daughter.

The pale, childlike face of Preeto began to swim before his eyes and her plaintive cries echoed in his ears. He was seized by a shiver, a cold and uncontrollable shiver that seemed a precursor to certain death. The shivering, he felt, could be stopped only if he picked up the red-hot iron from the fire and clasped it against his heart. But why was his head on fire? The entire blazing furnace seemed to have entered his head. He/pressed his head with both hands and the fire came onto his palms.

He was going mad. He would end up doing something terrible. He must run away, far away from all this. He opened the window and jumped out. For a long time he wandered aimlessly in the fields. The afternoon had now become evening. On the horizon, someone had murdered the sun. The blood of innocents had spread across the sky and had dissolved into the waters of the streams and canals. Would anybody eat the sugar cane that had been sprayed with blood? Or wear the cotton which had been irrigated by blood? What kind of wheat would grow in this blood-drenched soil? And what kind of a harvest would it be after this bloody season? The shower of blood that had reddened everything had been caused by the axes he had fashioned. This crop of bones and flesh had been sown by spears made by his hands. And he had just finished making axes for the handful of villages that were still left. Those, too, would be gone by tomorrow night.

He was guilty. Heavily, deeply guilty. Bashir's mother had been right. At least he should not let them lay their hands on the new axes. His sins would not be wiped out even if he prevented that. But what else could he do?

And then he started running, like a man possessed, towards the village. He wanted to reach home before Bashir's men. He wanted to throw the axes in some well or canal where they would never be found.

When he reached the village, it was dark. The indifferent light of a hazy moon threw faint shadows onto the lane. The previous night's rain had left a muddy slush everywhere. Again and again his feet caught in the thick slush, but he kept walking quickly through the lanes. Suddenly, he stopped. He could hear voices coming from a short distance away. In fact, they were coming from his house. Had they already come, then? Was he too late? He could clearly hear Bashir's vulgar laughter.

He stumbled against some heavy object near his house and fell on his face. He tried to get up, but couldn't. An icy-cold grip had clasped his feet. He tried to free them but the grip only seemed to get tighter. A terrible fear clutched at his heart and a cold sweat covered his forehead. With a strong jerk, he turned to look back. In the dim moonlight, he saw a thatch of white hair rippling in the wind. The old woman's wrinkled forehead bore a long gash from an axe. And there was a curse in the wide open, frightened eyes. He looked at his feet. They were caught in the chain that was entangled around her forearms.

He screamed once and fainted. That night he was gripped by a high fever. All night he tossed wildly on the bed; all night his delirious shouts echoed in the silence of the village. 'Don't kill me, don't kill me with those axes! Get this chain off my neck! Oh, my daughter! Don't harm my daughter! Don't harm Preeto! Oh, these chains! In Allah's name, don't use those axes! Don't kill me!'

Translated by Navtej Sarna

THE CHARITY COAT

NAVTEJ SINGH

There were only three quilts at home; all of them were very old and worn out. And it was biting cold outside. The middle sisters used one of the quilts. The other quilt was used by the eldest sister, Seeto, and youngest, Munni. The third quilt was exclusively for their father, Master Ishar Das. Bhagwanti, their mother, would make do by layering a thin cotton blanket and a carpet together. But for the last few days, her bones had been aching due to the unending chill. It was the sort of ache that paralyses and makes one not want to do anything.

The younger ones had gone to sleep while the elder, Seeto, was awake. She had such a bad cough that she was struggling to draw breath. This relentless cough had made her miserable since her youth.

One day, Master Ishar Das had had her examined by a doctor whose father was known to him. The doctor had advised immediate surgery for her throat. He said that any further delay could damage her vocal chords and would have an adverse impact on her heart as well. The doctor had prescribed a diet that included milk, eggs, leafy vegetables, fruits, and vitamin supplements.

Seeto had been coughing like this for the last few years. But he could not bring any medicine for her except some local medicinal herbs. An operation and milk, eggs, fruit, etc., everyday—how could he afford all this? For over two years he had not been able to buy a quilt with his monthly salary of seventy rupees.

He called out to her. 'Seeto...Seeto....'

Seeto could not hear him due to her wracking cough. The

doctor had said any delay in the tonsil surgery would also affect her ears.

Once she finished her work in the kitchen, Seeto's mother started putting together her worn blanket with the carpet.

'Seeto's mother, you should take my quilt today. I will use the cotton blanket,' Master Ishar Das said.

'No, Seeto's father, I bask in the sun all day long. You have to go to the next village for work early in the morning. Thereafter, you go to Rai Sahib's bungalow for taking tuitions and return in the evening. If you don't have the warmth of the quilt even at night, then how will you go in the morning and discharge your household responsibilities?'

Today, despite the extreme cold, Bhagwanti had been washing the children's clothes and the bedding. Aching all over, she started tucking her children's quilts tighter around them.

Wearing just three layers of clothing, Master Ishar Das was trembling in his quilt. He would travel three miles to his job early in the morning. For several years he had owned no coat or sweater. On reaching the school, his fingers were so numb that he could barely hold a pen to mark attendance. Earlier, he would escape the biting cold of winter because he would reach home before dark. But now he got late because he was tutoring Rai Sahib's son. The boy was seldom ready to sit for his studies as soon as Master Ishar Das reached. Sometimes, he was sipping tea and at other times he would come to the tutor only after eating snacks prepared specially for him. So although the teaching time was only one hour, Master Ishar Das had to stay at Rai Sahib's bungalow for two hours. The two mile-diversion from the main route, taxing his brain for two hours, and then shivering on his return in the evening would fetch him only fifteen rupees a month. Since he was engaged for three months, it would amount to forty-five rupees. It would allow him to buy a quilt for Seeto's mother. It would mean he could afford to buy milk for Seeto, maybe even get her the tonsil surgery. As per the doctor, he had till March to do something about her health....

Lying on her cot, Bhagwanti said, 'When you get paid for the tuition, bring me some wool. I will knit a sweater for you. You have to do with just three winter clothes in such freezing temperatures. God forbid you also fall sick....' Shrunk in her frosty bed, Bhagwanti was shivering; her voice shook with the cold.

'I don't need a sweater. I have bought a coat today.'

'Where is the coat? How did you buy it? You have not received your salary nor your tuition fee....'

Seeto coughed unrelentingly. Bhagwanti went to her daughter and rubbed her chest.

Master Ishar Das had not shown the coat to anyone in the family. Had he come home wearing the coat nobody but Bhagwanti would have recognized him. Ever since the youngest three had come of age they had never seen him in a coat. He had had a warm coat stitched on the occasion of his wedding. It had stayed with him for years but had been left behind in Pakistan during Partition when they moved to this side of the border. After that, he had not managed to get himself a new coat. And, today he had brought home a coat but had not shown it to his wife.

The coat which he had left behind in Pakistan had a buttonhole into which a flower could be inserted on the left of the collar. Shortly after their marriage, Bhagwanti had tucked a flower there and asked, 'Do you know which flower this is?'

In spite of knowing he had shaken his head.

The then young Bhagwanti had coquettishly said, 'Ishq-e-pechan.*' Saying this, she had blushed.

And Master Ishar Das had so far not shown Bhagwanti his coat.

He put it on as he travelled from the school to Rai Sahib's house, and then on his way home. But before turning into his street, he had wrapped it up in a newspaper. He hid it after

---

*A species of ivy; ishq in Urdu means love.

entering the house because he had not purchased it but had got it in charity. Just yesterday!

When he had been a school student, his father had told him a story:

'A boy used second-hand books to study and ended up getting tuberculosis. The earlier owner of the books had been a TB patient. And the germs of the dreaded disease still lived in the books.'

Ishar Das's father had slapped him when he had eaten some sweets he had received after pleading for them from a neighbouring house. His father had then got him a full platter of sweets and said, 'Eat as much as you want but never ever beg for anything from anybody.'

It was a stern warning.

In a way, he had begged for this coat yesterday.

Seeto's cough subsided to some extent. Bhagwanti sat on Ishar Das's cot.

'Please show me what colour it is. Did you borrow it from someone?'

'No, no, there is no coat. I was just talking...' Ishar Das said with anguish in his heart. 'We are not destined to get a coat.'

'For God's sake, don't curse your destiny,' Bhagwanti tried to say with firmness. But she could not hold her resolve and burst into tears.

Bhagwanti was a woman of fortitude. She had never cried over trifles but now she could not restrain her tears. She placed her head on her husband's chest.

A tattered quilt lay sandwiched between them. Bhagwanti's warm tears fell on the man's covered hands and disappeared into the quilt. She kept crying for some time.

With great tenderness, Master Ishar Das covered his wife with his quilt. The tears welled up in her eyes as spontaneously as sleep. The warmth of tears seemed to melt the frost that had settled into her bones for ages. It was like every part of Bhagwanti's body, aching with bone-crushing toil, was getting a gentle fomentation. Now rather than shivering in the cold she felt the cosy warmth of more than one blanket as if there was sunshine and not cotton stuffed in them.

The next morning, as Master Ishar Das left for school, he had the wrapped charity coat hidden under his arm. It was very cold but he wore it only after crossing his street. Although a charity coat, it kept him warm.

Rai Sahib's wife had said while giving it to him, 'Rai Sahib got it stitched in vilayat.'

'For the illiterate, every country is vilayat. I had it stitched in Austria. Masterji, you must have heard of a science called psychology. Austria is inhabited by the doyens of psychology,' Rai Sahib had said and retreated to his room with a thick volume on psychology in his hand.

Mrs Rai was a goddess. Had someone else given the coat to Ishar Das, he would not have accepted it so readily.

The day before it had been windy and the cold too was very harsh. Moreover, Master Ishar Das had been feeling under the weather. Once the lesson ended, he didn't want to leave the warmth of the fireplace.

When he got up at last, he sneezed repeatedly and felt a little dizzy.

Just at that time, Mrs Rai happened to go past that room.

'Are you okay, Masterji?' she asked.

'It's nothing at all. Just the cold.' Master Ishar Das said.

'But you have to go four miles in this frigid weather. Why don't you wear a coat?'

The teacher first looked at Mrs Rai and then replied helplessly, eyes downcast, 'Mataji, I don't have a coat...not even a sweater.'

Mrs Rai had shuddered as she looked into the eyes of the teacher.

Never before had the teacher addressed Mrs Rai as Mataji, although he had noticed earlier that she reminded him of his deceased mother, in looks and nature.

Like a mother she had led him to the fireplace inside and herself gone to the kitchen to send him a cup of tea. He had been enjoying the heat of the fire all by himself for some time. Then a servant had come to serve him a cup of steaming hot tea along with some snacks. The teacher hesitated to accept this hospitality but the servant said this had been sent by the mistress. Ishar Das accepted the cup of tea hesitantly. It had a thick layer of cream on its surface.

He had hardly finished the last sip of tea when Mrs Rai appeared with a warm coat.

'Masterji, this is for you.'

'No, Mataji....'

'Take it as an order from your Mataji....'

Just as at drill time, when you have to obey the orders of your commander without giving it a second thought, the teacher accepted the coat. Overwhelmed, he could not say anything. Not even a few words of thanks.

In the meantime, Rai Sahib had also come. That's when he mentioned having the coat stitched in Austria and spoke of psychology as well.

Since the day before, he had been going home with this very coat protecting him from the chill. But before entering the home he wrapped the coat in an old newspaper and when he went out wore it again. He had concocted some story about the coat to his colleagues in the school who too had no coats of their own. But how could he explain it to Bhagwanti?

He tried to come up with something but in the end he had no choice but to wrap the coat in an old newspaper and hide it from her as if it was stolen booty.

He ultimately decided to return the coat to Mrs Rai. After tuition that evening when he asked the boy about his mother, he told his master that she had gone to visit her brother in Amritsar. Her affectionate words, 'Take it as an order from your Mataji', echoed in his mind. So he could not return it to anybody else and waited for her return from Amritsar. She would return after a week. Maybe she would refuse to accept it after so long. How would he tell Seeto's mother about this coat? For a week he would keep it wrapped...in old newspaper....

The coat had built a cage around Master Ishar Das. He tried his best to divert his mind from it. He had been teaching the boy for fifteen days and there were two and a half months to go. He would be paid a lump sum of forty-five rupees for three months, close to the exams in March.

Seeto's surgery had to be the top priority. A quilt would also have to be made for Bhagwanti. She had already arranged enough cotton for that using her homely wisdom.

In school, he did not think of the coat all day but whenever he heard a boy cough in class, he was reminded of his daughter.

'Don't worry, Seeto. This time I will definitely get you the surgery.' He would visualize Seeto before his eyes and address her in his imagination.

'Fifteen threes are forty-five, fifteen fours are sixty'. The boys were trying to memorize the fifteen times table by chanting in chorus.

'Yes, fifteen multiplied by three is forty-five....' Master Ishar Das kept thinking. Fifteen for January, in February it will be thirty, and in March it will be forty-five. Operation and quilt—both are necessary expenses....'

While teaching the boy in the evening he noticed a change in the behaviour of his student. Usually he was not a docile child. But there was a strange look in his eyes today. Ishar Das thought it was because his mother was not there.

So the teacher started checking the exercise book in a very gentle manner. But the scion of the affluent family did not sit at peace and kept touching his coat. Then all of a sudden, he asked, 'Masterji, Daddy brought me a very interesting magazine. It had a very good joke...would you like to hear it?'

'Okay, go ahead,' the teacher said without raising his eyes from the notebook.

'A teacher asked a shirker student to hold his ears. The student rose from his seat and held both the ears of his teacher.' Finishing the joke, the student guffawed.

Then the boy said to Master Ishar Das, 'May I ask you something? It's not a maths sum. Will you tell me?' And, without waiting for an affirmative response from the teacher, he said, 'Masterji, what is the difference between a teacher and servant?'

The boy had just asked the question when a servant came saying,

'Masterji, Rai Sahib has called you in.'

The teacher followed the servant. Rai Sahib was busy playing cards with some of his friends. The servant asked the teacher to stand in a corner of the room.

It was a gorgeous room. Once, in his childhood, Ishar Das had gone to see the museum in Lahore. This room was also well-decorated like that museum. Two braziers made it feel as though it were summer inside the room. The servant informed Rai Sahib that Masterji had arrived. Rai Sahib signalled him to wait. The game appeared to be taking a long time. This was what made the Rai Sahib look so thoughtful.

To the left of where Master Ishar Das stood was an almirah full of books. The books in this almirah outnumbered all the books in his school library. An English label announced that they were all on the subject of psychology.

Ignoring the books, Master Ishar Das started listening to the conversation between Rai Sahib and his friends.

'Rai Sahib, the weather is very cold these days. It pierces even the citadel of two sweaters, one coat, and one overcoat.'

'Dear friends, you are just like the frogs in the well—all they see is the sky above them and think that it's the entire thing. This is no winter at all. The winter I am referring to was what I experienced in Austria. It was in 1930 and I was in Vienna.'

Master Ishar Das felt his feet sinking into the carpet he stood on. How big it was! As big as three quilts—no even bigger, as big as four quilts. Four quilts...the fourth one for the mother of my daughters....

Rai Sahib came up to the teacher. Master Ishar Das folded his hands in respect.

'Please take a seat, Masterji.' Seating himself, Rai Sahib gestured to chair nearby. 'See, what I want to say to you today is a bit difficult to say but still I must say what I think. Why don't you sit?'

Master Ishar Das took the chair. The chair he sat in felt thicker and softer than all the quilts of his house.

'All the books you see in the almirah are on human psychology. I haven't just kept them for show. I have read them all and, in a way, squeezed out their essence. And I make use of this essence in my practical life also.' Rai Sahib paused.

'My vast study in psychology tells me that a student cannot learn anything from his teacher unless he has deep respect for him. Now ever since you accepted this coat the day before yesterday....'

At the very mention of the coat, Master Ishar Das felt as if a nail had poked him from the cushion of the chair he sat in.

'...I mean from the very moment of this acceptance, my son has lost all respect for you. Regular parents are unable to grasp these subtleties but I am a man of psychology. These things cannot remain concealed from me. Now, he won't be able to learn anything from you. He was asking me today, "Papa, what's the difference between our sweeper and the teacher. Lalu, the sweeper also wears your coat and now Masterji is wearing one too...."'

Not one but many nails arose from the cushion of the chair under him.

Master Ishar Das said with folded hands in utter humility, 'Rai Sahib, I had to do so at the command of Mrs Rai and the next day she left.' Master Ishar Das started removing the coat saying, 'I was waiting for her to come back so that I could return the coat with thanks.' As he said this, he started folding the coat.

'No Masterji, you need not remove the coat. Please put it back on.' Rai Sahib said looking Masterji in the eye. This was also like the drill master's command and Master Ishar Das obeyed Rai Sahib and put on the coat.

'If you need it for any of your children you can take an old coat of my son's. It's not at all the question of a coat. Okay, take your fee for fifteen days—seven and a half rupees. From tomorrow onwards, you need not take the trouble of coming to teach my son. I hope you will understand the core of this whole issue. It's not your fault at all. You have worked hard. It's just psychology....'

Translated by Parvesh Sharma

IN-BETWEEN THE BOOKS

SUKHBIR

Shekhar was casually browsing through the books in the poetry section of the Central Library. This part was in a corner of the library building and Shekhar felt a mysterious sense of loneliness here. At times he thought it should be named 'poetry corner' instead of 'poetry section'. He was busy looking at the books lined on the shelves when a pleasant voice reached his ears, 'May I help you, please?'

He turned around and found a young girl standing close to him. She was a library official. He had seen her before, either sitting at the inquiry seat or issuing books to readers from the counter. She was a slender girl of average height with moderate looks. However, her brown eyes made her look exceptionally beautiful.

Shekhar fumbled for the right words to respond to her.

The girl asked, 'Which book are you looking for?'

'Nothing in particular,' he said, 'I was just looking at the books in general. Well, a new book of criticism has reportedly come out on Hemingway. It must be here.'

'No, that is in the other section. This is the poetry section. Let me show you,' the girl said and led him to the section meant for books of criticism. She took out three books from the shelf.

Picking one from among them Shekhar said, 'Yes, this is what I was looking for. I have already read the other two. Thanks.'

The girl put the two books back on the shelf. Then as if she had recalled something all of a sudden, she turned to Shekhar and said, 'We have also received a new book on Hemingway if you are interested.... It is a compilation of his reporting during the

120

days when he used to be a reporter for some French newspaper. Would you like to see?'

'Sure.' Shekhar said, 'I would love to read it. I have a special interest in Hemingway's earlier writings.'

'Come then,' said the girl and took him to another part of the library. Shekhar found her interesting and amicable. He found her very knowledgeable and liked the way she helped others. He thought that she must be a voracious reader and fond of reading good writers.

The girl searched for the book but could not find it.

'Sorry,' she said, 'Seems like it's not available at this time. Someone must have borrowed it. Doesn't matter. You reserve it. It will be held for you once it's returned. If you want some other author's book, I can show it to you. Which other writer is your favourite?'

'Maybe Sandberg?'

'That you will find in the poetry section. If you are interested in Lincoln's biography written by Sandberg, it will be in the biography section. It's available in four volumes.'

'No, I'm interested only in his poetry.'

'Okay,' the girl said and immediately went to help another man who seemed confused as he searched for a book.

'May I help you, please?' she asked. The man seemed even more perturbed on hearing this.

Shekhar looked at the man and smiled. He went to the poetry section and started searching through books as earlier. He did not pick up any of Sandberg's books as he had already read the ones that were there.

⌒

When Shekhar visited the library the next time, the girl was very excited to see him. Shekhar found her enthusiasm endearing.

'A new Hemingway has arrived—*Papa Hemingway*. Would you like to take a look at it?'

'Oh yes, I would love to see it.'

'Come then.'

The girl took out the book from the shelf and gave it to Shekhar.

'Thanks. I would like to read any new book on Hemingway.'

'You seem to be a great fan of Hemingway's.'

'Undoubtedly.'

Shekhar noticed an expression of surprise on her face as if she was unable to understand why he was so interested in Hemingway. Also, he could see a faint derisive smile on her lips. Shekhar wanted to know the mystery behind this reaction.

'What's your opinion on Hemingway?' He asked.

The girl hesitated, then replied. 'Actually, I don't like him. I tried to read three or four of his novels but couldn't complete any of them.'

'Not even *Old Man and the Sea*?

'No.'

'But I have read it several times.'

'That is very strange!' the girl said.

At that time Shekhar liked the expression of surprise in her brown eyes. After a brief pause, he asked, 'Who is your favourite writer?'

'J. D. Salinger,' the girl replied promptly. 'I have read some of his works twice or thrice. I have read *Catcher in the Rye* several times.'

Now it was Shekhar's turn to raise his eyebrows and to put on a faint derisive smile. The girl noticed it and asked, 'Well, what's your opinion about him? You must have read him, I suppose.'

'Yes, I have read him but I didn't like him.'

'Strange!'

'Yes, you can call it strange.'

The girl smiled and said, 'Okay, who is your favourite among the new writers?'

'Irwin Shaw.'

'I didn't like him much,' said the girl with an expression of dislike on her face, 'I find him quite boring. I have a great liking for William Saroyan. He has a unique and interesting style.'

'His writings are overly sentimental. Honestly, he sounds artificial,' Shekhar responded.

'And, what about John O'Hara?' the girl asked.

'I join Alfred Kazin in describing him as "the big American bore".'

The girl burst into laughter.

Shekhar liked her laughter and wondered whether she had laughed at him or his opinion.

'And, what's your opinion about O'Hara?' he asked.

'Very high opinion, indeed. He is very interesting. Did you watch the movie *Butterfield-8* based on his novel?' the girl responded.

'Yes, the film was good, but I couldn't read the novel. I got bored,' said Shekhar.

'But I liked the novel more than the film. I have read almost all the novels of O'Hara,' she replied.

'How strange that I have a great liking for Hemingway and a complete dislike for O'Hara whom Hemingway liked most among the next gen writers,' observed Shekhar.

'Similarly, I would say that I have a great liking for O'Hara and a complete dislike for Hemingway whom O'Hara treated as the greatest among the previous gen writers,' she replied.

⸱⟋

Whenever Shekhar went to the library, he had a brief conversation with the girl. They would say 'Hello' to each other and exchange pleasantries. This was followed by the mention of books. They would discuss the books they had recently read and their critical opinion on them. Then they would recommend those books to each other. Just as the girl took books out of shelves for Shekhar, he too would recommend books and take them out for her from the shelf of the relevant section.

'It's a beautiful novel—it would be more suitable to call it a novelette—by Carson McCullers,' he said, showing her the book *The Ballad of the Sad Café.*

'It has such a smooth flow and simplicity that you would like it even if you are reading it for the second or third time,' he added.

'I will definitely read it,' she replied. 'You must not have read Edward Albee's play *Who's Afraid of Virginia Woolf?* A film is also being made based on it.'

'No, how is it?'

'Wonderful! Come, let me show it to you,' she said and they walked towards the drama section.

They would each borrow the books suggested by the other but they did not enjoy reading them. During the next meeting they would express their dislike of the work with hesitation. In order to get out of the uncomfortable situation, they would change the topic of conversation. They discussed certain personal issues also but they would never go beyond a particular limit. They could not liberate themselves from the cocoon of formality.

Shekhar's liking for the girl grew with time. He had a desire to get close to her and to know her better. However, the intensity of this desire did not grow beyond a point. Sometimes he was enamoured by the slender and flexible physique of the girl. But at other times he thought to himself that she looked very frail and it was only her fashion style that made her look attractive. He also found her choice of books and authors to be odd. Not just odd but disgusting.

At times he thought that her choice of authors was not bad after all. Some of the authors that she liked were great writers. It was a different matter that he did not like them. Shekhar wondered why she did not like Hemingway. He was surprised at her reaction at the mention of Hemingway. Her nose crinkled as if she had smelt something foul. At the same time, he really liked when she crinkled her nose. He was enamoured with her eyes. Her brown eyes, which at times appeared green, fascinated him.

⌣

Shekhar felt that the liking he had developed gradually for the girl had reached a point of saturation now. What could be the reason for this saturation? He wondered but could not find an answer. The same must have happened with her also, he thought. Now whenever they met, the ambit of their conversation was limited. Their interactions did not seem to suggest the beginning of anything new in the relationship that they shared.

Four or five months passed this way. Now whenever Shekhar went to the library, he felt no excitement at the prospect of meeting the girl. Sometimes he found her busy working and would go past her, saying a formal 'Hello', and then return with his books. On such occasions the girl did not show any particular interest in him either.

One day, as they were talking, the girl asked him what he did.

'I am part of the editorial board for an Urdu daily.'

'Are you a reporter?'

'No, I write features under two or three different names. One of the most liked features is written by me under the pseudonym of a girl. Reading the feature makes you feel the beauty of the girl behind it.'

'That is very interesting.'

'Yes, I enjoy writing that feature.'

'What is there in the feature? I mean on what topic does the girl write?'

'This girl roams about the city and interacts with different kinds of people, particularly women, ranging from actresses to labourers, dancers and others and writes about them. She also writes travelogues about the places she visits. Not only this city, she writes about other cities also.

'She writes about the women of not just this country but

other countries as well. She seems to be restless and on the lookout for something. Wandering in quest of that "something" she meets a girl working in the library and now she plans to write about her also.'

'What is she going to write?' The girl asked with curiosity and her eyes widened with anticipation.

'It will be known only when it is written,' Shekhar said with a smile.

It was true that Shekhar wanted to write about that girl but he found himself unable to do so. He felt he needed to know more about her. Surprisingly he wrote about the women of other countries based on sheer imagination without ever meeting them, while he did not want to write about this girl without knowing her properly.

And there was no possibility of knowing her more beyond what he already knew.

However, how much further should I go? Shekhar thought. It should not stop here. One way or the other, it must go further. This could not be the end of his quest.

Finally, Shekhar felt a change in the status quo when he did not see the girl in the library. He was told that she had left the job. Hearing this Shekhar stood in the library nonplussed and felt a vacuum from her absence. Finally, he went to the poetry section of the library and sat there. Looking around with blank eyes, he started thinking about that girl. Without her, the library seemed quite desolate to him.

After that, whenever he went to the library, he felt a sense of desolation. The girl's absence saddened him. In this state of sadness, he felt closer to the girl. In solitude, he would think about her—right from their first meeting to her departure. And the more he wanted to write about her, the more he was afraid. He realized that she was not a fictional character but a part of his reality. And he found it difficult to present this reality.

He had started feeling closer to her. One of the methods was reading the writers she liked but he did not like—Salinger, O'Hara, Saroyan, Dorothy Parker, etc. He derived a peculiar pleasure in reading them. He was surprised to find that now they did not seem as distasteful to him as earlier. Two or three months went by like this.

One day, Shekhar went to the library and was surprised to see the girl there. He could not believe his eyes. Sitting at a desk, the girl was glancing through the pages of a magazine. Shekhar hesitated to go near her. He was thinking about how to approach her. In the meanwhile, the girl looked up from the pages of the magazine and focused her attention on the door as if she were waiting for someone. She was startled to see Shekhar. There was a glint in her eyes and a smile on her face. This smile seemed to be welcoming Shekhar.

Shekhar walked up to her.

They enquired about each other's well-being and chatted. They didn't have anything particular to talk about, but they wanted to talk to each other.

After some time, the girl asked, 'What are you reading these days?'

Showing the books he had in his hands, Shekhar said, 'O'Hara and Salinger.'

'Okay!' the girl exclaimed with astonishment and then smiled.

Shekhar noticed her expression of astonishment and the smile. He understood the astonishment but the meaning of the smile eluded him. She seemed to be concealing something behind that smile, but it looked like she wanted to say something as well.

Shekhar was about to ask her about it when the girl said, 'You know what I'm reading these days?'

'What?'

'Hemingway and Irwin Shaw.'

'Really?' Shekhar asked.

The girl pulled out two books from near her purse and, holding them out to him said, 'Yes, really.'

'Then let's go and have a cup of tea in a good restaurant,' Shekhar said, wondering how he was able to muster this courage. 'Let's go,' the girl replied. She was still smiling.

Translated by Parvesh Sharma

THAT WOMAN!

RAM SARUP ANKHI

Today I tell you the story of an old woman—Ram Kaur. One part of this story I have heard from others, the other three parts I have seen unfolding before my own eyes.

This story is from the time when poor farmers in Punjab's villages, suffering economic hardships, sold their daughters in marriage to better manage their own households.

Ram Kaur was her parents' only daughter. She had three younger brothers. She had been a beautiful girl in her youth, energetic and strong. She was short-statured and there was little chance of her growing any taller. But she was quite attractive, fair complexioned with sharp features. Short and sturdy, Ramo was like her mother.

A boy, Gurcharan, visiting his maternal uncle who lived close to Ramo's home, fell in love with her. 'You enchanted me, O beautiful damsel,' as the folk song goes.

Gurcharan stayed in the village for six months. Who knows why? Did he stay for Ramo or to help his maternal uncle with the farm? He was the seventh son of his parents, the youngest. His family probably had a small landholding and it is unlikely that there was any need for him at his home. Surely, there must have been some other reason why he stayed for six months at his maternal uncle's home!

One day Ramo said to him, 'My father is not going to let me marry you. Just take me away, take me anywhere. I will be satisfied with whatever little we have.'

He was almost on the verge of tears when he replied, 'Where

can I take you? I have nothing, I'm penniless. I'm absolutely nothing! I am broke.'

'Then, you shameless, despicable fellow, why did you entice me? Just wait, I'll smash in your head.' Ramo picked up a brick. He got up quickly and walked away, leaving her sitting alone. Had he not done so, Ramo might have considered strangling him there and then. The fool had not accepted her simple proposal! After he left, Ramo, who was ready to smash his head with a brick, who wished to strangulate him and kill him, held her head in her hands and began to weep bitterly. They never met after that. He left his uncle's home and went back to his village.

Ramo's father took 600 rupees from a family and gave her away in marriage. Two hundred were spent in buying some clothes and other accessories for the bride and for hosting the ten or twelve men who came as part of the marriage party. The remaining 400 proved helpful in helping run his household more comfortably. In those days, 600 rupees were as good as 6,000 today.

This much of the story I have heard from others.

Ram Kaur gave birth to five sons. All five were equally strong and sturdy. None of them had any ailments at all, no fever, no aches or pains of any kind. She had no daughters.

Chanan Singh, Ram Kaur's husband, didn't dare challenge her in any manner. He had only one weakness: he didn't work hard but was a hard drinker. He used to drink almost every day. Wherever he could he found a drink. He could not stop himself, could not resist the temptation. Ram Kaur somehow managed all of her household needs and arranged meals for the family. She had to look after the needs of her sons, had to bring them up. Whatever little land they had she gave it out on a sharecropping basis. All the other chores she handled on her own. Whenever Chanan happened to be at home, she would quarrel with him. She had even beaten him up a couple of times. She would threaten him with the dung scraper. But whenever he was unwell, she diligently looked after him as well, bringing him medicines from the village doctor. Still, she continued to abuse and curse him relentlessly.

Ram Kaur didn't care to maintain friendly relations with her neighbours. She would pick a quarrel on the pettiest pretext and would continue to shout obscenities for hours on end. Everyone was afraid of her. No one dared challenge her. The neighbours often said, 'She is a tigress, keep your distance from her.' But despite all the bitter fights with neighbours, despite all the arguments, she always joined them in their times of distress and shared in their moments of joy.

People often said, 'Chanan drinks because of the humiliation he faces from his wife. This tigress does not let him live in peace for a moment; provoking and taunting him all the time.'

No young man ever dared to take any liberties with Ram Kaur, or pass a vulgar, snide comment. All of them addressed her respectfully, calling her 'Aunt'. God forbid she caught a whiff of sarcasm or insult—the offending person had better run for his life.

One day, Chanan, brought to breaking point by her taunts, disappeared. She didn't bother about him for nearly a week. Then she started worrying. She sent men to nearby villages to look for him. Her sons went to different relatives to enquire about him. But he was nowhere to be found. Ram Kaur would fret about him. Sometimes she sat next to the hearth and started wailing in sorrow. The women of the neighbourhood accused her of hypocrisy and play-acting. They said, 'She never cared for him when he was around, now that he is gone, she is pretending to be grief-stricken.'

Many months passed and people started thinking that Chanan must have fallen into a ditch and died somewhere. If he were alive, he would surely have returned by now.

'Good or bad, whatever he was, he was the head of the family after all,' they would say.

'For this tigress, he was as good as dead even when he was alive. She didn't give him any respect even for one day.'

'He was treated the way one treats a stray dog—just throw him a roti now and then. Terrible! That was the life he had.' Most of them blamed Ram Kaur and cursed her.

The two eldest sons of Ram Kaur were grown up now, of marriageable age. She arranged their marriages. Both the sons, Angrej Singh and Gurjant Singh, were very obedient, and did as their mother told them. The brides were young and energetic, and always obeyed their mother-in-law. They took over all the chores of the house.

However, Ram Kaur started feeling that her sons doted too much on their wives; it was as though they were always with their spouses. It seemed as if their interest in working on the field was diminishing. She agreed that the axiom is true: 'Day for the fields and night for the wife'. But 'night for the wife and day for the wife' was a bit much surely. Worried that the wives would spoil her sons, she started scolding her sons. She began to behave very rudely with her daughters-in-law.

It became so bad that her sons had to leave home. They owned a vacant plot of land on the outskirts of the village, allotted to them at the time of reorganization of landholdings. The two brothers managed to construct two rooms there. They moved there with their wives. In due course, both of them were blessed with children. Both the brothers took land on annual lease from other farmers and made ends meet. Their mother would not let them go near their own land. Their share of land had not been allotted to them because there was no firm proof of the passing away of their father. Ram Kaur was holding onto everything.

But this woman, Ram Kaur, was a strange being. She would spit at her elder sons and their wives if she happened to come across them or she would turn her back on them but if one of their children ever happened to come to her home, she would offer him a bowl of warm milk, mixing a liberal quantity of sugar in it. And she would shower unmitigated affection on the child.

Then, she arranged the marriages of her younger sons, Ghichar and Dulla. They were married to two sisters. She didn't invite her elder sons, Angrej and Gurjant, or their wives to the wedding. Their children came on their own, uninvited. Ram Kaur looked after and fed the children well even as she abused and cursed their worthless fathers.

'Ve, you don't turn out like your father,' she would tell Angrej's son.

And looking crossly at Gurjant's daughter, she would taunt her, 'Did your mother allow you to come to my house?' Yet she would give the child lots of sweet delicacies.

Some two years after the wedding of Ghichar and Dulla, Ram Kaur bought a buffalo. She already had one but that was old now. She sold the old one and, adding some money of her own, she bought a newly calved young buffalo. And she started selling the milk of this buffalo to the milkman. She earned enough to buy yet another buffalo the following year.

And then milk became the cause of dispute in the family. Ghichar and Dulla argued that they should have enough milk to drink. They toiled all day in the fields but their mother sold all the milk to the milkman. They wanted their wives also to have some milk to drink, because they were busy looking after the buffaloes all day. Is the woman who clears the dung and urine from under the animals not entitled to a glass of milk?

The old woman was driven by greed. She wanted to save enough money to buy another acre of land. She replied: 'What do I save from the selling of milk? Just enough to pay for their feed. From where do I bring milk for you to drink? If there was some to spare, I could give you.' She would continue, 'I fed you so well before your marriages. And your wives should have got what they want at their parents' home. Now you are family men, with sons and daughters to look after. You are no longer bachelors to enjoy life as you please. If you start wasting money like this, how will you manage the household?' She even warned them, 'If you want to live as you wish, be ready to live separately.

Aren't two of your elder brothers already living by themselves?'

She gave milk to Ghichar and Dulla off and on but she never gave anything to her daughters-in-law. She didn't like them at all.

One day, Dulla slyly handed half a glass of milk he was drinking to his wife. Ram Kaur happened to see this. The old woman created such a storm! All day long she kept muttering abuses and cursing her daughters-in-law. Neither the sons nor their wives said anything. To respond to Ram Kaur would be like lighting gunpowder. They were afraid that while fuming with anger, she would just hit her head against the wall and die.

She would secretly give milk to her youngest son Harnek. He depended entirely on his mother, a youth stepping into adulthood.

To avoid the daily bickering and tension, Ghichar and Dulla moved out of their home as well. They built two rooms on the outskirts of the village next to those of their elder brothers and started living there.

All the four were waiting and hoping that the old woman would die soon. She did not die, nor did she share her buffaloes. She told Harnek, 'I won't get you married. What do you need a wife for? A girl born to someone else is not going to be friendly with me, and will never become mine.'

Harnek would not respond. But he wanted to say, 'Mother, my wife will not be coming here for you, but for me.'

Ram Kaur looked after the kitchen all by herself. She milked the, now three, buffaloes. Harnek cleared the dung and did the cleaning. She gave all their land on lease. Mother and son kept themselves busy taking care of the three buffaloes. They used the milk from one buffalo for themselves and sold the milk from the other two.

One winter day, she was sitting on the platform in front of her home and enjoying the sun. It was early afternoon. She noticed a man in the distance coming in her direction. He had a walking stick in his hand. He carried a small bundle on his head and was accompanied by a seven- or eight-year-old girl. Walking gingerly, the old man went past her, looking at her gate as he moved on. When he had gone some distance, she shaded her eyes with her hand and stared at him. Then she asked a woman walking by, 'Who is he? To whose house could he be headed? He went by looking at my home.'

He returned that evening. She was still sitting right there. This time he stood in front of her and asked, 'Are you Ramo?'

She immediately became attentive and sat upright and opened her eyes wide. She did not recognize him. He told her, 'I am Gurcharan Singh, nephew of Thaman Singh of your village.'

'What brings you here, Gurcharan Singh?' Ram Kaur went limp, as though someone had squeezed the life out of her. She went back in time. She went many years back, to a time when she was just a sixteen-year-old girl. Wrapping her warm shawl around her, she got up and brought him inside, to the inner courtyard. She placed a cot for him to sit down.

He said, 'There is a house of Sidhus here in your village. Their son was suggested as a match for my granddaughter. I thought I should have a look at their house and the neighbourhood.'

'And this girl?'

'She is the daughter of my granddaughter. She was adamant about accompanying me.' He continued, 'I knew about your village and asked the Sidhu family about your home too. I thought now that I have come so far, I should see Ramo also.'

Ramo noticed that Gurcharan Singh looked quite old now. His beard was absolutely white, like the egg of a hen. His eyes did not have the same sparkle. Four lower front teeth were missing. Stooping, he walked with the help of a walking stick. Old memories surfaced in her mind, one after the other. She brought three bowls of warm milk from the courtyard, sweetened each with a handful of sugar.

Gurcharan said, 'Ramo, I won't be able to drink so much. Bring an empty bowl. Some of it I'll drink, the rest I'll give to this girl. Take one bowl back.'

After drinking milk, they started exchanging family news. They talked about their sons and daughters, then they began to discuss other relatives. They avoided talking about themselves. Then he said, 'Okay, I'll leave now. I'll reach my village by sunset. There are enough buses available.'

Ram Kaur pressed him to stay for the night, saying they would talk at length. But he was in a hurry to leave.

Standing at her door, she watched him for a long time. Then she went in and lay on the bed, covering herself with a quilt. She was feeling very low.

In a few days, she slowly came to feel as if she had no complaint against anyone in life. All her belligerence melted away like mercury spreading and losing itself in the soil. One day, she told Harnek to take one buffalo each to the houses of her two sons. And then she invited four elders of her neighbourhood and divided her land into five parts. A few days later, she called Harnek and told him, 'You take control of your home from now on. I am not going to live much longer. Get married now.'

Translated by Paramjit Singh Ramana

DOG AND MAN

GURDIAL SINGH

'Today is Tuesday,' Isra remembered suddenly while twisting off a bit of dough.

'Chandi used to feed roti to the dog on Tuesday.' The wet dough clung to his fingers. So he dusted some dry flour onto it and began rolling it with the pin on a wooden board. The roti expanded to cover the whole of the circular rolling board. It looked like it had been flattened out very unevenly with irregular ends. It was thick in some places and thin in others. But Isra slapped it onto the insufficiently heated iron tawa.

'Oi, go in and bring the oil lamp,' he said to Ghunna, who was sitting in front of the hearth, fiddling with a piece of burning straw. Ghunna refused, saying, 'I won't go!' and ran out, taking with him the straw with one lit end.

Isra got angry. He shouted at the boy, threw a stick after him, and swore. Screwing his eyes half shut, he roared, 'Get back here! You bastard!'

But Ghunna had gone out and started playing with the children in the street. Raging, Isra got up and brought the oil lamp from the kothri, the small inner room. He removed the roti from the hot tawa and smeared the uncooked side with his fingers dipped in oil. He put the roti in the reed basket and sat back against the wall as if there was nothing more to do.

Next to the wall, close to the haari, Dabbu, the pet dog, settled down, placing his muzzle on its front paws, and looked at him. Its ears sagged like a goat's. The ashen light of the hearth fell on its dappled body and at times its black eyes lit up like glow-worms. Tucking its scraggy tail between its hind legs, it sat motionless, in a pensive mood, as though it was lost in thought just like its master.

Isra felt sorry for it. For the last five days, Dabbu had not touched even a morsel of food. The buttermilk that had been poured into the earthen bowl too had not been touched and had been spoiling for the last three days. Its stomach was nearly touching its spine due to starvation and the ribs had become noticeably visible. For the first time in seven years, Isra had not felt jealous of Dabbu. And it was the first time he felt comfortable and familiar with the dog.

Dabbu! He remembered that it was Chandi who had named it and it had come along with her as if a part of her dowry. Perhaps it was a stray dog that she had looked after. Only she could feed it roti and buttermilk. It would keep circling around her, wagging its scraggly tail. Sometimes, when Isra felt it was unfriendly, he would hurl a stick at it or even feel jealous as though it was a former husband of hers. Dabbu would then limp away, with one leg injured, crying. Then Chandi would scold Isra who would go silent. But in his heart of hearts, he felt as if she was totally devoted to her husband from an earlier life when she protected this pariah. As Dabbu came in again it would start growling at Isra and wagging its tail defiantly as it looked towards Chandi. It made Isra seethe with rage. Mumbling to himself he kept swearing at the innocent animal. And Dabbu occupied the courtyard, as though he owned it, prowling back and forth.

…Now see. This is the same Dabbu.

Isra touched the oiled roti and realized that it was still warm. Picking it up, he waved it in the air a few times and made a puch-puch sound, calling Dabbu. Dabbu's only response was to move its ears and twitch its eyebrows, but it did not rise. Isra raised the roti a little higher and puch-puched again. But the dog did not pay him any heed. Isra was hurt but he kept the roti raised and kept looking at Dabbu.

After a while the dog got up on its own and moved slowly, as though it was ill, towards the door of the kothri, as if it had forgotten its way.

'Oi! This side!' Isra called Dabbu. Dabbu reached the door but turned to look towards its 'master'. Isra could not see its eyes in the dark but seeing the emaciated body, he was afraid. For a moment he stayed silent but then tried another encouraging puch-puch. Dabbu looked at Isra who said, gently, 'Come, eat.'

The dog looked at the roti listlessly, then sniffed it a little and turned to looked at Isra.

'You son of a bitch! Why are you bent on starving yourself to death? She is no longer here to feed you choori made with sugary crushed rotis. So don't expect that now.' It was as if by talking to Dabbu, he was actually talking to himself.

Then Dabbu picked up the roti unenthusiastically and walked slowly as though ill, to come back again to its place near the haari and sat facing away from Isra. From this angle, Isra could not tell if Dabbu was eating or just sitting there.

Just then he realized the fire in the hearth had turned into nothing more than dense smoke. He pushed the moist fuel wood deeper into the fireplace and started blowing air into it. Despite trying his best, the wood refused to ignite. Instead, the smoke spiralling out of it thickened. He kept wiping away the tears that the smoke caused with the end of his kurta. But with each puff, his eyes would start watering again.

'Now what revenge are you taking on me, you witch? Do what you can,' he said, gnashing his teeth and thrusting a bigger log in but the fire did not catch. Frustrated, he sat back, resting against the wall. Wiping his smoke-embittered eyes with the end of his kurta he placed his head between his knees. He stayed in that position for a long while. Just as he was about to break down crying, the fire flared up on its own. The conflagration lit up the entire courtyard.

It was quite late at night when he tried to appease his hunger with four misshapen rotis and a bit of pickle which Chandi had made. The flames arising from the hearth leapt upwards and started licking the plumes of the peahens Chandi had drawn with soot on the low wall of the oven called the kandholi. She had drawn them just a month ago. Chewing on the dry roti with his decayed teeth, Isra looked at the artwork. Suddenly he felt terribly thirsty, as thirsty as a dying man might. He filled a bowl of water from the pitcher lying nearby. He could not quench his thirst with the lukewarm water but he swallowed it all. He stared at the fire again and at the peahens and a popular adage came to him: 'When the rotis are done, the fire burns. When the grain is husked, the wind rises. When the husband is consumed, the woman awakens.'

Then he looked at Dabbu who still lay near the haari, its head on its paws. He watched the dog for a few moments and after eating he cleared the used vessels from near the hearth. He got up, went out, and started calling out to Ghunna.

'Oye! Come in, boy. Are you also an enemy set upon taking revenge on me?'

Ghunna shouted 'coming' from a distance and then ran away in the other direction.

It was a cool moonlit night in the balmy month of Assu. Children from all the houses were playing in the glistening cold sand. Earlier, during such pleasant nights, when Chandi would call out to Ghunna over and over, he would say, 'Let him play. He is just a child....'

But today, that same child seemed a rebellious brat. Someone who never listened to what was said, and never obeyed his elders.

'Now are you coming or should I come to drag you from there?' His voice had become hoarse from shouting at the boy.

Ghunna walked towards him slowly, looking behind him at every step. With each step Ghunna took, Isra calmed down. So, he asked gently, 'You fool, will you have roti or not? Little beast.'

Ghunna turned a deaf ear—he came in, went straight to the

fireplace, and took some rotis from the basket, and started eating.

'Dal...Bapu?' the boy asked in a tearful voice.

'Eat the rotis as they are. Don't expect any vegetables or dal now.' Isra erupted again angrily.

The boy protested and whispered, 'I won't eat.' This only added fuel to the fire of Isra's wrath. He swore at Ghunna. 'Making a fuss! Who do you think you are....'

Ghunna put the rotis back in the basket and, rubbing his eyes with his hand, started crying.

'Now let me see how you...' Isra swore at him and rushed at the boy who ran out, screaming in fear. Isra picked up his shoe from the veranda and flung it at Ghunna. It missed the boy but hit the wall.

'Vay! What's happened to you?' Sadho, a distant aunt of Isra's came out of her home hurriedly, wondering what the commotion was about. She first saw the boy running away, then at the fretting and fuming Isra, who stood in the doorway.

'No, no, son, don't do this.' Panting hard and coughing she said, 'Don't take it so hard. Take it as the will of God. Vay Ghunnu! Come here, son, and sleep with me. I won't let your Bapu beat you. Come. Come here, my son.'

Isra, his fury still unabated, came in and settled himself on the cot that was in the courtyard. But he continued cursing God knows whom...he didn't name anyone in particular.

The fire in the hearth was still burning. The lamp in the kothri had dimmed and the mess of clothes on the cot looked lifeless.

Lying on the cot Isra looked to the left. His work spot used to be there. The tools were lying in utter disarray. He could not remember whether he himself had left the tools like this. The pokers, scraper, hammer, shoe stretcher, etc. were all scattered like the bones of dead cattle in the skinning yard.

There was a bitter taste in his mouth. Isra coughed, spat out the phlegm and, lying supine on the cot, stared at the sky. A crescent moon as yellow as a maize roti seemed to touch the parapet of the kothri. Above it floated a dark cloud. Resembling an enraged bear, it looked like it was advancing towards the moon, its mouth agape, while the moon seemed to be fleeing in fright from it.

Suddenly the moon-gazing Isra became afraid. He heard a piercing scream from inside the kothri and he sat up with a start. He stared towards the kothri. The flame of the lamp died down slowly. He heard the scream again and imagined that he saw Chandi running out. Her hair was open and dishevelled, she looked like a demon.... Shrieking, she continued running.

Isra started to sweat in fear. His legs trembled. He clasped his knees firmly with his arms and buried his head between them. He fixed his gaze on the embers of the fire dying down slowly.

For five nights he had been seeing Chandi running out of the kothri shrieking and shouting. This phenomenon had convinced him, that after leaving this place, Chandi had fallen or tripped and drowned in a pond or well. People don't see ghosts of the living, he thought.

It was a well-known rumour in the village that Chandi had eloped with a boy from the potters' family of Nandpur. But Isra did not believe this. No woman can abandon her home and beloved five-year-old son without a very good reason, he thought. Also, there was no apparent reason why she would be fed up with Isra. He had given her all the space and freedom she could have desired. She could go where she wanted and return whenever. So, he ruled out any possibility whatsoever of her running away.

Sadhu Meerab had chided him the very next day. 'You stupid Chamar! What were you thinking when you sent her all alone to the fields to pick cotton? Did you think she was praying there? You must have mistaken her for a pious woman.'

Not only Sadhu Meerab, everyone he met pounced on him for not only being guilty of seducing someone else's wife, but also for being on the receiving end this time.

'Were you blind when that lecherous potter attired in a

chequered lungi and with a plumed turban on his head would come and sit for hours on end at your shop? Actually, dullards like you harm yourselves by trusting your wives too much. Even God has never trusted women! Moreover, things would have been different if you had brought her home as a traditional bride. What does a bought woman care for a dunce like you? Why didn't you notice when she stepped outdoors with kohl-rimmed eyes and new clothes? How can you expect that a soft, beautiful woman will live with a rustic fool like you? She is one to live life to the fullest. She has squeezed you as much as she wanted and then thrown you away like a sucked out sugarcane. Now she has found another able-bodied young man. She will use him as long as possible and then throw him away as well—like an Arab eats the dates and throws away the seeds.'

Such public advice pricked Isra like a poker. Sometimes, he got ready to argue with the other but how could a man as passive as him fight? He was not brave enough to even speak rudely to anybody. No one had sympathized with him when he had bought Chandi for 750 rupees.

'You low caste, when does a wicked woman like her settle down with a good-for-nothing man like you? For six months, at the most, one year—this is the maximum they will stay with the likes of you,' Basanta had predicted. So Isra took all precautions in this regard for the first two or three months but then when she established her fidelity, he relaxed. He had finally become a 'householder'.

But who knows the ways of God? Isra heaved a deep sigh and, lifting his head, he looked to the left. He felt his sunken cheeks and long nose had shrunk like dried wood. He sighed deeply again. He smelt the fragrance of moist clay. He glanced at the parapet and found it gleaming white as if painted afresh. Just last month Chandi had coated the kothri and walls of the courtyard, freshening them by making several trips, carrying the troughs of clay mixture on her head. She had also raised the kandholi and whitewashed it. In short, she had spruced up the whole house, making it gleam like a memorial.

But nobody knows the ways of God. Who can say what Chandi was thinking? Isra breathed deeply again. Gathering the few strands of hair on his half-bald head he knotted them into a small bun and after dusting off the turban lying on his pillow, he started tying it as though he was getting ready to go somewhere.

Sadho's voice could be heard from the other side of the wall. Perhaps she was talking to Ghunna because he was responding to her.

Isra attempted to get up but then sat back clasping his knees. Perhaps he missed Ghunna. Chandi had left five nights ago and ever since then Ghunna had been sleeping at Sadho's. He would play with his playmates during the day, come back in the evening to eat, get annoyed with his father on some pretext, and run out again. He had been aggressive even when Chandi had been around. He did not care for Isra even then and had never obeyed him. After all, he is the son of the bought woman! The serpent's child is essentially still a serpent, even if we feed it milk and rear it at home, he thought and sighed resignedly. It reminded him of Bakhtaur's Billu who was also the son of a bought woman. As a young man, he had run away after breaking Bakhtaur's legs. Nothing was ever heard about his whereabouts after that. Bakhtaur had been laid up in bed for two years and then died like a cripple. Nobody took care of him.

Isra started perspiring, perhaps due to fear. What kind of a woman was Chandi, he wondered. He thought for a while and then felt as if all his limbs had atrophied. He lay back on the cot again with tears gathering in his eyes.

After a while, his legs started shaking with cold. He realized that he was lying on the cot without any bedding or blanket covering him. The kothri's door was still open and the lamp was still aglow with embers. He wanted to get up and bring a khes, a thick cotton sheet, from inside to cover himself but he could not move. After a few moments, he folded his legs and tucked them into his belly and, turning to the right he clutched the edge of his bed tightly as though afraid he would fall. He started dozing off. He opened his eyes and saw that all was dark and desolate in the courtyard. For a moment, he thought he was lying all alone in some wilderness with ogres prowling around remarking about 'the smell of man'!

He looked around and found Dabbu panting near the haari. For a few moments he watched the dog. Then he stopped clutching the cot and folded his arm under his head like a pillow. He covered his face with the other arm and thus hid his face between both his arms. He then cradled the nape of his neck with his hands locked together behind it and bent his knees so they touched his chest. He felt the prickling of his sparse beard on his knee and the friction caused a sensation that made him close his eyes and doze off.

Was he dreaming? He felt as if some creature was racing towards him. Panting hard, hurting his ankles and knees as he stumbled, he ran recklessly through the jungle. He had spent his whole life in search of the princess of folk tales. To protect her from the giant, she was turned into a fly and made to sit on a pillar in the palace. But he could not find her. Now the same princess was sitting in a window of the palace, laughing at the sight of this fleeing creature. But instead of the proverbial flowers that fall from the mouth of a captivating beauty when she laughed, she was spewing sparks of fire which fell on his head.... His head and his body were burning and erupting in blisters wherever the fire fell.

'Ah...I'm burning...' Isra screamed in his dream and woke up and looked around, his eyes dilated with fear. A frightened Dabbu had retreated a little at this expression of panic. Standing at a little distance from the cot, very wary, he was looking at Isra. Isra's heart was heaving like the bellows.

When he regained consciousness after some time, his body

seemed to have been drained of all vitality. He felt cold and lay again in the same posture with his knees folded against his chest and his head held between his arms.

His eyes opened for a moment. Dabbu was still standing silently before him. Isra beckoned Dabbu with a puch-puch. The dog took a few steps towards him slowly. One more puch–puch and it came closer to the cot and placed its muzzle on the side of the bed.

'Why are you being shy now, yaar? Now you too are like me,' Isra said in a hoarse voice. He put his hand on Dabbu's head and started caressing it affectionately. The dog moved its head closer to Isra until its muzzle touched Isra's knees. The warmth of its breath made Isra feel that the biting cold had somewhat abated.

Translated by Parvesh Sharma

THE SURVIVORS

SUKHWANT KAUR MANN

The surroundings have turned desolate. I don't know why peacocks don't call any more. The day before, the feathers of the wild fowl lay scattered all over the road. It used to flutter around that big acacia tree and would roost in the same tree every night. How bright and vibrantly coloured its feathers were! But that morning, its feathers lay scattered on the road. God knows which hunter found him. Perhaps some dog or cat got hold of him. It was the last wild fowl that sheltered in this acacia.

This village was earmarked to be demolished. But its residents were not willing to vacate it. The expanding city was almost touching it. Many notices had been issued ordering the villagers to clear out. But most of them had not been allotted any land to resettle. Some of them had been running dairies from their premises and some had set up small businesses within the city. And a few elderly people were too attached to the village to leave. High Court, and then Supreme Court. After the final notice, a thundering bulldozer appeared on the road beside the village. The village was in turmoil. Men and women desperately tried to salvage their possessions and carry them to safety. Driving their cattle and opening the door of the coops...the chickens fluttering their wings and squawking in alarm...the goats bleating...trunks, utensils, cots...pushed, pulled...men, old, young...cursing, crying, shouting...running away.

'May God destroy you, wipe you all out, may you die, you who uproot us!' Bhanto Mehri was shouting, cursing; looking like a reincarnation of Goddess Kali; her hair dishevelled, mouth foaming, she was staggering away, pushing her goats ahead by beating them with a stick. The boisterous granny, badly out of breath, was leaving, dragging her cot along. The bellowing buffaloes kept returning to their shelters again and again. The mud huts, brick houses, piles of wheat chaff, and stacks of dung cakes were all disintegrating in the face of the bulldozer as if some big tornado had struck.

They were saying new flats would come up here, big showrooms would be set up, metalled roads would be laid. At first some people tried to stop the bulldozer. Then, squabbling, blaming the government, they started to salvage their belongings from their homes. Watching their houses collapse, staring at each other's faces and noticing the gloomy visages of their parents, the village children were stunned and mesmerized in equal parts. They felt a strange restlessness. Despite their parents' warnings, they started following the bulldozer. 'Look, Kalu's room...there it goes,' Bhinda shrieked.

'Curse you, shameless!' Kartaro scolded Bhinda.

'Look, Dheere, there goes your kitchen. It goes dher, dher, thaah...' the boys could not help laughing.

'Ve! Why does it make you so happy to see our house destroyed?' Dheera's mother was furious.

The boys were drenched in sweat. They ran about madly, trying to outpace each other, to help people take their belongings out of their homes and towards the outer road.

All through the night, dogs, sitting on the mounds of debris, whined and howled in a strange manner while mewing cats roamed around the demolished village. Bhanto Mehri's rough voice— sometimes she could be heard shrieking, sometimes crying, then clapping and guffawing—cut through the silence, a frightening sound.

At daybreak the contractor arrived, accompanied by workers carrying saws and axes to chop down the old peepul, banyan, and neem trees in the village. The workers were residents of the village who had become urban labourers. The government had been very kind to the villagers: all were given temporary jobs.

'Ve! You will all be damned, don't cut down the peepul.' Bhanto Mehri shouted, raising her arms. For a moment, the workers were taken aback.

'What's the matter?' the contractor asked authoritatively.

They looked at each other, then their axes swung into action.

'Your mother...' one of them cursed the tree trunk for being too hard.

With their eyes filled with anger, sometimes they stared at the sky, sometimes at each other or the contractor. They spit on their calloused palms and struck the trunk again and again, wiping their sweat as they continued to work, badly out of breath.

Now they stood around a pitcher of water. Kartara said, 'That was our house; my great grandfather planted that neem...look how thick its trunk is! My mother used to sit under it with her spinning wheel. Grandmother used to spin yarn under it....'

'Come on, get going,' the contractor yelled.

'Your mother...' Kartara cursed him under his breath.

Bhinder and Shishu laughed out loud. They raised their axes and struck at the trunk of the old peepul tree. Peepul is very hard; Kartara, Bhinder, and Shishu were soon out of breath.

'Ve! The whole clan will be wiped out...don't cut the peepul, it is a sacred tree,' Bhanto Mehri protested, shouting warnings. The people of the village say that she has gone crazy. First the wells were closed and then the hotels took away the work traditionally done by her Mehra community. Her son also took up a job in a hotel and moved to Chandigarh. Bhanto did not go there. Or, perhaps, she went but returned since she would not have liked it there. She lived in her shack in the village. A bit crazy, sometimes she would heat up her bhatthi, the public hearth, for roasting corn. No one else would come to get their grain roasted. People would laugh at her, but she continued to feed the fire. Sometimes she would pretend that she really was roasting something.

'Ve! Lachhoo, come, see how fine the popcorns are!' she would say, as she continued to sieve the sand.

'Come, Tai, give us some corn,' passers-by would keep up the charade and laugh at her.

Her husband, Lachhoo Mehra, had a big herd of goats. Being a water carrier, he supplied water from the well to the whole village. Then he would take his herd of goats to the acacia grove. The goats loved the young acacia saplings and would munch on their fresh shoots. Lachhoo would start singing hymns to the goddess and then verses from 'Bego Naar', the folk tale. The land, called shamlat, was common to the whole village and so, other people would also bring their buffaloes there to graze on the tall grass under the young acacias. The buffaloes would graze and their young minders would wrestle with each other or play kabaddi. The boys would take turns looking after the cattle.

'Why, Taya, you have grown old but you have still not changed your ways,' the boys would tease him when he sang verses from the romantic folk tale 'Mirja'. But when he sang hymns to the Mother Goddess, he became ecstatic and started dancing and jumping around in a trance.

In such moments, Lachhoo's goats had a habit of wandering into others' fields. 'Oye, stupid!' the farmer Gehlu bellowed one day as he drove Lachhoo's goats off his field, beating them mercilessly. The frightened bleating goats ran to their master and stood around him. Lachhoo patted every one of them, caressed and embraced them. When he noticed that a goat had a cut on its body or leg, he became speechless and tears sprang to his eyes. Once he returned home, Bhanto counted the goats and found one to be missing. They counted again and again…losing count in the process. A fight ensued during which Lachhoo thrashed Bhanto and pulled her hair. The house devolved into chaos.

'May you be wiped out, Gehlu!' Bhanto shouted at the farmer. 'May you die…you stole my goat!'

'Listen villagers, listen, today he has stolen my goat, tomorrow he'll try to lay his hands on my daughter…I'll cut him to pieces. Considers himself a big shot!' Bhanto went on cursing Gehlu, calling him a Jat as she wielded his long stick used for herding goats.

'I'll cut you down just like the soft shoots of acacia!' Bhanto ran after Gehlu as she cursed him. Lachhoo ran after her, abusing her using filthy language, but Bhanto evaded him.

That evening, mutton was cooked in Gehlu's house. The pot sizzled, and the scent of frying meat could be smelt in half the village. Mutton dishes were served in many houses in the area. Gehlu got drunk and rushed towards Bhanto's house.

He abused her using filthy language and threatened to kidnap her daughter. Bhanto retorted fiercely. Lachhoo pulled her back by her braid and locked her in.

In the morning, Lachhoo went to Gehlu's house to lodge a protest. Crying and whining, he begged other respectable people to help him. The panchayat met to decide on the matter.

'No! This amounts to cutting the poor man's throat…' a rival of Gehlu declared in support of Lachhoo.

'My lord, that is right….'

'His goats have ruined my mustard crop. I'll claim damages,' Gehlu countered.

'Yes, Bhai, he is a devotee of the goddess…when he reaches a frenzy singing the hymns, he loses his senses.'

'It has to be admitted our Lachhoo is a real devotee….'

'I noticed him day before yesterday during night prayers, he completely lost himself dancing….'

Everybody laughed.

'Okay, Lachhoo, you should take better care of your goats,' the sarpanch advised him. And, making fun of Lachhoo, the panchayat dispersed.

Earlier, whenever there was a wedding in the village, Lachhoo would slaughter a few goats and cook mutton so delicious that everyone was left licking his fingers. His mutton was very popular in many surrounding villages.

But slowly the city hotels took away this business from him also.

Lachhoo's goats disappeared one after the other and finally they were all gone. One night, he hanged himself from a branch of the acacia tree in front of his house.

⌣

'Bravo! A little more effort!' the contractor was encouraging the workers.

'Well done! Cut down the young acacias, only a few remain.'

Tiny agile birds were chirping, dancing in the air in a flurry around the young acacias, where their nests were, where their chicks—opening and closing their beaks—looked rather helpless.

'Sardarji, these tender chicks evoke a feeling of pity,' Sheru said, pausing.

The contractor had already moved away and paid no attention to Sheru.

'This is a shameful job! Killing innocent beings! How will we attain salvation after all this!' Kartara said and wiped the sweat from his brow.

'Look at these weaver finches crying, see what a cacophony they have created…. O God! What a job we have been assigned!'

Crushed chicks lay among the destroyed nests in the felled acacias in the village shamlat. Shattered eggs lay scattered and weaver finches clamoured above them.

'Bhai, this is real brutality….'

The women who had come to get some hay for their buffaloes stood there helpless. Both Baba Lekha and Chetu looked at the ruined, devastated shamlat and returned to the village, tapping their walking sticks, their backs bent.

The young children were collecting weaver nests.

Bhanto Mehri returned again. She kept coming back…nothing could keep her away.

'Oh God! May they be wiped out!' Sitting by the ravaged

acacias and broken nests, she started venting her spleen.

'Tara has brought a truck,' someone announced.

Kalu, Golu, and Manna hurriedly loaded their things onto the truck. Other villagers stood nearby talking about land, enquiring about prices. When the truck left, they all looked sad; some had tears in their eyes.

Bhinda, Mehna, and Bilu came running from somewhere far away. They were entirely out of breath. They said the estate office people had locked the buffaloes away and were beating the animals mercilessly. Bellowing buffalos ran backwards and were hit with sticks. They had taken some seventy to eighty heads of cattle away with them. 'Look here, Jungy is injured, they twisted Jora's arm.... Gehlu has been hit on the head, he is in hospital. We have just come to let you all know that he may die.' Gehlu's wife ran off, crying bitterly and his aged parents headed somewhere tapping their walking sticks on the ground. Bhanto Mehri came running like a mad woman exclaiming 'Oh God!' and scolding the children.

The estate office people were demanding that a fine be paid. Otherwise, the starving buffalos would die of thirst in their lock-up; their milk would dry up. Sweating profusely, the cattle owners ran here and there, trying to find some little ornament to pawn to Dharmu, the moneylender, or borrow money at exorbitant rates of interest. Then they left for the estate office. They couldn't understand why they were no longer allowed to graze their cattle in their own lands. Much of it was still lying vacant; only a few bungalows had come up.

'This is tit for tat.... Gehlu stole Lachhoo's goat and ate it... now those men....'

A mild whirlwind hit the ruins and crossed the metalled road scattering the vivid, bright feathers of the wild fowl all over the place.

'That neem remains to be felled,' the contractor said to the workers, 'come on, men, come on.'

'Yes, sir.'

'Get your axes ready then.'

'Come on great-grandson, chop off your ancestral neem...'
Shishu took a jibe at Kartara.

'It is so thick, Bhai.'

'Nothing will be left standing,' Kashmira guffawed.

'Come on. Hurry up.' The contractor was in a great hurry.

The workers readied their axes. Spitting on his palms, an
angry Kartara frantically swung at the neem. He suddenly felt
a great burst of energy go through him as chips of wood flew
off the neem.

The workers left after their shift. The now subdued young
children looked at the felled neem. Then they started digging up
little neem saplings that had sprouted on their own under the tree.

'Bibi, look, neem saplings. Where can we plant them?' Preetu
asked his mother.

'What? We have no courtyard of our own any more.' Preetu
was saddened by this.

Amru's grandmother sat on the debris of her house and poured
her heart out by yodelling. Some distance away, a dog howled.

Young puppies had been buried under the rubble and died.
Now the dogs were digging them out and dragging their corpses
around. Vultures hovered above this scene; a rat could be seen
disappearing under the debris.

Gehlu's grandmother came to Amru's grandmother. Both of
them covered their heads with their shawls and began complaining,
sounding as if they were on the verge of crying. Women and
children tried to retrieve whatever they could from the ruins of
their homes. Finding some small objects, the children happily ran
over to their mothers to show them their treasures.

Tents sprouted up overnight all along the road around the
village. Putting together their broken hearths, the women started
dung-cake fires and put pulses into pots to cook. Glum-looking
men sat nearby slurping hot tea from bowls.

The children got hold of a stray donkey and tied a broken can to its tail.

Some people from the village, who had gone to the hospital earlier to enquire about Gehlu's health, returned. They were low-spirited.

'For many days now the dogs have been howling at night at the sadhu's mound.' Ambo, Karo, Beebo, and Bhanti sat atop the rubble and recounted the ominous signs they had been seeing.

'Once I happened to wake up at midnight...an owl was hooting from the tamarisk tree.'

'These things long for ruins, friends.'

Jeeto and Rano brought some kittens from somewhere. The kittens had not opened their eyes as yet.

'From where have you brought these?'

'Their poor mother is dead.'

'Oh my God! The poor things.' Bhanti's heart ached with pity as she commiserated with them. Rano brought some milk from her mother in a small bowl. She fed the kittens using a ball of cotton dipped in the milk, squeezing out sustenance for them drop by drop.

The boys hit the donkey with a stick. It ran, the tin rattling behind it, and the boys enjoyed the spectacle and laughed.

'Look! It feels as if a marriage is taking place.'

'Yes. Look how our Kalu is running around.'

'They haven't been to school for three days now.'

'Look there! Kalu is riding the donkey.'

'He is siting facing backwards.'

'Shame on you!' they all chortled with delight.

'Paint his face black now,' shouted Ambo.

The bowls slipped out of the hands of the men drinking tea. The women were doubled over with laughter...shouting, laughing, dancing, clapping. The boys chased the donkey around gleefully.

Translated by Paramjit Singh Ramana

GREEN SPARROWS

AJEET COUR

It was the month of Kartik. The hot sun blazed throughout the day. Clear and sharp, its glare was unbearable.

He wore dark sunglasses when he went out. Still, in a couple of hours, he would get a headache, his eyes would be tired and he would return and seek solace in the darkness of his room.

He had come home after almost seven years. Life in a foreign land moves along a set rhythm. The morning passed in a rush: getting up, shaving, a quick shower, pulling on one's clothes with an eye on the clock. Then, running for the subway to his office. A sandwich and coffee for lunch. Then, back home in the evening.

Sometimes, a pub. Drunken gossip with friends and then home again. Heating up something out of a can—beans mostly, or scrambled eggs, toast. And then, bed.

Only Saturday and Sunday were different. On both these days the morning alarm would be silent. His impotent irritation with the alarm would also ease. He would sleep until late. Then, he would go for a walk and meet Emma.

Sunday afternoon he would cook chicken and manh ki daal, with a garnishing of ginger and green chillies! The back door of the kitchen would remain closed so that the sharp pungent aroma of the tempering would not pervade the neighbourhood! Shopping! Groceries for the week would be bought. Then, a long and vigorous bath. Laundry. House cleaning! Watching television or listening to music!

Saturday afternoon to Sunday evening, Emma would be with him in his flat. She would go back home on Sunday evening.

Only her toothbrush, nightie, and towel would be left in his flat. Her towel would hang on the rod, drying in his bathroom, for the next two days.

Abruptly, after seven years, he was back home, and free. Free of work, and free of worries. Every day was like Saturday and Sunday for him now. He was totally idle, crowded in by a host of Saturdays and Sundays.

He had nothing to do. No rush to wake up, he slept till late in the morning.

His room was on the rooftop, a barsati, a terrace apartment. It had been his own place since childhood. When he had been young, it had been his study. Later, he had also started sleeping here.

Years ago, the family had slept on the terrace, during summers. They slept indoors during winter. He had slept in his mother's room; he and his younger sister Ashu. Bauji, his father, slept in the next room.

∽

Biji, his mother, put the stuffed paratha and a glass of milk on the table and sat down on a chair near him....

It seemed as if she wanted to say something, but could not decide how to begin the conversation.

As he broke a morsel of paratha, he felt as if his fingers had lost some of their nimbleness.

'Are you not eating?' he asked, trying to overcome his hesitation.

'I can't eat parathas now. Bad for the stomach...' Biji replied diffidently. She felt strange talking to her own son, who had come back home after such a long sojourn abroad.

What is it that has come between us, he asked himself. This feeling of alienation!

Perhaps it was the distance of seven years that stood between them, frozen and still like ice.

They had lived these seven years differently, fighting different battles. He and Biji. Why only Biji and him? All of them—Bauji, Kamal, and Ashu.

They had asked him to come home for Ashu's wedding! Ashu had written to him, appealing to him to come! But he couldn't. He had been studying medicine, and had to work in the library for three hours daily to pay his fees. Later on, he had got a scholarship, but the two years in between had been extremely difficult. It had meant studying for long hours, attending practicals and dissections. Then, in the evening, working in the library, on his feet for three hours, to earn a living. Life stretched out as a long journey of weariness, exhaustion, and running about. All the threads of his life seemed to be strung to the hands of a clock. And the clock was running faster than he could!

No, he had not been able to attend Ashu's wedding.

After that, he did not know how, and when, the letters from home had become cold and distant.

And now he was looking at his old life from beyond the seven years he had lived abroad. Distance had made many things hazy.

Even now, there were things, which, when seen at close quarters, pierced the heart like shards of broken glass.

He did not know why, but he was upset with himself as he ate the paratha. As if he had stolen something from his family in broad daylight. His feelings surprised him.

He thought…arre, this is your own mother! She who sits in the chair near you. Sad, but looking at you with tolerant eyes. The same mother with whom you would quarrel for four or eight annas, new socks, or a new pen. Who had looked behind your ears to see if they had been washed properly or not! Who had pulled your ears, and also smacked you—and sometimes had hidden you to save you from Bauji's beatings.

This is the same mother whose bed you would stealthily creep into at night when you felt scared!

But ever since he had come home, an awkward distance yawned between Biji, Bauji, and him.

Ashu was with her in-laws in Chandigarh. Her husband was an IAS officer and was posted there. He had forgotten whether he was with the Punjab Government or Haryana Government, though Bauji had told him. But what difference did that make?

The day after his arrival, Ashu's husband had called from Chandigarh. Ashu had also talked to him. After a couple of minutes, he had felt that there was hardly anything to say on either side.

'Achcha then,' he had said.

This was the same Ashu whose plaits he used to pull, wrestle with, crack jokes with, squabble with over marbles or crayons or books, or scold for cheating at cards, and with whom he fought over comics.

What had happened to him that he was no longer fit even to quarrel with anyone! Not to fight, not to be upset, and not even to have the pleasure of making up.

Biji sat on one side of the table, and he on the other, trying to eat the paratha.

Finally, Biji said softly, 'Maybe you could visit Ashu for a few days….'

Visit Ashu's in-laws' home? What would he talk to them about? What would he say to anyone there? Ashu's husband! A stranger who was married to his sister! The same Ashu, his doll-like sister. Ashu, in bed with that stranger….

He was upset with himself, his own thoughts.

You cannot talk to your own mother, you sit silent reading a newspaper with your father! What will you talk about with those strangers? he reproved himself.

'We can invite Ashu here,' he suggested.

'But what will her in-laws say? Why don't you go and fetch her? Spend a day there and then come back with her and Bubbles the next day. If Kuldip can get leave from work, invite him too.'

There was neither any claim in Biji's voice nor any demand.

Request? There was no request either. It was as if she was talking to a neighbour, asking him if he was going to the bazaar, and if he was, could he get a box of matches for her.

Yet, there was, perhaps, a trace of some mild entreaty in her voice.

He stayed silent, taking refuge in sipping hot milk.

꜀

After breakfast, he took a round of the veranda outside, and then came back into the sitting room. Bauji was reading the newspaper. As he walked into the room, Bauji held it out and asked, 'Newspaper...?'

He took it.

The pages of the newspaper fluttered like the wings of an injured crane in the air swirling under the ceiling fan. He opened the paper and looked over the printed words, conscious of Bauji's eyes on him through his misted, thick glasses. There was a strangely helpless and bemused look on Bauji's face. Trying hard to make sure that nothing would offend or upset his foreign-returned son.

Wasn't Bauji avoiding him these days? As if he were a special guest who could not be disturbed.

He realized that he was not reading the newspaper, but was merely trying to hide behind it. He felt dismayed to see his father, who had always had such a regal and dignified aura about him, look so vulnerable. He felt a sense of fear grip him. This fear was absolutely different from the fear he used to feel in his childhood, which had driven him and his sister to hide in their own secret haven when they heard him come into the house. At that time, it was Biji's kitchen which seemed the safest place to hide in; rather like a 'no-war zone' under UN observation.

This helplessness of Bauji's he could not bear. It was like the wretchedness of a torn quilt from which clumps of cotton wool escaped from the rent fabric. But the arm that he could extend in support hesitated; it was difficult for that arm to reach his father, because a wide distance of seven years sprawled between them, frozen over, and hard like the ice of the South Pole!

A desert of snow!

A piercing ray of bright sunlight had penetrated the glass panes of the window and, peeping into the room from behind the curtains, stretched out across the worn-out old carpet.

Even otherwise, there was a naked brightness in this room. Upstairs, he had put up thick dark coloured bedcovers over the curtains on all the windows of his terrace barsati. Thick covers and curtains, both had combined to preserve the darkness of the night inside, keeping the bright glare of the October sun out of the room.

But, here, under the brilliance of the sun, and under Bauji's eyes, he felt strangely conspicuous and exposed.

In a daze, he gave the paper back to Bauji.

'Have you read it?' Bauji asked in a manner which held no question.

'Bas!' he answered softly, tiptoeing out of the room and towards the stairs.

'What should I cook?' Biji walked out. She stood at the back door, which opened into the backyard. Actually, it opened on to a veranda, which spread out to the backyard. The stairs to the terrace were in the backyard.

'Whatever you like,' he replied and hurriedly went up.

He felt very safe in his room. Safe and secure.

Lighting a cigarette, he fell on the bed. Suddenly, he noticed a cobweb in the corner of the room. 'Arre! Still there?' he thought. Since the day he had come, whenever he lay on his back on the bed with a cigarette, he noticed the cobweb. Every time he thought: I will sweep it away with a long brush or broom when I get up. But, once the cigarette was done, he would turn on his side, close his eyes and fall asleep, forgetting the cobweb.

'Surely, today...' he decided.

He was eating a paratha. Bauji sat near, listening to the radio, and looking at him. Biji sat on a low stool, her chin resting on her palm, and head leaning on the kitchen door's jamb. The skin of her face was like dried strips of turnip—her face, her hands and elbows too. Like a crumpled sheet of waste paper.

He thought that in these last seven years her eyes had shrunk. They had always shone brightly, like brilliant lights. Now they were shrivelled and bleary. Like the small puddles of wet mud dotting the road after a heavy shower.

...If you think of it, it is nothing. You hardly feel the passing of the years. Mornings, evenings...and time goes on. Till you look in the mirror and see someone else's face! You are taken aback, perplexed. Then, the realization of time gone by, clear and sharp, pierces your heart just like a shard of broken glass.

Suddenly, he thought of Emma. If he wanted to share this sensation that he just experienced—of the glittering dagger-point piercing him—with Emma, would she understand it? Did she understand him? Perhaps not. One cannot convey the intensity of one's emotion to another.

'Poor words...' he thought.

Bauji switched off the radio. The news was over. He was surprised that the room had all along been filled by the newsreader's voice, yet he had not heard anything.

Bauji said with a slight laugh, 'I am also getting parathas to eat these days—stuffed with cheese, cauliflower, radish, and methi! Otherwise, your mother doesn't cook. She just gives me a glass of milk, that is all. And boiled eggs.'

'What to cook for two people...and what not to cook!' Biji replied with a deep sigh.

He thinks: all this is not being said to Bauji. She says it to you but it is meant for me.

'When the sabziwallah comes to the lane I buy a few vegetables and cook, otherwise we make do with dal. Sometimes, I do not have the strength even for that. Bas...then we just eat some bread with milk.' Biji seemed to be in the mood to talk today. Less with him, more with her own self. Biji…who had always been so silent….

Perhaps this was her way of telling him: 'Come home. Stay!' The obvious.

He understood, yet persisted in pretending not to understand the obvious.

Every day the sparrows raised a hue and cry at the break of dawn. His first morning in Delhi—when he had got up early in the morning—he had thought that he was hearing all this clamour in his sleep. Drifting in and out of sleep, the tumult of the sparrows had seemed mysterious. As if his childhood had come back and was standing near his bed, laughing at him.

Those days, Biji would wake him up with a laugh, 'Even the sparrows are up and about, but this boy is still in bed! Get up, don't you have to go to school?'

Implying that the lesson that even the unlettered foolish sparrows had learnt—getting up when the sun is not yet out—was wasted. Why couldn't he learn that lesson?

And he would sheepishly get up.

Lying on his bed, he peeped into his childhood and smiled.

Now that he had been here for all these days, he was used to the clamour of the sparrows.

The day of his departure was also drawing closer.

After eating the paratha, he again came back to his room on the terrace.

The room wore an extremely forlorn look.

Gradually, it seemed as if the roof of the room had disappeared. The roofless room seemed desolate in the vast blue expanse of the dusty huge vacuum of space. Then, slowly and softly, even the walls of the roofless room seemed to recede. He lay on his bed, alone, in endless vastness, in eternity. Then, he did not know when even the floor from under the bed disappeared. And, it seemed to him that he was floating in the air. A vagabond, like a leaf fluttering in the gusts of wind...like a scrap of paper in infinite space. Who was he? Why was he? Where were his roots? And who were rooted in the soil of his mind? He did not know.

Solitary! A non-entity!

A sparrow twittered. He floated down to earth, like a rag of muslin. The bed came down. The floor under the bed came back. The walls also came back from their wanderings.

The sparrow seemed to be chirping only for him. Full of wondrous joy. When it twittered, its whole body quivered, the shiver starting at its beak and weaving through the last feather on its tail. It sang in happy abandonment, full of extraordinary intoxication.

It seemed to him as if he were a king and the sparrow his slave singing only for his pleasure.

Suddenly, an idea came to him, 'Don't these sparrows grow old?'

It startled him. He had seen dogs growing old, and also seen old cats. Horses, lions, all of them grow old. And gradually become helpless and die...like human beings...dependent, lonely, and colourless. Slowly breaking away from life. Dying bit by bit.

But these sparrows.... He had never seen an old sparrow, friendless, sitting quietly, with its beak hanging open listlessly. He had never seen a sparrow walking with halting steps, half bent. He had always seen sparrows singing and hopping about, with a flutter of wings, their bodies quivering with an eternal thirst for life. Always in a group, with other sparrows, singing—wanton and enraptured! Full of life! Intoxicated! Forever celebrating life! Evergreen sparrows!

When they die, they must be dying suddenly. Singing away, he thought to himself.

Why doesn't man die suddenly? With a song on his lips!

Translated by Ajeet Cour

HOPES SHATTERED

GULZAR SINGH SANDHU

The all-knowing old matriarch, Bebe, was indispensable for any ritual in the village. Weddings or funerals, nothing was complete without her. She was consulted on all matters: the site to be chosen for the construction of a new house or the digging of a new well; what offering was to be made to the rain god if the monsoons failed; what herb was to be given to a pregnant mother to induce labour; which shaman to invite when a young woman was possessed by an evil spirit. And her advice had been gratefully accepted by three generations of people.

Bebe was also the living chronicle of all that had occurred in the village. She even knew the compensation price that had been fixed for every yard of land, for every well, and every tree at the time of consolidation of landholdings in the village.

She knew everything that took place. She knew which girl the village schoolmaster was eyeing and whom the village patwari had had an affair with. She also knew that an upper-caste boy was trying to get close to a thirteen-year-old Dalit girl. She had once overheard the boy at the well, commenting mischievously to the girl that her slim waist would bend under the weight of a full water pot. Bebe had also heard the girl's reply—to the effect that he needn't worry, she could even lift him if she had to.

Now, of course, she was no longer the same old Bebe. She had been struck with paralysis. The right half of her body had become numb and lifeless. She could not move even her little finger on that side. She lay in the barn on an old charpoy, flies swarming around her. Her sons avoided her; her daughters-in-

law would not even offer her a glass of water. She groaned and
gasped in her bed. She had to wait for hours before anyone
would come near her.

She now saw everything through the prism of her broken
mind. It all looked distorted. She felt that everything in her house
was going to pieces. She thought the animals were being fed on
poultry feed and the poultry on animal fodder. The hens were
being milked and the cows were being beaten for not laying eggs.
She imagined the younger daughter-in-law sleeping in the elder's
bed and the elder one lying in the younger's. How far had the
Jat boy gone with the waterman's daughter? She did not know.
It had all become hazy after she became disabled.

Her sons had done their best to find a cure for her. They
spent a fortune on injections prescribed by the local doctor.
Someone suggested that she should be fed a wild pigeon's liver
and her sons immediately shot down all the pigeons around the
village. Being prosperous landlords, they spent lavishly on her
treatment, demonstrating their wealth and prestige. Nobody in the
village could accuse them of stinginess. But having exhausted all
possible sources of remedy, they were now sick and tired of her.

The old woman had realized that there was no cure. She lay
for hours, staring at the ceiling, and shouting for her sons and
neighbours. Utter dejection had driven her crazy. Images and
past events flew through her mind like bits of straw in a strong
wind. Her shrivelled body and her dull eyes—sunken deep in
their sockets—frightened children. Nobody would come near her.

Nasib was not like the others. He always called on her
whenever he came to his native village from his place of work
in Calcutta. These occasions gave the old woman a chance to
give vent to her pent-up feelings. She had so much to say to
Nasib when he called on her this time. She cast a tired look at
the tall, bearded visitor and complained, 'Ah, my son! Everything
is going to pieces. The crops have been poor. The rains have
been too heavy. The hairy caterpillars attacked the crops and the

locusts ate up what was left. Be seated near your poor mother.'

This was the year the astrologers had forecast ashta-graha, the collision of the eight planets.

Nasib sat on the charpoy, which creaked under his weight. Bebe blessed him as he held her shrivelled hand. 'My son, the astrologers have forecast that the eight planets will collide.' She raised the issues that were troubling her. 'Doomsday is approaching. Nature is going to unleash its fury and life as we know it is going to be destroyed.'

Nasib dutifully nodded and kept up the pretence. She had built up these fantasies from the bits of local rumours tossed her way. Nasib knew that newspapers had flashed the ominous warnings of some astrologers. Wheat prices were fluctuating and heavy rains had been drumming on the roof. The villagers gossiped about these things, and yet went on with their lives. As always, farmers tilled their lands, children played hide-and-seek, and women gave birth.

But Bebe's mind had magnified and distorted everything. The astrologers' forebodings had taken the shape of reality. Confined to her bed and paralysed, she had compensated by letting her mind become overactive and fanciful. Since she was dying, she thought the world was coming to an end.

She had heard that the waters of the great lake, artificially created by submerging hundreds of villages in the hills, were threatening to break the Bhakra Dam. The rain was pouring and water was rushing down into the lake with all its fury, forming muddy whirlpools. How could a man-made dam resist the wrath of the gods? It would crack and wash down the villages, cattle, huts, fields, and chickens. Rivers would change their course and ponds would turn into seas....

But Nasib held no faith in these rumours. Visiting his village for the wedding of his sister, he had gone about making arrangements and meeting his relatives, friends, and elders. He had invited them all to the wedding. He had walked the streets where children were merrily playing marbles. When he asked a young boy, 'Why are you playing silly games on the eve of doomsday?' the boy replied, 'The world is coming to an end anyway. Why not enjoy the last few days?' Nasib was amused at the response.

He had come to Bebe for a friendly chat, a regular feature of his visits home. Bebe had heard of the wedding plans along with news of hairy caterpillars and locusts and the impending collision of the stars with the rising waters. Suddenly she emerged from her reverie and said eagerly, 'I hear the stars are colliding.... I am happy you have fixed the wedding of your sister and you have come to invite me. I have blessed hundreds of marriages. Your father touched my feet before he left on horseback to marry your mother. You cannot imagine my excitement at the idea of attending the wedding. My jewel, parrot of the royal orchard, my precious son, you must have me carried in a palanquin to the ceremony. I shall put on my silver-buttoned dress which is lying in that wicker chest in the corner.'

She tried to lift her hand to point to the wicker chest, but it lay heavy and limp. She saw a phantom hand, conjured up by her will, rising and pointing at the corner. In her half-numbed senses, desire and reality had blurred into one. She again tried to raise her arm but could not. The thought flashed through her mind that Nasib, being so well-travelled and educated, would know a cure for paralysis. 'You have come from the big city of Calcutta,' she said. 'There must be doctors there who can cure me. Do you know any? You are a great man who commands machines. Why don't you command a machine to snatch away my disease?'

Nasib replied, 'Yes, old mother, machines today can do everything. They poke the clouds to drop their burden of rain; they work like bulls tilling the earth; they fly through the sky like a magic carpet. The machine is the miracle of our times. Surely it can heal you.'

Suddenly Bebe's face fell. This reassurance disheartened her. She was a dethroned queen of the village and nobody paid her respect in the same way as they did in the old days. Even if she could walk to the wedding, she doubted she could command the same old prestige. What was the use of getting well? She started picturing the doomsday that was to come in the wake of ashta-graha. She saw the muddy, swirling waters of the lake crashing through the Bhakra Dam. The bursting deluge…the people fleeing, overrun by the billowing wall of water sweeping away the sand dunes, houses, cattle, and chickens before it….

'Haven't you heard about the cracking of Bhakra Dam?' She wanted to share her fears with her young well-wisher. 'The dam is not going to last long, they say. Maybe a few days more. Then it will collapse and the waters will drown everybody.' She seemed concerned.

Her ailing heart wanted destruction, and surely nobody could stop it. After all, the earthquake in Quetta was not all that far away. She had felt unhappy then. But now she knew that the world was a miserable place and God was not so unkind as to allow his creatures to suffer incessantly. There had to be an end to this suffering. So God, in his great wisdom, had inspired engineers to build this dam so that he could destroy the world.

Nasib could not gauge the depths to which the invalid had sunk. He wanted to get rid of Bebe's groundless fears, which her wild imagination had created out of rumours.

He declared, 'Don't bother about such nonsense, Bebe. The Bhakra Dam is firm, rock-solid. It is not some foolish village masons who have built it with clay bricks, but trained engineers commanding machines. Some bastards in the village have spread false rumours.' He used harsh words for the rumour-mongers to help wash her fears away. 'Dear Bebe, there will be no flood, no destruction of villages, no collision of stars. The world will not end so soon. Don't worry, the Bhakra Dam is strong….'

Bebe's face grew pale. The world was slipping from her hands. She did not want the dam to remain intact. Nasib's unwanted assurances upset her greatly. She felt betrayed, as if someone had swindled her.

The very news that the dam would not fall struck her like a thunderbolt. She collapsed on the bed. The other half of her body also became paralysed.

Translated by Balwant Gargi

THE WIND

GURDEV SINGH RUPANA

Madan was shocked as the sudden cries of a baby rent the air. Behind a bush, a six or seven-month-old infant lay face down, crying. At times its crying was muffled, at other times it was clearer.

Madan stopped his camel cart, picked up the baby and cleaned its face with a corner of the tail of his turban. Then he looked to see it was a male or female child. It was a girl. She stared at him. Close by lay a milk-white burka as though the wind had blown it there. 'Some mother has deserted this poor thing,' he thought. 'What an evil time this is that even mothers can no longer look after their babies.' He unfolded the baby's arms and drew them around his own neck. Just ahead, he saw a man sprawled in the shallow ditch. On nearing the ditch he realized that he was looking at a corpse. On his forehead was drawn a moon and a star with black ink. His face showed signs of torture, distorting the drawing of the crescent moon and star. A bunch of entrails protruded from his abdomen. Near his feet, the earth was churned up, showing his death throes.

After killing him, the brutes had flung him away, abducted the woman, and abandoned the baby. Careful, he cautioned himself as he imagined what might have happened. The baby took after her father. Staring at the burka, he imagined that the woman must have been very beautiful. Her beauty must have been the cause of someone's enmity with her husband. He speculated that she would gradually adjust in her new home, call it her own, and accept her captor as her husband. Surely, she would have other children. Who knows, she may forget this baby! But if they had taken the baby also, what harm would that have caused? 'Babies are divine, the image of God, and man fears to commit sins in front of them,' he recalled his mother's statement. Yet what had been done here was not virtuous. Now his mother's view seemed false to him.

The baby began to cry. He recalled his wife's wish. Durgi used to pray that God would bless her with a daughter to share her joys and sorrows. 'See, God has sent a daughter! She knows nothing yet...she is neither Hindu nor Muslim. She will play with Biloo, they will be sister and brother.'

Madan's wife, Durgi, had had three children. All were born through cesarean and two of them had died. Biloo survived but the doctor had said that his wife would die if she conceived again. So her longing for a daughter remained unfulfilled.

'Will you take Durgi as your mother?' he asked the baby as he tried to console her. He then took her towards the water channel. Having helped her sip water, he untied a cloth parcel in his cart, put a bit of gur in her mouth, lay her on the seat, and started urging the camel forward.

About two furlongs ahead, he looked around and came across two more dead bodies. And then he saw a few more. He looked ahead and saw that the road was littered with dead bodies. He remembered what his mother used to say, 'Madan, you don't drive properly. Like a sheep, you look down. If you do so, you see only half the world.' Today, for the first time, he agreed that his habit of lowering his eyes was worrying. At the waterway, if he had looked ahead properly, he would have backtracked. But where could he have gone? Would anyone have taken him in for the night? Hans Raj had forced him to leave his shop with the assurance that the caravan had passed and there was no need to fear anyone any more. Yet the people were afraid and so doors were closed. In the bazaar everything was shut; he did not see a single shop owner. Even Ramlal was not at the toll booth. If the booth had been open he could have made some arrangements to stay there.

Wherever he looked, all he could see was dead bodies. Even the camel got restless.

'Water...' he heard someone. A yet-to-be corpse tried to sit up.

Madan approached the man. 'Water.... We are from Mardana's tribe. May you have Baba Nanak's blessing!' The man had a head wound and there was a lot of blood congealed in the back of his head. He struggled to sit up straight but fell back on the ground. Household objects lay scattered on the road. Machine parts for kneading flour, a broken flask, parts of a damaged spinning wheel. Some dented silver utensils but no copper or brass vessels were around. Madan picked up a silver bowl and went to the pond to bring water.

Some corpses were hidden in the water and others lay half-submerged. He counted about thirty of them. The water had been reddened by blood. He circled the pond, but couldn't find a clean spot anywhere. Bending down, he filled the bowl with water but could see that there was blood in it.

'If you have a long life, you attain something. In this water is mixed the blood of someone like you.' Madan stooped to wrap his turban around the man's head. Before the final turn of the cloth, he tumbled, shuddered in fear, and walked away from the man.

'Water!' He turned to look and saw movement some distance away. He picked up the bowl which still had a bit of water in it. The man lay flat on the ground. Blood was flowing from the left of his torso and had congealed on the ground. Madan supported and propped him up. The water that the man drank seemed to pour out of his side as blood. He asked Madan to wrap his wound tightly, 'Now help me sit against the trunk of this kikar tree or the military men might just bury me alive.'

He helped the man as quickly as possible. The sun was about to set and Madan wanted to reach home before sunset. He was still very fearful. He mounted his cart and the camel started moving ahead. They had only moved a short distance before the wheels of the cart went over the leg of a corpse. From the cart, Madan took a long stick and hit the camel. It leapt forward and the vehicle ran over three or four more corpses. With no trace of anger, he got down, grabbed the camel's reins and began to guide the cart so as not to trample any others.

The baby began to cry again. He realized his error and said to himself, 'From the start, I should have carried water for the baby.' Halting the vehicle, he lifted the baby into his arms. She stopped crying. But he could still hear the sound of a baby crying somewhere. He spotted four or five children huddled together under a rosewood tree. They all began to cry bitterly at his approach. The oldest among them was clinging to a corpse.

'Have no fear...I am not going to kill you,' he said. He asked the oldest boy, 'Is this your father?' The boy nodded. All the children quietened. Madan kept wondering what to say to them. Some children were sitting under an acacia tree. A few of them were crying. One was sobbing with his head on his dead mother's breast. The wounded ones were asking for water. What to do with them? Whom to care for? From where could he alone bring water for them? He had just crossed a caravan of corpses. A bigger caravan of this sort lay ahead. Getting across that, he had to reach home and that too before sunset. He could see a long line of living children that extended twenty miles.

He stood there for some time. Then he laid the baby by their side and hurried away lest he change his mind. Holding the camel's reins as before, he guided the vehicle safely over the corpses. Even so, some foot got trampled or the wheel passed over a leg. But he did not get upset with the camel. The helpless animal was not to blame. He had no choice but to let the cart's wheels go over these hurdles.

He reached the waterway that showed that he was halfway through his journey home. He felt tired now. The arm that had been pulling the camel's reins to either side was exhausted and could not hold itself up any more. So far, he had covered two-and-a-half miles; he had as much more to cover. Half a mile of it was unpaved, kaccha, which would be a better path to be on today. The sun had set and on reaching the bridge, he found that the canal was overflowing with corpses, pushing the water out onto the pathway. He stopped the cart.

The camel relaxed as he let its reins loose. They rode along like this. If he saw a corpse, he pulled the rein to one side. Otherwise, the vehicle went its way. Gradually, it became darker and he could see nothing.

He only knew that they had gone over a corpse when a wheel went over something with a thud. After covering a mile, he could tell from the sound of the thud whether the corpse they had run over was that of an adult or a child. From the sound of the camel's feet he could tell whether the ground they were on was dry or soaked with blood.

Now his fear was gone and slowly he began singing a song that was usually sung during a nighttime journey:

What a terrible mistake you have made, O Saihban!
Your lover you have got killed.

He felt his song was lacking in feeling.

Today he could not imagine the swords flashing, or hear the clash of steel or see the blood flowing. He stopped singing.

Once the journey on the hard road ended, the camel paused for a little bit. Then it continued on its way on the kaccha track.

When he reached his village, his neighbours, who had been waiting for him, exclaimed, 'He has come! He has come!'

He could hear sounds of weeping emerging from his house. When he came closer, they became silent. He unlatched the camel from the cart, and tied it to a post so it could move around in the courtyard to graze. On one side, there were numerous women weeping and keening. His mother got up, came to him, and, embracing him, began to weep, 'Son, we are ruined.'

'What is the matter?' he asked his mother.

'Biloo has died after falling off the roof,' he was told.

Stunned, he fell to the ground. Everyone present was silent for a while. Then someone said, 'Madan! Let us go and cremate him. We were waiting for you.'

'Wait for a while, we shall do this work as well,' Madan said. 'But first, I am very tired and hungry.'

Holding him by his shoulders, his mother screamed. 'Brute, you call this work, and you feel hungry?' She began wailing and beating his chest with both hands. 'Someone bring a lamp!' she yelled.

Someone brought the lamp.

'People of this village, we are ruined. I was mourning the younger one. But something has happened to the elder one! See how he just looks on blankly!' They gathered around her.

Something evil has him in its thrall! Call a shaman!

Biloo's dead body lay in the yard, covered with a cloth. Madan stared at him unblinkingly and couldn't turn away. He thought that this corpse that lay here was just one of the many other corpses he had seen on the other side, just a mile way. That was all. The wind did not care.

Translated by Tejwant Singh Gill

I AM NOT GHAZNAVI

GURBACHAN SINGH BHULLAR

To meet Jassi after so many years was like crossing the protective boundary I had drawn around myself.

There is no special reason why I had not seen her for so many years, nor had I taken any firm vow about it. I had just decided, a casual decision taken almost unconsciously.

To be clear, I never felt like she was cut off from me. She has always been close to me in a unique manner. Physically away but very much still a part of my thoughts.

I can't even imagine that I could consider my relationship with Jassi an insignificant incident or a finished chapter of the book of my life and turn the page and move on. Rather, in sharp contrast, whenever I remember her, I unconsciously start humming lines from a film song: 'When you call me your own, I begin to feel proud of myself.'

Sitting next to Jassi, whenever I would hum this song, she would remark that I knew only one song to express my admiration for her. Or she would tell me that I would never be able to fool her no matter how hard I tried. She might taunt me by saying that she was not sure if I was praising her by singing that song but that I was definitely thinking of myself as the hero of a Hindi movie. She knew how much I disliked the heroes of Bombay-made Hindi movies.

In reality, I never tried to fool her nor ever considered myself a hero of a movie. I was really proud of my friendship with her.

Jassi was a beautiful girl, very beautiful. To call her exceptionally beautiful would be no exaggeration.

It is said that beauty is not an attribute of an object itself. Rather, beauty lies in the eyes of the beholder. But Jassi's beauty is not a result of my perception. Even if it is because of my perception, it is a totally unrelated issue. Because she is pretty even without my eyes appreciating her. Very pretty, exceptionally pretty.

Whenever I think of her, I take out from its box a pen she gifted me and write something new, or read her comments, some sincere, some naughty, written in the margins of my books. I always also take out a one-line letter that Raju wrote to me. I have already read this letter a hundred times. Now I don't have to read it, I just have a look at it. I like to look at that letter. By now it is completely etched in my memory, commas, full stops, and all.

Many years after she separated from me, Raju saw her once at Ludhiana railway station. Raju is my bosom friend and he knows very well what my relationship with her was like and how significant she was to me. She had met Raju once or twice, but she was not so friendly with Raju that she could discuss with him her relationship with me. Jassi had been accompanied by a man. Maybe he was her husband. Without any doubt, he must have been her husband. So, Raju didn't talk to her. But there on the railway station he wrote and posted a one-line letter to me.

He had written: 'I saw Jassi at the railway station just now, I wanted to send my eyes to you.'

I had replied to Raju that there was no need to send the eyes. I have the ability to see her from where I am. To have a glimpse of her, I have never felt the need to open the album and to look at her photograph. The imprint of her features is as fresh in my consciousness as is the idol that is always in front of your eyes. She is no less than an idol placed on the shelf of my mind.

Many girls are beautiful. In a sense, every girl is beautiful, one way or another. But some are very beautiful. And a few rare ones are exceptionally so. But what is the meaning of the beauty of the flower that has been given prominence by trimming the foliage around it. Then that flower dances arrogantly in the wind as if that flower alone exists in the garden. The real beauty is that the flower should be as and where it is. Anyone looking at its splendour should exclaim spontaneously, 'What a miracle of nature! Wah, Kartar! Bow to the creator!'

In addition to being very pretty, Jassi was an aberration of a commonly believed rule of nature. It is often said that the girls who are blessed with beauty are often denied the gift of intelligence and wisdom by the Almighty. But human beings often break such rules of nature; perhaps sometimes nature itself does not follow its own rules. Along with a matchless appearance, she had been blessed with a highly perceptive mind as if she were a golden bowl filled with amrit.

The inner and outer beauty of Jassi was highlighted by her sheer simplicity. She had no vanity, made no use of her looks. She combed her hair if she felt like it, otherwise just ignored it. If she felt like it, she ironed her clothes, otherwise wore them as they were. Once she gave me a photograph of her with dishevelled hair and her chunni carelessly thrown over her shoulders. She said that she had got that photograph taken because she needed one for some form.

'You must have had this snap taken from a tripod camera, where the photographer ducks under a cloth cover to take the photo,' I teased her.

'Yes, I had this snap taken at a fair,' Jassi replied in a similar bantering tone.

'Then, like the women going to a fair, you should have displayed your arm with the wristwatch,' I continued, extending my left arm forward!

Today, when Raju called me as I got ready to leave to see Jassi, I had an urge to look at her photograph again. But I only had to think about her and her image appeared in front of my eyes, full and clear. Even today her image was as clear and fresh in my mind as it was when we used to see each other every day. The same graceful beauty, the same intelligence, simplicity, and innocence. Thinking of her, I had a unique feeling and experience—as if someone had suddenly switched on the lights in a temple and a smiling idol stood in front of me.

Then I was already married and Jassi had been engaged to be married. After completing her MA she was going to be married. But as it had turned out she would leave me much earlier than that. Her father had got a transfer because of a promotion. They were just waiting for Jassi's exams to finish.

Because of my very emotional temperament, I always find ordinary day-to-day events dull and meaningless. I move around like a cascade of water, battering against mountains, falling headlong downstream, flowing as fast as possible, breaking into two and uniting again. But whenever I was in Jassi's company I always felt as if I had entered a smooth, unruffled space and would noiselessly, calmly, and patiently move on.

When Jassi met me for the last time before she left, I could not tell her that I would die without her. Neither did Jassi cry hysterically with her head on my chest and cling to me, nor did she beg me theatrically to accompany her to some faraway unseen land. Yet this was our first meeting when we were quite sentimental. But even during this meeting we didn't lose our composure.

While leaving, she had said that she would write to me.

I told her the story of the girl who, because of some exceptional circumstances, became my adopted sister and treated me like her brother. She used to send me a rakhi, a ritual token of affection between brother and sister, every year. At the time of her marriage, she wrote with a heavy heart, 'Brother, don't write to me now, what do we know of the attitude of that man?'

I told Jassi that I wouldn't write to her. I would only pray for her happiness wherever she was. She too had not dwelt on the sentimental idea of meetings through letters.

And we went our separate ways.

Jassi wrote to me a few times and I did reply to her letters. She wrote for the last time just before her wedding. She had not even felt the need to extend a formal invitation.

After that she never wrote to me. My story about the adopted sister might have made her even more cautious. There was no question of me keeping track of her. Whenever I thought of her, an image of her bright broad forehead, innocent big eyes, sharp nose, and full open lips emerged in my mind and then I didn't want to fall like a stone in a calm pond.

After she went away for all those many years, I got only one piece of news about Jassi in the form of that one-line letter from Raju—a letter that I had read more than a hundred times and which was completely etched in my memory.

In this life full of chance meetings and this world full of accidental reunions, Jassi had now reached Raju's city. Her husband had been transferred there. When Raju learned of it, he wrote to me. It was more than a letter; it was an invitation. He was going to explore the possibility of my meeting with Jassi when I got there. He would find some way.

Reading Raju's letter, my heart began to beat faster despite all my efforts to stay calm. I felt there was no harm in casually meeting Jassi one more time, calmly, without any hassle or trouble. There was no harm in just once crossing my self-created protective line, my Lakshman rekha.

As I get closer to Raju's home, my heart starts beating faster.

I knock at Raju's door. A middle-aged woman opens the door. She carefully studies me, then smiles and greets me. I accept her greetings like a stranger and walk in.

Raju has sprained his foot. He is sitting on the bed, back supported against the wall and legs out in front. One of his feet is badly swollen. He shakes hands with me, smiles and presses my hand. He calls out, 'Bring some water.'

His wife appears to have gone somewhere. The other woman brings me a glass of water; greying hair on the head, dark circles around the eyes, discoloured lips, sagging breasts, and a sickly body.

Handing me the glass of water, she smiles again as she did at the door. Noticing her smile again, I am confused. I think I have seen her somewhere, but I can't remember where.

'I think you both have not recognized each other,' Raju interjects.

Instead of replying, I look at the woman again. But I am not able to recollect who she is.

She says, 'I have recognized him, but brother has not recognized me.'

I find her voice familiar but still cannot place her.

Seeing my confusion, Raju says, 'She is Jagjit, my cousin, Bua's daughter.'

I look at Jagjit again but still can't place her. Raju laughs, 'No. Not Jagjit, she is Putli, brother, Putli!'

I stand up and, placing my hand on her head, bless her, 'You silly girl, you are Putli? Why didn't you tell me earlier?'

Hearing the word Putli, the image of a slender girl floats into my mind—like a mulberry dangling from a branch reaching towards the ground. Just as her thick shiny black hair does. A fair complexion, doe eyes, rosy lips, and a strong supple body.

Putli had done her B.Ed. while staying at her mother's paternal home. Whenever I went to see Raju at his home, I heard only one name, Putli, her nickname, lovingly given to her because of her beauty. And a putli she was. The entire family addressed her by that name. I too called her Putli, the doll.

Bhabhi, Raju's wife, comes into the room and joins the mirth caused by my inability to recognize Putli. Then she goes to cook and Putli starts serving us our meals. Time and again she comes into the room to serve us some dish or the other and time and again she goes into the kitchen to fetch something or the other. When she comes into the room, I see her as Jagjit: greying, faded lips, and body. When she goes out of the room, Putli appears in my mind's eye: a slim, lively girl with long shiny black hair almost reaching the ground.

After we finish eating, Bhabhi and Putli join us with their plates. We all continue talking to each other. They finish their food and put the plates down. I look at my watch and ask for their permission to leave.

Surprised Raju says, 'No, brother, you go tomorrow.'

Bhabhi too objects, 'What is this? Returning so soon! We won't let you go like this.'

Putli says, 'Brother, stay here for one day at least. We have luckily met after so many years.'

'I'll catch the 2 o'clock train.' I answer them all. 'I have to go to my village today. It is very important. They had written to me. There is some family problem. They will all be waiting for me.'

Raju looks puzzled. He wants to say something. But Putli and Bhabhi are there; he can't say anything in their presence. Because of his sprained foot, he can't come out to talk to me. Sitting there he tries to dissuade me.

I say, 'I'll come again. Today I came to see you because I happened to be passing through. I thought I would spend some time with you and board the next train.'

I pick up my attaché case, greet Bhabhi, stop Raju from getting up because of his sprained foot, look at Putli once again, and head out and hail a rickshaw to the railway station.

Translated by Paramjit Singh Ramana

DOE'S EYE

MOHAN BHANDARI

It was perhaps Saturday. It must have been Saturday, yes, a holiday. No, a holiday was declared. Otherwise, why would this have happened! I had no idea at all that it could happen this way. I wasn't frightened, but I was puzzled, confused. Such were the times. My mind was under stress. Besides stress and haziness, there was another thought in my mind. What I was thinking of I cannot tell. Dread and foreboding was all around. How can such a distracted person even remember what day it was?

If a person is killed, forbearance follows. If the soul is killed, memory ceases, nothing can be done. And so it happened then. Memory ceased to function. All was forgotten—what day, what month.

Now memory has revived. It has happened gradually. It is restored. One by one, the events of the day are coming back. It could be that the mind was not in proper form. Wait a minute… what happened slowly comes to mind. One by one, I remember what transpired. It was the month of November. It had just begun. It was the second or third day. Likewise, the date. Saturday was the day the unlucky incident happened. It was night, riots were taking place. A woman was killed. Then more killings followed. Riots were taking place and no action was being taken. Discipline bound us. No order, no action. Riots continued to happen. There was utter disorder. No sleep during the day or at night.

On the third day, an order came through. The jawans were to stay in the barracks. The officers were to stay in the barracks and rest till further orders. The words struck like a hammer in

185

my head. To take rest, I went to my kothi in Defence Colony. The area was out of the danger zone. In the order, rest carried ambiguous meanings. Of course, we were used to getting such orders. No discussion, no objection could be raised. Such words as why, how, but, no—these did not figure in our dictionaries.

My wife and children were out of station. In the house, I had been alone for the last month. Except eating, drinking, and sleeping, what else was there to do!

Parade? Obeying orders was not new! Forget this talk of before and after. A break happened during the previous days. There was no rest. Day and night, over and above, hung the ominous dictum of 'till further orders'.

I phoned Major K. Malhotra. 'Hello, how are you? Hello from this side. Yes, yes, myself.'

In reply I said, 'Come on friend, you can spend the night here…. For a couple of hours only! Bring Major Dube also. You are both welcome. I am rather bored all alone. Yes, till further orders.'

Laughing, I hung up the phone. After some time, they arrived. They were mutual friends, bachelors in the bargain. Our company was known as the triad. I invited two more friends from the neighbourhood. Earlier too, we used to spend time together. This evening however was different…. I was about to fall over when Bunny held me. Malhotra asked what the matter was. I said, 'Earthquake!' It seemed to me that the roof was shaking. 'Major Dube seemed hysterical. 'Oh, no. This cannot happen. This is mere illusion. Be steady, man, don't lose heart.'

The others, feeling shaken, watched us.

From the city, flames were rising. We could not keep standing there for long. We went down the stairs and sat inside. Then we began to drink rather fast. Of the two of us, only one talked. After uttering some yesses and noes, we became quiet. There was no sensible talk. Silence prevailed. To me it seemed as if we drank silence and not whisky. Right from the start.

'We should sound an alarm,' I thought.

Suddenly, the doorbell rang. It was very faint. Silence prevailed. The bell rang again. I went towards the door and said, 'Who is there?' There was no reply. I repeated, 'Who is there?'

'It's me, sir. Makhan. Your Makhan Singh. Open the door, sir.' The voice was hushed. I recognized the voice of my former servant.

'Why at this hour!' I exclaimed as I opened the door. He stood there and with him was a middle-aged woman. I signalled him to enter. It was dark outside. First, he stepped in and then the woman. I shut the door quickly. Startled, she clung to the wall. I saw her look at me. Then with her head lowered, she stood still. When she had regained her composure, I found that she looked rather youthful. Beautiful. She had an oval face and a dark mole on her chin.

Taking me aside, Makhan Singh said, 'Sahib! Her husband was killed as well as her son. A gang of rioters attacked them. Somehow, she escaped and came to me. Danger still lurks but so far she is safe. I also escaped...the madness is everywhere.' Both were trembling.

He ran his hand through his dishevelled hair. Desolation and despair prevailed.

'I have brought her here so that she can stay safe. So long as you are around, no one will dare harm her.' As he explained this, he became emotional and tears began to flow from his eyes.

'You did well, remarkably well,' I commended him. I was in two minds. I felt proud that so much confidence had been reposed in me. How could I betray his trust and faith! When someone seeks shelter, you should perform your duty even if you have to pay a heavy price for that. The military man in me was fully awakened.

'I have to go back,' Makhan said even as he undid the bolt and stepped out without giving me a chance to react. In this situation, I should not have let him go but nothing could be done anyhow now. I, myself, was lost in thought.

I picked up courage to talk to the woman and assured her I'd help. She did not say anything but kept standing, her head bowed, not uttering a single word. Already, I was engrossed in silence. I was in a dilemma. What to do—I failed to decide.

I went to my friends and told them what happened and pointed towards the girl. They had already been staring at her. Of the four, two of them smirked on hearing me.

Their smiles seemed strange…. They undid the door's bolt and went away. All this happened mechanically. Their actions intrigued me.

They laughed loudly. Major Chadha said, 'Good luck, my chap.' His words sounded vulgar to me.

'What is your name?' I asked the woman. She shuddered but said nothing.

'What is the harm in telling me your name? After all, I don't wish you any ill.' She moved her lips and trembled. But she couldn't speak.

'Don't be upset. Don't fear. Tell me,' I said gently and with great sympathy.

'Nasib…Nasib Kaur.' She uttered her name with hesitation and fear.

'Eat something, you must be hungry,' I said, so as to calm her. She shook her head to denote her refusal. To my later queries, she gave no reply. She was not in a proper state of mind. The blow had completely shaken her. Perhaps I could ask her all this the next morning.

With this idea in mind, I sent her to my bedroom. After some time, I saw her lying huddled like a bundle. Her knees were stuck to her stomach. I took two blankets and came out of the room. Suddenly, I remembered that my revolver was inside the room. In the state of mind she was in, she could do anything. I rose, went in, opened the almirah, picked up the revolver, checked it, and turned to leave. Seeing the revolver in my hand, she trembled, her big eyes widening as she looked at me with fright. With folded hands, she seemed to mumble, 'Don't kill…don't kill me!'

I had invited divine wrath. But I felt responsible for her. How could I let her down? The tear, lurking in her big left eye swelled and gently flowed onto her cheek. It was as though a doe's eye was gazing at my face. Outside the room, sitting for a long while, I mused over the eye gazing at me from the table, roof, walls, from every object I could see.

I remembered an incident from my childhood. I was perhaps ten or twelve years old. One day, some people went hunting in the jungle close to the village. I also went with them. For the whole day, they searched in vain for some animal to hunt. No partridge or quail was to be found. The dogs tried their best but no prey emerged from its hideout. Evening was setting in and we were tired and returning to our village. Suddenly a doe sprang up from behind a hillock, and the hunters were overjoyed to see it. Getting down on his knees, the rifleman took aim but the doe leapt to one side. He tried again but in vain. This fight between life and death went on for some time. At last the doe, ignorant and innocent, came and stood right in front of us. The shot was fired and the doe collapsed on the hillock. It writhed in pain and the hunters headed towards it. I also went and stood nearby but did not get too close.

The doe was writhing and looking at me. Its wide eyes had grown bigger. A tear came out and began to flow down its cheek. Still the eye was staring at me from each and every object in the room. Seated outside, I kept thinking. My state of mind was that of the hunter who could do whatever he wanted. The poor, helpless, and hapless woman lay in my bedroom like the doe. That night, several thoughts came into my mind. Thoughts of virtue and sin. Pondering over them, I fell asleep.

When I got up in the morning, I found the door of the bedroom closed. I had a bath and kept arranging and rearranging the objects around the house. Her door was still closed. Who knows for how many nights she had remained awake! Now she was fast asleep. 'When she gets up, we shall have tea together and talk about life's pains and pleasures.' I was wondering how I would initiate the conversation I was thinking about.

I peeped inside and saw that she was lying stiff, eyes wide open. Like an unhinged man, I began to roam around. Picking up courage, I rang Major Malhotra. He and Dube reached in no time. The neighbours were also called. We went into the room and Major Malhotra closed her eyes.

News of her death was conveyed to Headquarters. According to them, I have committed a sin. I don't care whether I am jailed or set free. However, there is one thing that will never let me feel free. It is a deep sense of regret that I didn't offer her the warmth of my body. I didn't comfort a creature so obviously in distress. Had I done so, she might have remained alive.

Translated by Tejwant Singh Gill

ERADICATOR OF SUFFERING

BACHINT KAUR

The Divine Presence watches all deeds, good and bad.
Every action gains merit, some actions cause one to
draw closer to Him, others push one away.

The last couplets of the Japji Sahib were yet to be recited
when the rear tyre of the bicycle of Hazoor Singh, the retired
BSF soldier, burst with a bang. Many devotees and worshippers
were going to Gurdwara Dukh Niwaran Sahib at the break of
dawn. Many women were walking barefoot; others were riding
their bicycles. A few were on their motorbikes.

Soldier Hazoor Singh had hardly crossed the Baradari gate
when the tyre burst. His bicycle refused to go even a yard further.

After wondering what to do, Hazoor Singh decided to drag
his bicycle along. He started walking slowly towards Gurdwara
Sahib. What else could he do? His home was further than the
Gurdwara Sahib from where he was. Walking along slowly, he
reached the railway line exhausted. Just as the light was spreading
across the sky above, his face too lit up with hope. He had just
noticed a cycle mechanic spreading his old tattered mat by the
roadside and setting up his repair shop.

Hazoor Singh approached him, and as they saw each other,
their faces began to glow like fresh blooming flowers.

'Come, Babaji.'

'Fix this little puncture, young man. By the time I reached
the Baradari, the rear tyre burst all of a sudden.'

Before touching the bicycle, the mechanic bowed to his toolkit
with such reverence as if those few simple iron tools were his

Gurdwara Sahib. Then he placed the bicycle on the ground as if he were about to fix the hooves of an ox. With the help of two big levers, he pulled the tube out of the tyre and pulled the bowl full of water closer to him. But the old tube was already full of repaired punctures. It was not a small cut that he had to repair. This time a big chunk of tube had been ripped apart.

The cycle mechanic very swiftly and deftly repaired the tube and handed the bicycle over to Hazoor Singh. He got busy inflating the front wheel of the bicycle with a hand pump.

'How much, young man?'

'It is early morning, Babaji, and you are my first customer... pay me whatever you like.'

When Hazoor Singh put his hand into the front left pocket of his old army shirt to look for money, the pocket turned out to be completely empty. Nothing there.

Perplexed and troubled, so many expressions flitted across on Hazoor Singh's face.

'What happened, Babaji?'

'Son, I forgot to bring money from home. Normally I don't need much money for myself. My family usually gives one or two annas every day and that I donate at the gurdwara while paying obeisance. At the most I might need to inflate the tyres on the way. But today my poor bicycle got a puncture. And Nand Kaur forgot to give me some money!' As he was saying this, Hazoor Singh's glowing face had turned pale.

'Baba, you are my first customer. If the first customer does not pay, how will I earn anything during the rest of the day?'

'This is your delusion, young man. Please give me my bicycle. Believe me, I go to Gurdwara Dukh Niwaran every morning; I will definitely pay you tomorrow.'

'Baba, you are my first customer, it is my first earning of the day, I cannot give you credit. I am helpless, honour bound! You stay here with me for some time. When someone known to you passes this way, you borrow money from him and pay me. You come to the gurdwara every day, many people will be known to you.'

Hazoor Singh had never cared much about money. He served for forty years in the army and every month he handed over his entire salary to his family. He never felt the need to carry any money. Even now he got forty rupees as pension every month, but today he couldn't even find some small change. Not even one or two anna coins.

For a long time, Hazoor Singh stood by the barbed wire next to the road near the railway track, carefully studying the faces of the people going past. But such was his luck that today it appeared as if nobody known to him lived in Patiala city. Five-thirty, six, and now it was going to be six-thirty. The recitation of Sukhmani Sahib was going on at Gurdwara Dukh Niwaran Sahib; it could be heard clearly:

In all forms He himself pervades.

Through all eyes, He Himself watches.

All creation is His body.

He Himself listens to His own Praise.

He has created the drama of coming and going, of life and death.

He has made Maya subservient to His Will.

When he used to work, he never paid much attention to money. He always believed there would be enough and that one need not hoard money nor should one squander it. That is why he never thought about actually saving any. But today he was caught off-guard by his lack of money. All three sons of his had good jobs and they were quite well off as a family. But Hazoor Singh's family never let him have more than a few coins in his pocket, as if he were a child. But this issue of money didn't matter much for Hazoor Singh since his needs were so few, just like a yogi's. He had his meals at home, tea at home, and had plenty of old military uniforms.

But sometimes he did have a secret wish—to buy a lottery

ticket! At least once. But how could he do this? He was never
alone. Even when he went to withdraw his pension, his wife,
Nand Kaur, or his son, Niranjan Singh, accompanied him. This
was virtually his only indulgence.

He had been waiting and thinking for more than an hour,
and he had a terrible headache. In the gurdwara, the recitation of
Sukhmani Sahib had been completed and the singing of hymns,
the shabad kirtan, could be heard. Today he would not be able
to listen to the singing of hymns also. He thought about leaving
his bicycle there and walking to the gurdwara. But he realized
immediately that it was too far to go on foot. It would take a
long time to go and as much time to return. He thought about
his weak, tired legs.

Lost in such thoughts, he stood next to the gate which
guarded the railway crossing. All kinds of ideas crossed his mind.
Suddenly he noticed an aged blind beggar sitting on the other
side of the railway track. She begged for alms with her old
dupatta spread before every passer-by and blessed every one of
them in her piteous voice.

Hearing Hazoor Singh's footfall approach, the old blind
woman's voice became even more plaintive. She started blessing
him, using an overly compassionate tone of voice as she asked
for alms.

'Babuji, may you always roll in money. God will bless you
with every gift. Please spare a penny or two for this old hapless
blind woman also.'

Just as the footsteps came to a stop next to her, she was
gripped by a strange feeling of fear and excitement. The beggar
woman hadn't lost hope. She spread out her dupatta, which had
a few coins lying on it.

Looking at those coins, Hazoor Singh lost his sense of decorum
and concern for the distinction between honour and dishonour.
He spoke softly and gently to the old woman.

'Woman, I haven't come to give you anything…. I…I have

come to borrow some coins from you.'

'But you don't appear to be a beggar like me.'

'No, I am also a beggar.'

'That is a lie.' The old beggar woman was confused and she tried to hide the few coins she had.

'I am not lying.... I am telling you the truth.'

'Why are you making fun of an unfortunate blind woman, Babuji?' There was a tinge of pain in the beggar woman's words.

'I am not making fun of you, old woman. I am telling you the truth. Every morning I go to Dukh Niwaran Sahib Gurdwara. And paying my obeisance only once, I secretly ask Him for all kinds of alms in my heart. I bow my head there only once and ask for so much. The only difference between us is that you beg for alms openly, in loud clear words and I beg secretly, not letting anyone know. Here, on the way to the gurdwara, I see only a few beggars sitting by the roadside, but inside the gurdwara there are long queues of beggars and I am one among them every day. Today on my way to the gurdwara the tyre of my bicycle got punctured and I had not a single penny on me! Nothing.'

For a moment, a third eye appeared to emerge on the old blind woman's forehead. She felt as if God himself had come to visit her today, to test her devotion. Her heart was trembling because she had never faced such a situation in her life.

'How much money do you need, Babuji?'

'Only two annas. I have to pay the cycle mechanic. Because it is his first earning of the day, he cannot give me credit.'

The old blind woman immediately collected all the coins she had in that dirty old cloth, put them in a cracked brass bowl and pushed it towards Hazoor Singh.

'Take whatever is here.'

'What will I do with all of that? Just give me the two annas which I need.'

'Take them, take them all, they are all your blessing.'

'No, woman, give me two annas as a loan with your own

hand; I will return it to you tomorrow for sure.'

Giving in to Hazoor Singh's insistence, the old beggar woman rummaged through the coins with her fingers, picked up two one-anna coins from her bowl and handed them over to him. The melodious sound of hymns could still be heard from the gurdwara.

'Thank you very much, old lady. Money is also a small god. Today I have understood this fact.'

Hazoor Singh took the two one-anna coins from the blind beggar woman and handed them over to the bicycle mechanic.

And he turned his bicycle towards home and hurriedly cycled away.

Translated by Paramjit Singh Ramana

TO EVERYONE, HIS SHARE

WARYAM SINGH SANDHU

Ghuddu took the buffalo out into the courtyard and tethered it at the manger. Running his hand through the fodder, he looked at the vapour rising from the buffalo's nostrils and called for a bucket to milk it. Then he set right the dung-smeared tattered old rug covering the buffalo and, trying to control his own shivers, looked to the east for any sign of sunrise. But the fog had completely overpowered the sun, much like a strong wrestler pins his rival down with a knee on the neck. Instinctively, his own hand went to his neck. Many years ago, when he had been a wrestler, he had often experienced the pain caused by his coach, Jinda Podriwala, or some other wrestler, when they pinned him down by the neck during practice and in the actual bouts. In any case, his reputation was more of a loser rather than of a winner. It was because of this that a village elder, Baba Gharal, had jokingly remarked to him, 'Oy Dharam! You fool, what a huge frame you have! If you are going to lose every day, it would have been much better if your body had been cut into two and two men fashioned out of it. One of them would have ploughed the fields and the other looked after the cattle. God really is a fool....'

The youngest of the three brothers, Dharam had remained 'Ghuddu'. He was no longer a wrestler. There was no fear of a knee pressing down his neck. But still he felt as if there was a pain in his neck. Whose knee was it that was pressing down on his neck?

His sister, Bachno, brought the bucket and the wheat flour

to mix with the fodder. She had come from her in-laws on learning of their mother's death and had been staying here since then. She handed the bucket to Ghuddu and went to sprinkle the flour on the fodder.

Ghuddu patted the buffalo and sat down to milk it.

'Listen brother...look.... Our two elder brothers will be here soon. The eldest must have stayed last night with Karam Singh. Look here, you should sort things out with them.... Look...the last rituals for mother have to be arranged.... You have to take the ashes to Haridwar.... The wise say...it is better to arrange to settle the daughters as well. See.'

Ghuddu was very irritated.

Big granny! Who is she to advise me...?

Thinking about Bachno, who was younger than him, he swallowed the anger with his spittle, 'That witch...'

Bachno went on talking, 'Look, I know you are financially tight. But one has to perform these duties anyhow.... I have told the elder brothers too that they are well off, they can afford it.... Nevermind. Anyway...they replied saying, "We take nothing more than the grain for food...he gives us nothing...." See here... everyone cannot be like your brother-in-law.... All over the country, women take their share of land but he has not even once suggested that I do the same....'

Ghuddu, who had been controlling himself with difficulty, now shrieked, 'Go, you take your share...let them also take theirs.... This wretched land has made me a king!'

Frightened by the loud shouting, or perhaps because Ghuddu had pressed too hard, the buffalo jumped away. Ghuddu fell back and, despite all his efforts to save it, the bucket fell over, spilling some of the milk. He stood up and, picking up the wooden dung scraper, started beating the buffalo mercilessly.

'See...can't even talk straight....' Fuming, Bachno picked up the bucket and walked away grumbling.

'What harm has this poor dumb animal done to you?'

Ghuddu's wife Ratni was shouting from near the hearth. 'Why do you take your anger at others out on this poor animal?'

The frightened buffalo, her ears raised and eyes terror-stricken, stood trembling near one corner of the manger in the posture of someone seeking pardon.

The sound of an approaching motorcycle could be heard in the distance. Ghuddu started running his hands through the fodder in the mangers before the cattle. As the sound of the motorcycle came closer, neighbouring dogs began barking louder and louder. After a while, the motorcycle came to a stop in front of their house. Ratni covered her head before opening the door. The elder brothers of her husband, Swarn Singh and Karam Singh, were standing before her. They drove their motorcycle through the doorway and parked it in the mud plastered courtyard. Swarn Singh, the elder of the two, took off his goggles and wiped them clean with his handkerchief. And then, wiping away dewdrops on his overcoat with his glove-covered hand, went into the front room towards the bed of his father, Bishan Singh. The younger, Karam Singh, wrapped his warm shawl tightly around him again and rubbed the sole of his embroidered handmade footwear against the edge of the raised platform of the front room to wipe off the dung sticking to it. Then he turned towards Bachno and asked, 'Where is Ghuddu?'

Bachno took her arm out of her shawl and pointed towards the cattle where Ghuddu was trying to catch the calf that had been so frightened by the thunder of the motorcycle that it had pulled out the peg it was tethered from the ground.

'Come, brother wrestler, come here! Let us discuss a few things. Brother cannot get leave every day...and I too have a hundred things to do.... Then we have to take the ashes of the old woman to immerse in the Ganga...you go if you want to or I'll go....'

'Coming,' Ghuddu replied nonchalantly. Untying the rope from the peg uprooted by the calf, he called his son, 'Oye Kaku, pick up a cot and place it in the veranda for your grandfather....'

Before Kaku could take the cot out, old Bishan Singh said to him, 'Kaku, bring the chair.' He moved to one side on his cot, leaving space for Swarn Singh to sit. But Swarn Singh kept standing near the cot, adjusting his turban and caressing his beard with his hands.

Swarn Singh was the eldest of the three brothers and the most educated. He had completed his education on his own and succeeded in getting a job as an overseer. He had a good income and was living comfortably in his own house in the city. His only daughter was happily married into a prosperous family. Both his sons were well settled. He had good connections with the rich and prosperous of the city, he spent his time with them and was friendly with them. He had his own special social circle. He rarely visited the village. His share of two-and-half acres of land that he owned in the village was cultivated by Ghuddu and he took nothing more than the grain for food over the year from his younger brother. He used to tell his friends and relatives that he had given the land to Ghuddu for free.

Kaku brought an iron chair, which was the only chair in their house and had been there for a long time.

'Son, clean the chair a little,' said old Bishan Singh as he placed his faded cotton quilt properly on the bed, tied his hair into a knot with his trembling hands and began tying a dirty old turban around his head. Whenever Bishan Singh faced Swarn Singh, he went through the same experience, as if he were a petitioning farmer waiting upon the tehsildar, the revenue officer. Swarn Singh appeared to him to be made of different stuff, something that was rather good, fine and strong in quality. The stuff that was perhaps used in making dolls and toys. Compared to Swarn's way of living, his sophistication, he felt rather rustic and coarse. So, whenever he happened to visit his eldest son's home in the city, he had never been able stay for too long in that rather urbane atmosphere. He felt as if he was not able to take the right steps in that house; his daughter-in-law and grandchildren appeared to stare at him as though he was a stranger. He felt completely out of place. He felt as if someone had taken a rabbit playing near its burrow in the fields and forgotten it in a marble cave.

Kaku cleaned the chair. Bishan Singh was still in a dilemma whether to address Swarn using the plural pronoun, as was the custom when talking to 'big people', when Swarn went and occupied the chair. On such occasions, Bishan Singh often felt very irritated with himself. His inner self would mock him, 'He is not some viceroy's progeny.... He is my own son.... Why do I...?'

Karam Singh brought in a cot on his own. He was two years older than Ghuddu. As a student, he had been careless with his studies but naughty to the core. He would hide his satchel in the fuel wood of Santi Mehri and run off with his friends to play hockey. He would then pick up his bag when school closed for the day and go back home. Being younger, Ghuddu was always with him. Both of them joined the school together and both dropped out at the same time. They started helping their father at home and in the fields.

By the time Karam crossed his adolescence, he had started moving about in society; he became a conduit for carrying supplies for smugglers. Ghuddu, on the other hand, being well-built and stronger, decided to become a wrestler. Karam's efforts proved worthwhile and by and by he began to earn a share in the smuggled goods. Black money was easy money. Within days, he was transformed. He built a house in the central square in a nearby town and was leading a comfortable life. He owned a dairy and a poultry farm. He lacked for nothing.

And the wrestler Dharam Singh remained the Ghuddu that he was. His father's plough had been passed down to him. Baba Gharal had only jokingly remarked to Ghuddu that it would have been much better if his body had been cut into two and two men fashioned out of it; one of them could have ploughed the fields and the other looked after the cattle. Ghuddu had really been trying to do his best as a farmer. But like someone trying to run in a nightmare, he could not move forward. It was as if some supernatural power had caught him by the waist and was pulling him back.

Driving the peg for the calf into the ground, Ghuddu felt as if every one of the blows was landing on his own head and he was being driven deeper and deeper into the ground. He was thinking about the discussion he was going to have with his elder brothers…. Thinking about them both, he was shaken…and then this Bachno, his sister! Oh God! What kind of siblings were they!

He was annoyed with the eldest because in front of relatives and friends he always talked about him in such a condescending tone, as if he were an orphan. Even after taking his share of the crop, he would talk about the land as if he had given it for free to Ghuddu. And Ghuddu could not let go of that piece of land. Perhaps he would find it even more difficult to make both ends meet without it. But he could not bear the burden of the obligation: that he cultivated his land for 'free'. Karam Singh, on the other hand, always took his share but complained that Ghuddu was not doing as well as he should. He felt he was not earning enough from his share of land. Just the previous day, when they were all collecting their mother's ashes, Karam Singh said to Bachno's husband, 'Brother, this year I plan to use a tractor and sow fodder for the buffaloes in my two acres of land. I hardly get anything from it now.'

'Not bad, not bad…it would be good…' Bachno's husband said.

Ghuddu knew that their conversation was targeted at him. He was fuming with anger but didn't say anything. The landholding was already rather small, what would he do if two acres were taken away? He was worried.

He hesitated broaching the subject on his own. It was only his sister and her husband or his father who could intercede, in whom he could confide, share his problems with, or seek help.

But his brother-in-law had been advising Karam Singh in his very presence to get the possession of his share of land. And his sister Bachno was not going to come to his help in any way. She held a grudge against him—her elder brother and sister-in-law treated her much better than he did. They maintained regular contact with her, visited her and shared in her every moment of joy or grief. They found time to be with her and to help in her hour of need. They gifted her clothes every six months or so. But Ghuddu hardly ever visited her or came to her rescue when she needed it. She felt that Ghuddu did not treat her son properly when he came to visit once or twice a year. She used to grumble:

'Oh my God! So indifferent! He gave a few useless clothes at the time of the birth of my son...and that's all.... May I suffer in hell if I lie. He has never given a single gift or any money to my son since then. See...we don't need his gifts of clothes or money...but still there should be some sense of responsibility of a brother towards his sister....' And she would start wiping her eyes with the end of her dupatta.

Ghuddu was really cross with Bachno. The day their mother passed away and she was being given her last bath, Bachno took off her gold earrings and handed them to Karam Singh's wife, as if she had been looking after their mother all her life.

For a moment he felt irritated with his mother also. But then he remembered her wrinkled face and shining bright eyes, and he was overcome with affection for her. She was the only one who really loved him and always stood up for him. If he raised any issue in the family, she used to argue on his behalf with great passion and persuasiveness. It was she who used to say about Ghuddu, 'He is my beloved son, so simple, so innocent... just like Shiva. You are all too sharp....'

Ghuddu was unhappy that he had not been with his mother when she died. All her life his mother had been with him, but at the time of her death she had been taken away. She had suffered an attack of paralysis two months ago. Swarn Singh came to enquire about her health and, despite her reluctance, took her away to the city so that she could be treated in a big hospital.

She stayed in the hospital for treatment for about one-and-a-half months, but her old, weak body could not recover from the attack.

And only old Bishan Singh was left who understood Ghuddu's problems, who felt Ghuddu's privations as though they were his own. He had lived and suffered all his life as a farmer. But he was such a humble farmer, so badly cowed by his deprivations, that he just could not assert himself or say anything with force and conviction. Or maybe he felt inferior when faced with the prosperity of his eldest son.

'O mother's Shivji! Will you go on fixing the peg...we have other work to do....' Karam Singh called out to Ghuddu.

Ghuddu stood up, wiped his mud-soiled hands on his clothes, and slowly walked across the veranda into the room and stood next to them.

'Sit down,' Karam, said pointing to the cot. Bachno came too, settling her shawl around her and sat next to her father.

'Father, our elder brother came to me last night and we are here to discuss....'

'Discuss what you want to...what is the matter...' Bishan Singh spoke softly as he scratched his beard.

'Look, whatever we decide after discussion...with consensus... would be best for all of us....' Karam Singh waited for a moment and looked at all those sitting around him. He continued, clearing his throat, 'The thing is that we want to have a proper final prayer and condolence meeting for our mother...we'll invite all our relatives and friends...the old woman was very fortunate, she had such a long life...had children and grandchildren...we have to give her the due honour.... What do you think?'

'Son, what can I say? But what is this attempt to honour small poor people like us?' Bishan Singh spoke hesitatingly.

'I also told Karam Singh that all this is a sheer waste of money. But he does not agree,' Swarn Singh expressed his opinion.

'O brother! What will the relatives say? The sons are well-to-do, prosperous, earning well...what has come over them? It may be a waste of money for educated people like you.... But then it does not affect you so much...you live in the city.... We will have to bear the taunts and barbs of others...' Karam Singh was still going on when Bachno interrupted him.

'No, no, brother. What are you saying? That is no way to talk!' She went after Swarn Singh. 'Brother Karam Singh is right. My in-laws are ready to come...my sisters-in-law will mock me and won't ever let me forget this....'

Ghuddu knew that it was he rather than their father, Bishan Singh, who was being addressed. He wanted to give Bachno a tight slap. Swarn Singh was right, it would all be a waste of money. And Ghuddu knew his own financial position very well.

'Well, my dears, I'll contribute. Whatever is my share, tell me now...' Swarn Singh said, agreeing to the expense.

Ghuddu had hoped that Swarn Singh would oppose the idea. But now he fell into the deep well of worries and tension. He was furious and rage began to build up within him.

Karam Singh detailed the expenses involved. 'It'll cost five to seven thousand easily. And then brother says that he incurred an expense of 2,700 rupees on the treatment of mother. So every one of us has to contribute 900 rupees each.'

Ghuddu was shocked to hear that the money spent on their mother's treatment was also to be included in the shared expenses. He started biting his lips. He could not decide whether he should speak up or not, or if there was anything he could do.

'You incurred some expenditure on the treatment for your mother? So what? This poor fellow looked after her all his life, fed her....' Bishan Singh somehow managed to gather enough courage to blurt out.

'Look, Father! That's not right...' Bachno butted in. She had taken her hand out of her shawl and was gesticulating wildly as she spoke. 'If he fed her, she too slaved all her life for him. She looked after his children, brought them up. See…he had mother's and your share of land too in his possession and earned from it….'

'You…you, shut up!' Ghuddu shouted at her in a rage, then muttered, 'Thinks herself a big advocate!' His nostrils were quivering and his forehead was burning even in that biting cold.

'See…I am like poison to him! Okay…I won't sit here any more,' Bachno exploded and left, waving her arms and fuming with anger.

Finding that the situation had become very tense, Karam Singh tried to defuse it. But Bachno turned and made another jab.

'See…I too have my share in the land! You are not special…. So, if I behave like an advocate, then fine, I behave like an advocate.'

'Oh! Stop it now. We'll talk about all that another time… just calm down….'

And Karam Singh addressed Ghuddu directly now, 'Brother does not have time. You tell me. Will you take the old woman's ashes to the Ganga or I should take them?'

Ghuddu remained silent for a minute or two. Many different ideas and sentiments were jostling for space in his mind. For a moment the outer fog appeared to have engulfed his insides also. Stunned, he sat without knowing what to say. Then the simmering fire within him burst into flames and suddenly he stood up, and said clearly.

'Look here! There's nothing that you don't know. I am almost broke…I can't afford to go to the Ganga or do anything else.' Then he stopped for a moment. Cleared his throat, and continued with a jerk of his head, 'If it is so important…you go and immerse Mother's ashes in the Ganga…. And this old man who sits here in front of you who is alive and healthy…' he pointed towards Bishan Singh, '…his ashes I'll immerse on my own.'

All three of them, father and the two older sons were staring at him, shocked. But he didn't stop.

'The fact of the matter is I can't afford it now.... Anyway, if you don't like this proposal, then, Sardarji, bring one third of the ashes, my share, and place it over there, on that peg. I'll go and immerse them when I can afford it.'

And without another word, he turned and went into the house. They were left staring at him open-mouthed.

Translated by Paramjit Singh Ramana

HOME

SUKIRAT

Yet another morning is unfolding in this home.

Manohar is in the kitchen preparing breakfast. Surjeet is on the computer scouring the emails that have arrived in his inbox since the previous night. Besides various banal messages, and a few official ones, there is also a personal message. It reads: 'Get ready to suffer me once again.' This is Kalyani's favourite and much worn subject-line for her emails. Whenever she comes to Mumbai, these are the words she uses to announce her visit.

'Your darling is coming to Mumbai,' Surjeet tells Manohar, sipping his coffee by the small table that they have set up in the kitchen. Manohar's ears immediately perk up at this—he had been absentmindedly slurping his cup of strong tea.

'When?'

'She is arriving by the evening flight, but hasn't given any details. She writes that there's no need to pick her up; if the flight is on time, she should be home by dinner time…. Otherwise, we should just leave some food out for her.'

Kalyani has been visiting Mumbai all by herself for the past many years. She usually came by the Rajdhani or some other train and Manohar went to Mumbai Central to receive her. He did that even when Kalyani had expressly said that there was no need to pick her up, that she was grown up enough to hire a taxi or catch the local train and reach home. But for Manohar she was still a child. Surjeet often taunted him for this by remarking, 'He can't brook even an hour's delay in meeting his darling child!' Unmindful of such teasing remarks, Manohar would wrap up his

208

work early and rush to the station to receive Kalyani. But this time, since Kalyani has not even provided her flight details, there is no point in going to the airport.

However, this minor disappointment does not last long. Manohar soon goes back to being his usual ebullient self, donning the mantle of an efficient and affectionate host. He starts planning the dinner menu which must include all that Kalyani loves: fried pomfret, bangda fish cooked in red coconut gravy, and beans lightly fried with mustard seeds. And suddenly he remembers something important—that Kalyani is visiting Mumbai for the first time after Bhai Sahib's death and, in terms of social customs, would it be appropriate to serve her non-vegetarian dishes?

'Now don't you start following these ghati ideas,' Surjeet retorted. 'It has been two months since Joginder expired. It's unnecessary now to bother about vegetarian–non-vegetarian norms. Cook whatever you feel like. And don't start condoling Joginder's death the moment she arrives. It is not required.'

Whenever Surjeet wants to express that Manohar's ideas on social norms are out of sync with modern life, he refers to the fact that he hails from the Western Ghat region of Maharashtra. The city-bred, urban Maharashtrians consider the Western Ghats as the backwaters of the state and disparagingly call the people from there ghatis. Initially, Surjeet would call Manohar 'my dear ghati' as an endearment. But with that romantic love gradually turning into domestic monotony, this epithet has regained its original sharp edge for many years now.

City slicker Surjeet had met ghati Manohar in an overcrowded local Mumbai train for the first time. At that time, Surjeet had arrived in Mumbai recently and was renting a room in Borivali. He would take the 8.40 local to his office every day. Manohar took the same train from Bandra. Since they often travelled by the same coach, they had started recognizing each other. And then, one day, reading a faint invitation in each other's eyes they had cut through the crowd to stand next to each other. In a coach packed like a tin of sardines, where bodies were rubbing against each other, they had felt their excitement rising in tandem and the need to conjecture vanished in that moment. Manohar was monosyllabic, merely saying 'yes' or 'no' always, as if it were an effort for him to converse in full sentences. He was probably a little shy, and so it was Surjeet who took the initiative. He first invited Manohar to meet him at an Irani restaurant near Churchgate and then to his one-room tenement at Borivali.

Surjeet had come to Mumbai from Delhi. He was an alumnus of the renowned St. Stephen's college and was well-educated. Rather early on he had come to the realization that he was not like the majority of people he knew. After struggling with himself for a few years, he had finally come to terms with his natural sexual orientation and hence felt neither guilty nor diffident in expressing his desires. But Manohar was rather callow in this regard. This could be attributed to many factors—his young age, the constricted social space in which he was brought up, or the limitations of his worldly experiences. It was his innocence, his inexperience, and his gawky responses that drew Surjeet towards him all the more.

Manohar lived with his parents and his brother–bhabhi duo in a crowded chawl in Bandra East. He was the younger sibling in the family and so was a little pampered too. Accountancy was his profession and going to the gym, his passion. He had chosen accountancy as a profession simply because thirty years back his father had become an accountant and a few years ago his brother too had opted for the same. Hence, Manohar had never thought of any other profession other than accountancy as his destined calling.

At Surjeet's invitation, Manohar came to Borivali feeling hesitant, excited, and guilt-ridden, all in equal measure. When Surjeet looked at his sinewy and well-built body, he was reminded of the statue of David sculpted by Michelangelo. That sculpture too showed a well-built, well-exercised physique with a face that carried the bewitching innocence of a child. Surjeet had invited many such friends to the privacy of his room earlier too. People had come and gone. But Surjeet had never wanted to establish a permanent relationship with any of them. Many came, provided a few hours of companionship and disappeared into the teeming crowds: Surjeet did not feel like keeping their contact details or retaining their memories. Transient mating of bodies floating in a mega city. But there was something in Manohar that captivated Surjeet. During their first meeting at his home, Surjeet did not proceed beyond touching his sculpted biceps, caressing his surprisingly soft palms, and brushing against his trembling lips. A child's clenched fist that could be opened if you wanted, without much effort, but it was much more gratifying to stroke it leisurely.

He decided to let this relationship develop its own dynamics in a natural and spontaneous manner. His conscious efforts to hold back his passion gave a diffident Manohar the much-needed trust and confidence in Surjeet.

'Would you like a cup of coffee?' Surjeet asked Manohar on his first visit.

'I find coffee bitter,' Manohar replied. 'I prefer tea. If you have tea at home, I'll prepare it myself.'

It was the first time Surjeet had heard three fully formed sentences from Manohar.

Like an experienced tea-maker, Manohar prepared tea for himself. He put the ideal combination of tea leaves, milk, and crushed cardamoms in the boiling water. He also asked for some biscuits. 'I don't drink tea without biscuits,' he quipped.

∫

Surjeet liked Manohar's free and informal movements in his room. And then it suddenly dawned on him that Manohar does know what to say, but in Hindi. He clams up when you talk to him in English.

Manohar started visiting Surjeet's tenement two–three times a week. Surjeet's office closed half an hour earlier than Manohar's. But he would wait for his friend at the station and then they covered the long distance to Borivali together. Manohar was fond of cooking; instead of the easily scrambled eggs and quickly cooked khichdi that were Surjeet's staples earlier, mutton and chicken dishes began to dominate their meals together. Soon the electric plate of Surjeet's makeshift kitchen was replaced by a proper gas cylinder. Manohar was not only a good cook, he also delighted in inviting people over. Surjeet introduced him to his other friends of similar orientation, to make Manohar aware that there were many more who lived like them and that they were in no way exceptional human beings different from other people. He also introduced him to his heterosexual friends who were comfortable with Surjeet's sexuality, to convey to Manohar that although there was no need to shout about their preferences from the rooftops, hiding their natural desires and feelings from friends who were heterosexual was also not required.

Manohar was gradually becoming more comfortable with Surjeet's friends; particularly with those who did not insist on conversing in English all the time. Not that Manohar did not understand the language; it was just that his education in an obscure local college had not equipped him with the required fluency in English. Surjeet's friends fell into two categories: those who considered Manohar below their and Surjeet's class; and the others, who appreciated the intrinsic warmth and affection of this guileless man. The latter became close friends of Manohar's, too; the former gradually disappeared, even from Surjeet's life.

Surjeet's own family had come to know about his sexual orientation right from the days of his struggle with himself to understand his true self. Like most families of their ilk, they could not accept his sexuality but neither did they put pressure on him to follow the normal track. They did not interfere in his personal life—they let him be. In any case, Surjeet's present habitat in Mumbai, hundreds of miles away from their native place, suited them fine in this respect.

It was only after Surjeet met Manohar in Mumbai that he began thinking of settling down in this mega city on a permanent basis. He had now come to realize that in Manohar he had found a life companion and he slowly began putting this idea to Manohar also.

Manohar's visits to Surjeet's room in Borivali gradually increased. In addition to weekdays, he would often visit him on Saturdays and spend the weekends there. Surjeet was well-acquainted with Manohar's people at home and they in turn were happy that their son had befriended a person who was intelligent and well-bred. Being essentially simple, unaffected rural folk, they did not suspect anything peculiar in this relationship. Surjeet wanted Manohar to let his family know about the true nature of their relationship but Manohar was hesitant. He knew that they would not be able to accept the reality and would feel traumatized. He argued that there was no need to do this as things were going on smoothly. Surjeet's arguments that 'we should be true to ourselves', 'we should not shy away from letting people know about our true feelings', 'it was the right course to take', all failed to convince Manohar. He argued back that he felt no guilt about his sexuality, nor about the course that life was taking, but why involve his family in it? They may not be able to understand all this. Why burden them with a feeling of shame and guilt to feel unburdened himself? Besides, Manohar truly did not feel any need to be 'open' with his family; these were compulsions of the over-educated mind of Surjeet. He and his friends were given to analysing every small detail threadbare, prone to reaching silly conclusions. They had a tendency to make mountains out of life's molehills. To Manohar, it was completely unwarranted to share every personal detail with others just to prove a point.

Manohar's resolve not to divulge the nature of this relationship to his family members despite repeated pleas and promptings only enhanced his image in Surjeet's estimation. He realized that behind a soft exterior, Manohar had strong willpower and Surjeet appreciated this aspect of his personality. From that time, Surjeet did not insist on his sharing the fact of their relationship with his family. On his part, Manohar wanted them to rent a flat where they could live together. For this, he said, he would not have to convince his parents. Since they were living in cramped quarters in a chawl, they would not mind if Manohar shifted to a better accommodation with his well-groomed and respectable friend.

Instead of just renting a flat, Surjeet went and made an outright purchase. He already had enough resources at his command and it only needed a more settled vision of life in Manohar's company to take this step. The flat was located on the seafront, near the village of Versova where lots of new apartment blocks were coming up. It was, no doubt, a little far from the nearest train station, but that was precisely why it was priced reasonably. Buying a two-bedroom flat with a sitting room did not pose an economic challenge. All its windows, including the kitchen windows opened onto the wide expanse of the sea below. Sunlight reached all the nooks of the house. Even the faint smell wafting from Versova's fish market found an easy entry into their abode. After some time they got used to it. The visitors were at times bothered by this permeating whiff, but Surjeet no longer felt it. Ghati Manohar, used to the odour of fish since childhood, had never found it offensive in the first place.

Soon the 'house' owned by Surjeet and Manohar was transformed into a 'home'. The two complemented each other well. While Surjeet, an architect by profession, knew how to rearrange spaces in the best possible manner, Manohar was an instinctive cook and a house-proud man. Visiting friends or Manohar's family appreciated their home's decor and upkeep no end. Eliminating a superfluous wall, Surjeet put in a sliding wooden partition instead.

The sitting room became much bigger and could be transformed into an extra bedroom if needed. He installed a small dining table next to the kitchen window, turning each mealtime into a seaside picnic because of the view. A mere 1,000-square-foot flat was so transformed that it could successfully compete with much richer and larger flats in Malabar Hill.

For his sister's wedding, Surjeet took Manohar to Delhi and introduced him to his family members and friends. Almost everyone liked him—those who took him to be Surjeet's friend from Maharashtra, as well as those who had an inkling of Surjeet's sexuality and surmised that Manohar must be more than just a friend.

From Surjeet's family in Delhi, the first person to visit him in Mumbai was his elder brother, Joginder. He was a well-established lawyer in the capital city and had come to Mumbai in connection with a legal case. At Surjeet's insistence, he decided to stay with them in their newly-acquired flat instead of staying at a hotel.

Manohar, as was his wont, left no stone unturned to provide excellent hospitality to Joginder. He asked him about his eating preferences. On learning that Joginder did not relish fish, he cooked a mutton dish to cater to his palate. He made dal the way Punjabis make it. Though he and Surjeet preferred rice, he prepared rotis for Joginder.

On one of the days during this sojourn, Joginder returned to the flat rather late in the evening. The three of them had drinks and then a late dinner. After dinner, while Joginder and Surjeet sat down for a brotherly chat, with glasses of cognac in their hands, Manohar retired to his room to sleep.

Joginder was older than Surjeet by seven years and Surjeet had a mixed feeling of camaraderie and respect for him. By this time, Joginder was getting tipsy but continued to drink out of a sense of bravado. Surjeet was feeling tired and wanted to put an end to the session but out of courtesy could not initiate the move.

After chatting about a slew of mundane things, Joginder's

attention turned to Manohar. He praised Manohar's culinary skills and congratulated Surjeet for having such a talented and loyal friend with him. By this point, Surjeet was of a mind to tell his brother that Manohar was not only his friend but his life companion too. But seeing Joginder in a tipsy state, he refrained from articulating this right there.

But that was not all. Joginder evinced too much interest in Manohar, more than what the context warranted. He wanted to know when and how Surjeet had met Manohar and how it was that Manohar was living with him. To satisfy Joginder's curiosity, Surjeet narrated the entire course of events to him in brief and then got up to take leave of him.

'Do you need anything in your room for the night...maybe, water?' Surjeet asked.

'No...nothing...but I'd like to have a taste of the pleasures that you are enjoying.'

'What?'

'To be frank, can I have a taste of the sex that you have with your friend?' Joginder asked, deciding to be direct with him.

'Bhai Sahib, stop blabbering,' a shocked Surjeet replied. 'It is time to go to bed and sleep.'

It was the first time that Joginder had shown any interest in Surjeet's personal life. He had remained largely indifferent even when, many years ago, Surjeet had approached him and, mustering up a lot of courage, had confessed: 'Brother, before you come to know about it from others, let me tell you that I am a homosexual and am prepared to discuss everything if you have any questions.' But Joginder had shown no interest in the subject at that time, nor did he choose to talk about it anytime later. Then why show so much interest in my relationship with Manohar, he wondered.

'I'm not joking. I mean it, yaar,' Joginder persisted. It was for the first time that he had addressed his brother as his yaar, his friend. 'You sleep in my room, and let me, just for one night, sleep with your friend. He is really so cute.'

'I think you are not in your senses,' Surjeet said. 'Get up and go to bed. It is time to sleep now. That's it.'

'Why get so upset, yaar? Can't you share your friend with me just for one night? I'm not going to snatch him away from you.'

'You don't know what you are saying,' Surjeet felt terribly let down. 'Just go to your room and sleep,' his short temper, shared by all in their family, had started rising.

'You seem to be too possessive of your friend,' Joginder said. 'Come, share him with me for just an hour. I promise, I'll leave your bed after that.' In his passion for Manohar, Joginder's mask of propriety and respectability had come off.

'If I ask you to share your wife with me, what will be your response? Will you agree to it?' Surjeet said trying his best not to explode.

'How dare you say such a thing? Have you no shame in talking like this about your bhabhi?' Joginder hissed.

'So this proposition about sharing your wife with somebody has indeed hurt you and rightly so,' Surjeet tried to reason it out. 'In the same way, Manohar is my life companion. He has also hosted you so nicely. How can you talk about him in this manner?'

'Life-companion, hunh! Do you even understand what this word means? Bloody homo!' Joginder said caustically.

Had such a nasty comment come from any person other than Joginder, Surjeet would have reacted violently. Joginder's status as his elder brother restrained him. But he could not help shouting back at his brother, 'Yes, I'm a bloody homo, a self-confessed one. But what about you? Away from your wife for a couple of days, and already drooling over someone else.... Do you know what it means to be a life companion? What are you—a bloody hetero or simply a bloody bastard?' Both had crossed a boundary and were now shouting each other down.

That was Joginder's first and last visit to Surjeet's home.

When Manohar came to know what had happened during the night, he tried to laugh off the matter. 'If in his sozzled state, Bhai Sahib had spoken foolishly, you could have kept quiet and the matter would have ended there. Why react so angrily to what he said? After all, he is your brother and it seems like reacting violently to trivial things is a tradition in your family.... Also, instead of feeling bad, you should have celebrated your brother's self-confessed homosexual tendency!'

But Surjeet was incapable of not taking the matter seriously and was not prepared to take it easy. He felt unhappy, and rather angry, at Manohar's mild reaction and wondered how he could take such egregious nonsense so lightly. It was a matter of principle for Surjeet.

'Oh, yes, must one learn from you to take everything seriously? We ghatis are used to taking matters lightly; not ready to fight over trifles. Should I learn how to bring matters of principle into each trivial argument and endlessly fight over it…hunh,' Manohar also stuck to his guns.

Their domestic spat was dissolved in the warmth of a hug by the following night but that incident created a chasm in the relationship between the two brothers. Joginder told everybody back in Delhi that while Surjeet was free to live the kind of life he wanted to live in Mumbai, he must not bring his 'concubine' to their home in Delhi ever. However, all that transpired on that fateful night at Surjeet's flat in Mumbai remained just among the three—Joginder, Surjeet, and Manohar.

Manohar felt bad about the turn of events in Surjeet's family. 'Why should you behave so egoistically,' he admonished Surjeet. 'After all, you are younger than him. If you show a little humility and say sorry to Joginder, he won't say no to patching things up. You ought to take the first step on the road to reconciliation.'

'You don't understand a thing,' Surjeet shot back. 'It's not a question of saying sorry. Joginder is in fact a repressed homosexual….'

'I don't understand these high-sounding terms,' Manohar interrupted him. Having come from a more conventional background, he always found such analyses of human sexual behaviours mystifying and beyond his comprehension. But Surjeet and his friends were fond of discussing all aspects of human sexuality, including alternative sexuality, and propounded their own theories on it. One of them said that the human race could be neatly divided into two categories—'homosexuals' and 'heterosexuals'—and all other forms of behaviour were eclectic mixes of these. Another friend opined that there was a third category called 'bisexuals' and these were people who were open to establishing relations with both men and women. Then a new friend, who had recently arrived from the US, confounded the confusion by adding terms like 'transgender' and 'transsexual' to the discourse. Even after listening to such discussions time and again, Manohar was unable to make sense of all these terms.

Even otherwise, Manohar was not interested in intellectual debates like these on issues of human sexual behaviour. He always felt that these things came naturally to people like human instincts and did not need to be discussed and theorized like Surjeet and his friends did. 'I think that these friends of yours just talk, talk, and talk,' he once told Surjeet. 'They come, gulp down a few drinks, and coin slogans like "Homosexuals of the world, unite". But in their own lives, they are not loyal to the companion they choose and keep on changing them like they change clothes.' But even after being a mute listener to these learned discussions in which he had become familiar with many high-sounding terms, he had heard a term like 'repressed homosexuals' for the first time.

'A repressed homosexual is a man who wants to sleep with a man but lacks the courage to do so,' Surjeet tried to explain it to Manohar. 'He feels guilty about his desire. But when he gets a chance to do so, his desire overpowers him…. Often even after satisfying his desire, he feels guilty about what he has done. To cover up their guilty conscience, such people confront homosexuality, often even vehemently. These people can prove dangerous. After satisfying their desires, they can even inflict physical harm on the object of their desire.'

'Your theories make no sense to me,' Manohar responded. 'This would mean that your brother is a criminal.'

'I am not saying that,' Surjeet said. 'But this much is certain— that Joginder is making too much fuss about this issue only to mask his own desires, to give a sop to his guilty conscience.'

Though the incident had created fissures in their relationship as brothers, it had not impacted the behaviour of other members of their family. In fact, in order to cover up her husband's mulish obstinacy, Joginder's wife showed more affection towards Surjeet and Manohar than was her wont. On each festival celebrated traditionally in the family, or on Surjeet's and Manohar's birthdays, she would convey her greetings without fail and send gifts quite demonstratively. But it was Joginder's daughter Kalyani who really linked the two sides together.

Kalyani had always been a favourite of her uncle's whom she called 'Sujju Chacha'. Later, after meeting and interacting with Manohar, she developed great affection and regard for him, too. When she grew up, she went to the National Institute of Design, Ahmedabad, for her studies. Often getting bored with her drab hostel life, especially the unpalatable food in the mess, she would make frequent forays to Mumbai where she was welcomed by Surjeet and Manohar who together provided the warmth of a home she missed in Ahmedabad.

After working as an accountant for many years, Manohar left his job and stayed at home. He treated Kalyani like his own daughter. Kalyani, who had stopped behaving like a child with her chacha long back, could still regress to her old impish self with Manohar. Kalyani called him 'Manohar Kaka', in deference to his Marathi lineage. Surjeet would usually return late from the office. So it was Manohar who would take care of all Kalyani's needs during the days she lived in their flat in Mumbai. So that Kalyani could sleep in on her holidays, Manohar would not allow the bai who came rather early in the morning to enter her room for cleaning; he would do these chores himself later. He knew that in her hostel, Kalyani could get only vegetarian food and she pined for non-vegetarian dishes. Manohar would go to the market and buy the choicest cuts of fish, mutton, and chicken, prepare her favourite dishes and feed her sumptuously. Although Kalyani protested at times that there was no need for such elaborate meals on a daily basis, this attention pleased her, too.

Kalyani never asked Surjeet and Manohar about their relationship—were they just friends or something more than that? It could be that like many people of her generation, she knew what alternative sexuality meant and was inclined to accept it. Or perhaps, like many of her generation, she never felt any curiosity to peep into people's bedrooms. But this could not be said of all persons belonging to her generation. For Kalyani had herself heard some unruly youngsters in the locality hissing pejoratives like chhakka and gur about Surjeet and Manohar when they saw them together. Quite sensibly, she chose to ignore these comments.

Manohar felt surprised and even elated at times when he saw on TV many learned people, including celebrities, discussing alternative sexualities and characterizing them as natural and acceptable. He also saw people from varied walks of life, including workers, artists, writers, doctors, and fashion designers coming out and frankly admitting their different sexualities. Many doctors, psychiatrists, lawyers, and religious leaders made statements on alternative sexuality and, perhaps barring the pious types, everyone accepted it as a natural part of human behaviour existing since eternity. The world was indeed changing. It may not be necessary to talk about one's personal life before all and sundry, but it was absolutely essential to accept one's natural desires and not feel a sense of shame or guilt about it. Watching all this, Manohar was invariably reminded of those discussions of Surjeet and his friends he had once dismissed as superfluous.

Manohar and Kalyani were eating. Manohar had cooked Bombil, a typical Mumbai fish that required considerable expertise on the part of the cook to prepare. It was wafer-thin in size and had to be dusted with flour to prevent it from disintegrating while frying. Kalyani was fond of Bombil and could eat as many as six pieces in one meal.

'You may be a Punjabi but you relish fish like we ghatis do,' Manohar quipped, quite pleased as he watched her eat.

'Manohar Kaka, you cook fish so well that you have made me a ghati too, I can't help but relish it,' Kalyani cooed. She was aware of all the shades of this word, of the various ways it was used in this home. Then, after thinking for a long time, Kalyani resumed in a more reflective mood, 'But, Kaka, sometimes I find that a relationship which looks refreshingly different from the outside ultimately gets sucked into the conventional mode.'

'What do you mean?' Manohar asked a bit surprised.

'For instance, yours and Sujju Chachu's relationship. It was meant to be of a different kind and yet it has fallen into the conventional groove. Don't you think so?'

'Don't talk to me in these high-sounding terms like Surjeet does,' Manohar said. 'I am a simple person and understand things conveyed in simple language.'

'I mean...I mean that Surjeet and you don't fall into the conventional categories of a man and a wife,' Kalyani said rather hesitantly. 'But now it seems this relationship has fallen into the same old time-worn pattern of a husband and a wife.'

'What's wrong with that?' Manohar asked. He was conscious of the fact that Kalyani had raised the topic for the first time with him.

'What is wrong is...that there is no equality of the two units in a husband–wife relationship. At least not in our country. You two have also got into that same relationship of inequality.'

'And according to your wisdom who is "husband" and who the "wife"?' Manohar asked with an impish smile.

'It is obvious that you do all the chores that a wife does in a conventional marital relationship—like cleaning, cooking, going to the market to buy vegetables, etc.'

'But Surjeet works from morning to evening. Won't you count that as work?'

'Exactly, Kaku, that's what I mean, all men who work and bring home a salary think that they don't have to bear any domestic responsibility, that bringing up children, cooking, cleaning, etc. don't concern them. And no one thinks that women are actually doing much more than an eight-hour job, which probably is much easier than this servitude. Similarly, while you are working much harder than Chachu in his office, your work is not counted or appreciated fully. You are quite capable of getting a regular job, instead of this drudgery…and I feel bad about it.' While arguing her case, Kalyani had suddenly become overwhelmed with the kind of passion that is peculiar to youth.

Manohar laughed away Kalyani's passionately pleaded argument saying, 'And if a person is content with serving others?'

'What do you mean?'

'I mean, dear Miss Revolution, that your thinking, too, is circling the same old grooves,' Manohar said, imitating the argumentative tone of Kalyani. 'Have you ever thought that staying at home and looking after things could be an expression of my own free will, my innate pleasure? That maybe I prefer it to the drudgery of working all day in an office?'

'But women don't have a choice in the matter. The domestic role is imposed on them by social conventions.' Kalyani's passion was ebbing, but some froth was still there.

'On that point, I agree with you,' Manohar continued. 'But right now we are talking about my situation…and my choices. To be honest with you, I had never liked my job as an accountant. I found that dull and dreary. I enjoy doing domestic chores…

frying fish for you. Now, please have some more…' Manohar closed the argument.

Kalyani's residual passion, too, settled after this calm analysis of the state of affairs by Manohar.

'But, Kaku, are there occasions when you disagree over something and fight?' Kalyani resumed the discussion on a different note now. 'I suppose all couples are involved in that.'

'Why? Are you bent upon igniting a feud between us? Why all these provocative questions today?' Manohar asked in jest. He was actually pleased that Kalyani, always child-like with him, was talking about adult issues in an adult fashion.

'No, Kaku, I sometimes marvel at your relationship,' Kalyani said. 'You have been living together for twenty years now. But I have never seen you fighting.'

'That doesn't mean that we don't fight. We do and quite frequently too. And when we fight, I have to accept the role of the submissive wife.'

'What?'

'It seems your uncle has inherited the khandani tradition of blowing his top on the slightest matter. When he gets into such foul moods, I keep cool to balance out things. At such times, I supress my ahm and act like the typical Bharatiya nari.'

Kalyani laughed over this skilful use of high-flown Hindi words to highlight the social reality in the country.

'And like the typical Indian woman, how do you supress your ego?'

'When your uncle gets adamant and refuses to budge, I step back and give him the pleasure of scoring a point. This happens even when I am right and he is absolutely in the wrong. I prefer this tactical retreat to having swollen egos, not talking to each other for days, etc. But it's not long before he realizes his mistake and concedes that he was in the wrong. So with a little patience and a cool head, I make him follow the right course. This is a strategy that I learned long ago and it has stood us and our relationship in good stead,' said Manohar winking slyly.

Kalyani was left wondering why her mother had never learnt this strategy!

Unfortunately, now there is no longer any need to learn this strategy. Joginder passed away in Delhi of a massive heart attack in his chamber in Delhi High Court. There was no time to take him to hospital for resuscitation. In the morning, he appeared quite hale and hearty. By the afternoon, he was no more. On getting the message, Surjeet flew to Delhi for his funeral and after the Chautha ceremony flew back to resume his work. This was Kalyani's first visit to Mumbai since that fateful day.

Manohar could not swallow Surjeet's argument that after the passage of two months, condoling Kalyani was no longer required. After all, she had lost her father and they were meeting in person for the first time since his sudden death.

True, he had talked to Kalyani and her grief-stricken mother on the phone and expressed his sorrow at that time but that did not mean that on her very first visit they should completely ignore the recent bereavement. Manohar found Surjeet's urbane indifference not just absurd but inhumane, too. He decided to follow his heart and leave Surjeet to his sophisticated mores.

Kalyani arrived; it was getting close to ten in the night.

'Hello, Kaku! Hello, Chachu!' Kalyani greeted them, planting a kiss each on their respective cheeks. 'There was a massive jam on the highway even at this hour; it took me almost an hour to reach here.'

'Go and freshen up. Dinner is on the table already,' said Manohar, pulling her strolley to her room.

Manohar had not cooked anything non-vegetarian, bowing to the tradition demanding that a meal after a bereavement must be vegetarian. Some customs, some mores were so entrenched in him that Surjeet had not been able to change those.

He chose to cook vegetables, Kalyani's favourite ones, and the way she liked them best.

'How do you manage to cook green beans so well? I have tried your recipe a number of times, but I can never achieve this heavenly taste,' Kalyani was enjoying her favourite vegetable.

'Well, Manohar cooks such delicious things only when you are here. In your absence, he feeds me only routine stuff, and the bland Marathi dal,' Surjeet retorted.

'Come on, Chachu,' Kalyani responded. 'You are like Papa—never satisfied with what you are getting. It seems that finding fault in whatever you get is also a trait that runs in the family. Don't you think so, Kaku?'

Manohar had been sitting rather subdued as he had not found the right opportunity to talk about Joginder's untimely death and to convey his condolences to Kalyani yet. Now that Joginder's name had cropped up, he seized the opportunity and said, 'Bhai Sahib left us too soon. It was a big shock for us. Must be very difficult for Bhabhi to cope with the loss. Her life companion has left her so soon.'

While saying this Manohar avoided looking at Surjeet. He knew that Surjeet must be squirming inside, cursing Manohar for not refraining from broaching the matter.

'Yes, Kaku, it was a big shock for all of us,' Kalyani replied. 'But Mama has reconciled to the loss. What can one do in such eventualities?'

Manohar's predicament was over. He felt that a big load weighing on his conscience had been removed and he became at ease. His conversation with Kalyani became more natural and spontaneous.

'So what about your new job?' Manohar asked. Kalyani had taken up a new assignment in an export house in Delhi recently.

'Well, I really can't say much right now,' Kalyani said reflectively. 'The job, no doubt, is challenging. But the owners are too money-minded. We are on different tracks. They are clueless about aesthetic design or the beauty of the product. In fact, they find my designs esoteric. All they want is that it should sell. Thankfully, our customers, most of whom are from abroad, like and select my creations. That satisfies our masters and that's how I'm still with them. But I don't know how long it can continue like this.'

'That's not too bad,' Surjeet intervened. 'If the buyers like your creations, then your masters will have no option but to produce what you design. In due course, they will accept your work quite readily. After all, it is a buyer's market; your employers are not producing garments to cater to their own wives. Isn't that so?' he said on the basis of his own experiences.

'I'll tell you something, Chachu,' Kalyani said. 'You seem to be repeating what father had told me.... You brothers lived far from each other. In recent times, you didn't have the best relationship. And yet you have a striking similarity in your ideas. Must be due to your common genes.... Papa was a liberal person. But I don't know why he carried some sort of homophobia. He never accepted the relationship between you two.'

'Now that he is no longer with us, it is better not to discuss these things,' Manohar said. He had sensed that the conversation was taking a perilous turn and it was essential to steer it in a different direction.

'Joginder's case was more complicated than that, he was not merely a homophobe...' Surjeet could not help entering forbidden territory. At this stage, Manohar threw a meaningful glance in his direction imploring him to refrain from getting into this sort of discussion, but Surjeet wilfully ignored that.

'What, Chachu?' Kalyani was mystified. There was something onerous in that half-finished sentence and Surjeet's demeanour; there was no way Kalyani was going to let it go at that.

'Kalyani, if Joginder had just been a homophobe, I'd have persuaded him to accept our relationship. Even our much older relatives have come to terms with my relationship with Manohar. Joginder's problem was that....'

'Stop it, Surjeet,' Manohar burst out in English, a language he used only at times of distress or anger. He wanted to put an end to this conversation at all costs. Manohar's outburst made it plain to Kalyani that Manohar was uncomfortable with the course the discussion was taking and he wanted to put an end to it. But why? What was it that Kaku wanted to hide from her?

'Kaku, please, I want to know,' Kalyani pleaded. 'It is important for me to know about Papa's problem,' she said. Saying this she looked at both of them one after the other, as though imploring them to resolve their differences, whatever they were, and to let her know the truth.

'The reason for Joginder's homophobia was the internal struggle that he was waging against his natural homosexual desires. This struggle instilled in him a feeling of guilt that he tried to suppress by taking a hard homophobic position. There was also a feeling of jealousy inherent in it—jealousy against people who were able to come out in the open and live life on their own terms. That explains the scorn that he poured on homosexuals. That was the reason he could never accept our relationship.'

Manohar was stupefied to hear Surjeet analyze a delicate subject like sexuality before the daughter of his recently deceased brother like he was doing it as a discussant at a seminar. What obtuseness! These so-called intellectuals think that all aspects of human life could be presented like empirical theses and that norms and sensitivity did not matter at all. How will a young girl, whose father had died only a couple of months ago and who was yet to get over the shock, take this devastating disclosure about him? Was Surjeet seeking revenge on his brother who was no more? Manohar felt disgusted.

Kalyani looked visibly shocked. In her discomfiture, she blurted out a series of questions, 'What are you saying…. But how do you know? How can you be so sure? You never told me about it? Was Mama aware of it?'

Manohar's heart overflowed with sympathy for this poor girl who had suddenly found out something troubling about her father.

The blame for this lay with Surjeet and he was determined not to let him speak further on the subject. 'Surjeet, have you said whatever you wanted to say?' he said livid with anger. 'Now leave this place at once. I'll handle the rest of the matter myself. Just get out!' Kalyani was surprised to see Manohar tackling Surjeet this way, as she had never witnessed this resolute side of his in all these years. On his part, Surjeet got up, picked up his glass of water from the table and, like an admonished child, quietly left the room.

Surjeet restlessly waited in the bedroom for Manohar to come. He wondered whether after his exit Kalyani had burst out crying and if Manohar had decided to stay there to offer her succour. But he had spoken the truth, he reasoned with himself, and there was no harm in sharing this truth with Kalyani who was a mature and intelligent girl. The truth does come out sooner or later, he argued, and the sooner it is known, the better it is for everybody connected with it. But maybe he should not have disclosed it so suddenly.

Not just his body, Surjeet's mind, too, was restless.

Manohar finally came to the room after a full two hours. He lay down on the bed, turning his back to Surjeet. This was his way of remonstrating and conveying that he was really annoyed with Surjeet. On occasion, when the two fell out it was always the one more aggrieved who turned his back on the other one. This was also to convey that the one who has hurt must make amends by crossing this 'no-man's land' that had emerged between them.

But this time things had gone too far and Manohar was in no mood to relent. He lay down at the far edge of the bed, almost lifelessly. As if conveying, 'I'm in no mood to forget. So please don't even try to come near me. No regrets, no persuasion, and no sorry, nothing is going to work this time.'

'Manu,' Surjeet whispered in a dulcet tone.

No response.

'Manu dear...' Surjeet slowly began crawling to cover this 'no man's land' between them.

No reaction.

'Are you angry with me?' Surjeet's leg touched Manohar's thigh.

'Don't try to touch me,' Manohar hissed back.

'Kalyani, is she alright?' Surjeet posed this question, unable to figure out what to say.

'Can she be alright? Did you leave anything unsaid? You have hurt her grievously,' Manohar replied in a biting tone. 'You may still nurse a grudge against Joginder and say whatever you like, but Joginder was her father. Do you even consider what you are going to say before opening your mouth...or is it that you suffer from verbal diarrhoea? You may claim to be intelligent, rational, even an intellectual but you do not even know what may be said and when. You have no regard for others' feelings.' In his agitation, Manohar got up and sat up on the bed. On gentler nights this indicated that Manohar was in a mood for a chit-chat, but on a night like this it could only mean that he was in a combative frame of mind.

'I had no idea that this disclosure would hurt Kalyani so much,' Surjeet pleaded.

'What, you thought that this revelation would please her no end?' Manohar said bitterly. 'Do you really think that the most important thing for her to know at this stage was why her father and uncle could not get along...I wonder if you have any sense left in your shitty head. She must be missing her father. Instead of making things pleasant for her, you are declaring that her father was a closet homosexual! What a nice thing to communicate!'

'Is there anything wrong in being a homosexual? We are normal people like everyone else, and you know that,' Surjeet tried to dodge Manohar's attack by turning the discussion in a different direction.

'Shut up, Surjeet,' Manohar screamed. 'Don't engage me in such silly arguments. You know very well that it is not a question of homosexuality being good or bad. It is a question of being sensitive towards the other person's feelings. It is a question of knowing what to disclose, and what must be left unsaid. You city slickers are fond of talking in abstract terms. But life cannot be measured in terms of formulations alone.'

'Now you are talking in abstract terms,' Surjeet said. 'Okay, what have you told Kalyani about her father?'

'After you had made the revelation, it was difficult to make a total retraction. So I had to take recourse to lies to neutralize the effect of your heartless declaration. I told her that in your younger days, you had a sneaking suspicion that Joginder had a tilt towards homosexuality. It was just a suspicion and nothing else. But since you were looking for some credible reason to explain your strained relations with Joginder, you created a theory out of mere suspicion. I told her that I've never believed in it and she too should never give credence to these silly conjectures.'

'Did she believe you?' Surjeet asked.

'Yes. Because she wanted to believe me,' Manohar replied. 'You too should never rake up this issue now. I am warning you, it will be disastrous, not for her, but for you…take it from me.'

'But Kalyani is a mature girl and knows that homosexuality is something perfectly normal,' Surjeet tried to get into discussion mode again.

'What a mule you are!' Manohar said in exasperation. 'Now, heterosexuality is also normal, isn't it? But suppose after my death you come to know that I was not what you were given to believe, that I was married, had a wife, children, a proper home in Jogeshwari, how will you take it? How will you take my duplicity, my lying to you all the time?'

'You being a heterosexual! Having wife, children, home! Impossible. I understand you too well to be deceived.' And saying this Surjeet held him in his arms and kissed him on the cheek. 'But, yes, what is possible is that you have another lover like me at Jogeshwari and you have been meeting him on the sly. Is that true?' Surjeet asked playfully.

'It's not a laughing matter, Surjeet,' Manohar said sombrely. 'It is not a question of homosexuality being good or bad. You have committed a big mistake by opening up an aspect of Joginder's life before Kalyani that she is no longer in a position to confirm or deny. She has an image of her father as a husband, no one has given you the right to break that. I don't know whether Joginder was a "repressed homosexual" or not. But for Kalyani he was a good father. He might not have been a good brother, but that's your problem. Why take revenge on Joginder by inflicting pain on his daughter? If it was that important for you, you should have confronted him during his lifetime. It is only a coward who takes revenge on a person after he is dead and that too by tormenting his daughter! This is downright despicable....'

'Sorry, that certainly was not my intention, but I am really sorry now, jaan,' Surjeet said using the endearment reserved for their tenderest moments and put his arm around his waist.

'Then, listen,' Manohar seemed to be in a reconciliatory mood now. 'Kalyani, on her own, will never raise the issue. But if the issue somehow crops up, promise that you will repeat the version that I've given her,' Manohar lay down, pushing Surjeet's arm away from around his waist.

'I promise you that, jaan,' Surjeet said putting his leg on Manohar's thigh and weighing him down. This time, Manohar did not push him away.

Night was finally falling over this home.

Translated by Sukirat Anand

WHITHER MY NATIVE LAND?

KESRA RAM

Day or night, in ones or twos, or larger groups, the Corona caravans were on the move. They walked and kept on walking....

This four-lane expressway is one of the busiest and most modern highways in the country. From the heart of Delhi it leads towards Uttar Pradesh and Bihar. It also has a by-pass so travellers going long distances do not have to enter the city and get mired in its traffic.

Things remained quite normal a few days after the imposition of lockdown. Perhaps the migrant workers hoped and expected that it would only be a matter of a few days. But when, after a three-week-long lockdown, the second phase was also announced, it created a wave of terror and commotion among them. They were daily wage workers who now had no work. They were tired and impatient after sitting idle for so long. More than Covid-19, they were afraid of unemployment and starvation. They were left with no money at all. When they heard the lockdown was going to be indefinite, they picked up their belongings, strapped them onto their backs, and set out walking for their hometowns.

The migrants thus started a huge exodus.

The highways became crowded with these long-route travellers. Everybody was impatient to reach home.

Meanwhile, the virus was also ready to explode on humanity like a bomb.

The migrant workers insisted on returning to their native places come what may. They had only one refrain: 'We want to go back to our homes.' Whether dead or alive, we will see!

The administration came down heavily on them. Yes, let us see! They retaliated by adopting stringent measures to stop the exodus. The entry and exit points of cities were sealed. Labyrinthine nakas, barricades, were put up on national highways.

This naka too is a part of this strategy. There is no link road nearby. Pinpointing the naka site, the Deputy Superintendent of Police had said, 'If we push them away from the highway, they will have a tough time getting back to it.'

The tent for the naka was pitched in the middle of the road. The tent was divided into two parts: one part was for the off-duty constables to rest in and the other was left clear for the passage of the people. Chairs were kept there for the on-duty constables.

Efforts to control the situation through the implementation of curfew orders and invocation of the Disaster Management Act began. Rules were made stricter and enforced quite brutally.

The incidence of the Covid-19 contagion was at an all-time high but people, especially the middle-class, were not ready to take the lockdown seriously. Many would take their bike or car for a joyride around the city. They would take along small kids also and when asked they had the audacity to tell the police officers on duty very unabashedly that the kids were bored because of the prolonged confinement. They were just going on a little outing....

Initially, the policemen would just chide such adventure freaks but when the situation worsened, they started using other ways. They would give them a light beating and send them back home.

The demand for additional forces in the city increased. For the fulfilment of this requirement, forces had to be called from the barricades. Now this naka had only four constables: Ramphal, Surinder, Ved, and Raj Kumar.

Ramphal said, 'As many as twelve constables need to display their art of wielding sticks day and night. Only then will there be efficiency in the performance. And now...?'

'The work never ceases. And what are we to do after all?

We have only to bludgeon the people. Two, three blows more or less don't matter.' This is what the migrants got.

Adjustments were made by forming two-member teams that would use their sticks and find time to rest as well. They manned the front so deftly that irrespective of the number of groups, they managed well. They had such strong dedication towards their duty that sometimes the four of them could weigh heavily on 400 people. At that time, it seemed as if it was not the victims but Covid itself that was screaming out loud.

One day, watching Ramphal beating the migrant workers mercilessly, Ved remarked, 'Ramphal, our brother, is a wonderful warrior.'

'What else...? Now a new name "Corona Warrior" too has been given to us.'

'The name has quite a flavour.'

'You see how we're stopping the workers from going to their own homes with their kids. We abuse them and swear at them and then push them back after thrashing them.'

'Even some of their bones might be broken...!'

Whatever it is, come what may, they didn't shirk their duties. Some of the workers would run back while some others would rush down towards the fields. Then crossing the boundary lines through the fields, they would come back onto the same highway. Some would lose their way and thus stray further away from their destination.

Beating the migrants seriously and purposefully would tire them out. When completely tired they would console themselves: 'Brother! How shall I....'

It had been nearly a month that they had been performing this duty. They were doing their work round-the-clock with great sincerity of purpose.

Prior to the pandemic, beating people publicly was banned. It was also not so easy to beat someone like this. The police officials knew that nowadays everybody carried the toy called mobile phone in their pocket. Who knows when someone might shoot a video which could go viral?

'In such a situation the officers also lose no time in ordering the culprit to be suspended.'

'Words also change their meanings with the passage of time. Earlier, people would call weapons like pistols and revolvers toys. Now the mobile phone with a six-inch screen has become a truly terrifying toy even for the police.'

'Covid-19 has really turned the traditional value system topsy-turvy.' Sometimes they would talk seriously among themselves about such things as well.

They also had a mobile phone which was their only source of entertainment. They would watch videos showing indiscriminate police excesses against women, children, the aged, and young men. They were doing exactly the same thing in real life even though no video of them had gone viral.

But they too were human beings after all. They belonged to ordinary poor families. They had not been brought up on a rich diet of milk and almonds. So, they tired easily. Also, they were bored with the same kind of duty every day—thrashing innocents. Who knew how their souls must have been cursing them?

They did not have much experience of the severity of such beatings, though they had done similar work earlier during the protests or agitations of farmers and employees.

In the beginning when constable Ramphal had come to the naka and heard that he would be given a free hand by the officers, he was very happy to have this freedom. He looked forward to not sparing anyone. Sometimes during a refugee dharna they would wield the sticks less forcefully.

One day, recalling his past actions, he said that he had served the maximum blows during a teachers' agitation.

'On teachers?' Surinder asked with a sense of utter disbelief.

'Yes, and I had not felt even a little bit of hesitation, Brother.'

'Why?'

'What do you mean "why"? I had my own grouse. Honestly speaking, I have never had a good teacher all my life. Someone asked for milk while someone else would ask me to bring him fresh fruits and vegetables from the field. If I didn't, they would beat me and my backside would be swollen.'

'We have also done this, like bringing milk or such other things, for teachers. But they were not bad as teachers.'

'Yet, you are also just a constable,' Ramphal taunted him.

'But what is the fault of teachers in it? And are all constables bad?' Surinder asked.

'Then are they ruthless?'

'Ruthless?' Surinder looked at him with dismay.

'Yaar, sometimes all this bludgeoning tires me out. After all, what is the problem?' Ramphal had suddenly steered the topic in a different direction.

'There is definitely a problem; otherwise, who would wander on the roads laden with their belongings?'

'And, what solution do we have for them?'

'We shall share it gratis if we find it.'

'Why not? Delivering a discourse costs nothing. Certainly, it doesn't consume as much energy as beating them up.'

'What else? We have a great message for the working class: ye workers of India. This is your path to emancipation.'

'Yes, the way comrades used to say, "Ye workers of the world, unite."'

Ramphal held his clenched fist high in the air and raised the slogan, 'Inquilab Zindabaad.' In his other hand he held the baton like a flagstaff.

'I don't know where the comrades have disappeared.'

'Why, do you feel any need of their presence?'

'I don't know,' the reply came in a very shaky, feeble, and fatigued voice.

When they are tired and a group of people slips past without the usual beating, they do not worry about it too much.

But officers consider this a huge lapse.

Something like this happened one night. The night was fast approaching dawn. Mostly it was only the trucks and trolleys which travelled at night. On the day eighteen workers were recovered from the drum of a jumbo concrete mixer truck, they had received orders to check movement very strictly. The labourers had started travelling mostly at night because the days were getting hotter.

That day, Ramphal and Surinder were on night duty. By midnight, they were exhausted after beating the workers and making them take to their heels. That night there were a lot more people on the road than usual. Let us see what happens! It we let fifty or a hundred people go there won't be much loss to the state exchequer!

To shake off their fatigue and boredom they switched on their mobile phone. They opened Facebook. It had the same old videos. Every now and then there were clips of the police doing noble deeds also. For example, of giving a gift, a rose, to a newlywed couple passing through the naka. To offer congratulations!

The situation was not unpalatable. And in one of the videos police were seen performing aarti of the lockdown violators in the lock-up!

In still another, the police were marching through the city with the portable speaker system that was playing a song: *O my motherland, I have given you my heart and my life is also yours.*

Surinder became thoughtful.

'Ramphal yaar, have you ever thought what we are engaged in day and night?'

'Duty. What else?'

'Tell me one thing, Brother, how long will this Corona continue? Will we have to do this as long as Corona lasts?'

Looking at his sanitized baton Ramphal said, 'What else would you do? Aarti? Om jai Jagdish Hare...saare bhagat jan corona se darein.—Let all devout people fear corona!' Then he coughed.

Getting serious all of a sudden, Surinder said, 'There is escape from this, Brother. We'll give up our jobs, Brother.'

'Wrong! How will you fend for your family after giving up your job?' Ramphal said, adding, 'Moreover, there is no chance of anybody's resignation being accepted these days.'

'Agreed, but why are we beating up these poor people so mercilessly?'

'Because we are ordered to do so and we are paid for this. Hunh....you big saint! You know what it is? Nobody knows anything about Corona all over the world. Also, there is no cure for it. Our government is wise. Perhaps it thinks one day it will solve the mystery of Corona. Meanwhile let us beat up the poor,' he said and chuckled.

'I'm just kidding, Brother. But just think about it,' he added.

Surinder was in no mood to joke at that time. So he picked up his water bottle and walked to where the caravans of workers were coming in, the ones headed for UP and Bihar from Haryana and Punjab.

A sweet and gentle breeze was blowing. He breathed deeply and felt the freshness. He felt good. After walking a small distance he sat on the road divider. He looked at the clean azure sky.

Has the sky become clearer than before?

Never paid any attention to this issue. What can be said?

Surely the air has become sweeter.

Drawing a long breath, he filled his lungs with fresh air and felt good. He wanted to forget everything by concentrating on the pure, rejuvenated, and infinite nature. He longed to be one with nature and forget everything else.

Perhaps the air was so salubrious that the very idea of violence forsook him for the moment. In any case, if he were to remember everything that they had done, it would drive him crazy.

Once again he looked at the star-filled sky and wondered: have the number of stars in the sky increased?

Who can say? Has anyone counted the stars? Caught in the the rough and tumble of life, he'd never thought about it.

But the air seems far clearer than before and the stars, too, look brighter, and there seem to be many more. Had it been like this earlier, we would have definitely noticed. How quickly we notice when a friend wears a new shirt!

The sky always looked clearer in the village than in the city. There is less pollution there. It must have become even clearer there now, naturally.

Thinking about this miracle of nature and the village his thoughts drifted to his own children.

Now when I go home, we shall all sleep on the roof. How nice it will be to look at the moon and stars and tell the children stories! They love listening as we make up the stories and name the stars!

Well, when we put the beds on the roof and sleep under the open sky I will have Rahul on one side and Chinki on the other.

And what about Chanda?

Oh yes! My Chanda! Her turn will come when the children get tired of listening to the stories and fall asleep with their gaze fixed on the sky, counting the stars and selecting from among them their own favourites. Dreaming thus he stretched out and yawned, raising both his arms; he felt a pain in his shoulders.

After all, how long does the age of enjoying beautiful and pleasant dreams last? They vanish in the blink of an eye.

So from the ethereal world of dreams he came crashing down to earth abruptly.

But...leave?

Getting leave would be difficult at this time. Disappointment engulfed his mind.

Then he comforted himself. Corona is not going to stay forever! What's this, after all, but a petty virus? The day it encounters the police.... Recalling one of Ramphal's funny remarks brought a broad smile to his face.

Well, let me discuss this with Ramphal, and maybe we can come up with something.

The three constables sitting in the tent were engrossed in a serious discussion. They were talking about the violence against poor workers. This was the only vaccine they had against boredom.

Surinder also joined the discussion saying, 'This is how we have been trained, brother! Are we to blame for it?'

Raj Kumar stated, 'People won't understand the gravity of the situation without having it enforced by the blows of sticks. They don't understand, nor do they listen to the voice of sanity or reason.'

'The people lose their cool in no time. And if there is a minor lapse on our part in handling the situation the government also loses no time to suspend us.'

'When are these workers flaring up, yaar? Two–three constables or the skeletal Home Guard jawans can brutalize them. If they get together and unite they can crush us.' Ved disagreed with him.

Surinder advocated Ved's viewpoint, 'They just want to go home. They call it "des", their native place, in their own language.'

'Yes, they call it "des". These daredevils are carrying their homes on their shoulders!'

'But they must follow the proper way of going back home as laid down by the government. There is a system for everything, brother,' Raj Kumar said.

'Now the only system is the force of the wooden staff.'

'Why? They should get their names registered. They will be sent home when their turn comes. This is what the government is saying.'

'Don't tell us what to do!' Ramphal said.

Supporting Ramphal, Ved added, 'The government doesn't want the migrant workers to leave. Who will run the factories once the lockdown is over? It is being done under capitalist pressure, Brother.'

Having finished eating, Surinder and Ramphal took their positions. A protest that started with around twenty-five workers soon swelled to about fifty as they tried to pass.

The police officials were now trying to scare them into

going back rather than press on forwards to go home. The workers would move back a little, then get off the road, go into the fields, and stealthily cross the naka and get back on the highway some distance from the barricade. Leniency had reduced the fear of the rod but they had to walk a longer distance to get past the naka.

After some time, the policemen at the naka came back to the tent to rest and opened Facebook on their mobile. This was the only pastime they had, in addition to chatting on WhatsApp, or using YouTube to play music—Sapna Chaudhary's for example. Sometimes there were new artists too.

They forwarded videos of police excesses on migrant workers uploaded by their friends on WhatsApp.

In the meantime, a group of workers passed by.

'What are you up to?' Surinder asked them without getting up from his chair.

Receiving no response from the scared group he asked again, 'Where are you going?' while his attention was focussed on the screen of the mobile phone he held in his hand.

'Apne des,' someone from the group replied.

'Apne des?'

'Haan, sahib. Bihar.' They had to answer this question everywhere. They could not make out if they were being ridiculed. The mere thought of the beatings caused them to forget everything. Only the diktat of the state—run…go back!—would keep resounding in their ears. Then they would run helter-skelter wherever their legs took them.

Some of them were getting ready to run back only to have a volley of sticks rain on their backs, the pain making them soil their clothes—they would forget everything but fear. With tears dried in their terrified eyes, they would move away to heal their wounded souls.

The lenient conduct of the police officials led the workers to think they must be drunk. Treading softly, they slipped away.

The policemen remained engrossed in watching their video clips and talking.

'The most backward states of our country too have turned into kingdoms and the chief ministers into monarchs. Just see....' Ramphal said, showing a video to Surinder. 'They have sealed their respective borders. The police parties of different kingdoms have been deployed against each other on the borders as though they were enemies.... And, between the two are caught the helpless hordes of workers.'

'Wonderful!'

'Still more wonderful are the rulers of these kingdoms. No ruler is ready to let his own subjects enter their home state. These workers would have never imagined this kind of tragedy—that at a distance of few furlongs from their homeland they will find themselves surrounded by the police of a self-styled king of UP or Bihar.'

'How can these barefoot and empty-bellied people produce a "Corona negative" report?'

'This one is even more wonderful. See how a police officer accompanied by two lady police officers and other constables is celebrating the birthday of a child in the lush green lawn of a palatial bungalow. He is cutting the cake by holding the birthday baby's hand. Standing at attention, the police party is singing "Happy Birthday to You" in chorus.'

'Unique! Isn't it? Everybody is wearing a mask! So proper social distancing is shown being maintained on this occasion.'

'This looks very stupid, yaar,' Surinder said. 'Is the duty of police officers to conduct birthday parties of such affluent people? He should have been at his place of duty at this time. How did he buy and bring the cake while the whole city is under curfew?'

'And here we are breaking the bones of the poor! We make them run so fast that their footwear or some other items are left behind. And, this...?'

'He is trying to refurbish the image of police. Hahaha....'

'This is what is called changing the diapers of the rich. He would never have thought of offering a glass of water to a poor man's child and here he is celebrating the birthday of a rich man's child and having it videographed.'

'You are right. These are the men who are then honoured with promotions.'

Meanwhile, a police jeep stopped at the naka. The DSP alighted from the vehicle. Ramphal and Surinder sprang to their feet and saluted the officer smartly.

'Playing video games?'

'No, sir, we were just watching a video. I don't know who has made so many go viral....' Surinder felt the DSP understood what he wanted to say.

'Do you also make anything viral?'

'No, sir, we have not posted even a single video.'

'How can you? It's possible only if you *do* something.'

The officer's tone was very harsh but his purport was not clear. So they could not decide what to say in reply.

'You are third-rate parasites. What am I asking?'

'Sorry, sir.'

'Are you on duty?'

'Yes, sir.'

'Why didn't you stop the workers who have crossed right now?'

'We had stopped them, sir. They might have run away through the fields.... Under the cover of darkness....'

'That is a lie. They themselves have told me that nobody stopped them at this naka. You were told in the very beginning that those loitering on the roads have to be treated as if they have Corona and you have to "check" properly the "immunity" of whosoever falls into your net. Do you follow me now? I am not speaking Persian.'

'Sorry, sir,' they said in unison as they stood to attention, wondering what the boss meant. Listening very carefully they tried to figure out what was intended as if their lives depended on doing what was required. 'First warn them from afar. When they come within range use the language of the weapon—beat them up! You also post a video.... Who is stopping you? When people see it.... They should think twice about flouting the law. Why are we here....' The DSP seemed to be under great stress. He also used foul language, of the kind that would even scare Covid-19 away!

'Sorry, sir...' But they were cut short.

'Duty is duty. Better understand that otherwise the fat will melt with a single departmental stroke. So take this as the first and last warning....' With this threat, the DSP boarded his car and sped off to wherever he had come from.

Repeating 'sir, sir' their throat had gone dry. They had not had any water when a group of workers arrived.

'Go back....' they fell upon them. Braving the blows, some of them ran here and there but one couple had big bundles on their heads and each had a small child. They were too tired, and could not move.

Trying to protect the child he was carrying, the man extended his arm. A strong blow struck his arm and the man shrieked, 'I've been badly hit.' But the torrent of blows continued and their cries rent the air. The man fell on the ground and the woman screamed and rushed to protect him from the blows. The police hit the man on his ankles. The belongings of the workers lay scattered all over. Nobody knew what happened to the children.

Due to the excruciating pain in the ankles, the man could not get up. He was no longer crying, he was wailing, 'Babuji, my hand is broken. How will I carry my baby now? I have to go very far.'

At first Ramphal and Surinder scolded him but then softened once he started crying. Then they examined his hand. They could clearly feel the break in the bone and his arm had started swelling.

The suffering was obvious. They were the perpetrators.

The terrified children clung to their parents, weeping bitterly. One of the parents said, as they cried, 'We were beaten at the last naka also. Not only the last, at every naka.'

The woman was sobbing, maybe because of her own pain or because of the agony her husband was suffering. Suppressing her own pain she pointed a finger at Ramphal, and asked, 'Why did you hit so hard, Babu?'

She looked into his eyes while addressing him as 'Babu', as if he were her brother-in-law.

Her words pierced the hearts of both Ramphal and Surinder. Ramphal froze in his tracks, overcome by remorse. He could not utter a word. Surinder, however, took charge of the situation, 'Run away now otherwise you will be punished more.'

The woman helped her husband lift the odds and ends onto his head. The man was still writhing in pain. She lifted the other bundle onto her own head and took the younger baby on her hip. The elder girl held onto her father's finger on his left hand and walked with him. The man's right hand dangled uselessly.

'Ramphal, we have made their journey so painful....' Surinder said, deeply anguished. But then unable to face himself, he ran, shouting at them: 'Run away! Go on! Run!'

The woman expected a strong blow of the stick on her ankles. She quickly turned around, saying, 'Babu, shoot us. Don't hit us with sticks. We won't be able to run....'

'I have never so far faced a situation when one transcends the terror of death or fear of the police stick,' Surinder thought. 'I have always been accustomed to seeing fear in the eyes of others. The fear of the police cudgel has been the primary source of that fear.'

He shuddered to read the questions in the woman's eyes. What power her eyes emanated and strength that single sentence from her lips had inspired! In one moment, it had castrated the power of the police.

His raised his hand, brandishing the stick but it became powerless. Dragging his feet he entered the tent where Ramphal sat crying. As Surinder came in, he burst into sobs saying, 'I have sinned, brother…it's a great sin. Really, we are both sinners. The eyes of those innocent girls are tearing my insides. The poor little ones didn't even have chappals to cover their feet.'

Surinder had never thought that a thick-skinned person like Ramphal could cry like this. It was as if he wanted to sweep away all his sins through these tears of atonement.

The woman's words, 'Shoot us, Babu, don't hit us with sticks', haunted Surinder also.

The limp broken hand of the man lurked somewhere in his consciousness. He concealed to some extent the wetness of his eyes and wiped a bit of it on the pretext of adjusting his mask. The flood of tears dammed in him for so long was about to spill over.

He picked up the water bottle and came out. He sat on the divider. He heard a terrified whisper close by.

As they were about to pass by the tent, their whispers and the flip-flop sound of their chappals made Ramphal rush out of the tent with a stick in hand saying, 'Who the hell goes there…?'

Before Ramphal could use his stick, Surinder, stopped him. 'Leave it, brother, I have already beaten them, their quota has been used up.' Then he mumbled in a voice choked with emotion: 'I have killed them.'

Tears welled up in his eyes. This time he did not think it necessary to wipe his tears. It was pitch dark, so no one could have seen him crying.

Ramphal's hand wielding the stick also froze at hearing Surinder's words.

'Okay then,' he said, and returned to his chair.

Just then he noticed Surinder's stick lying near his vacant chair. 'Then what did he kill them with?'

Translated by Parvesh Sharma

DEATH OF THE LUTE

GURMEET KARYALAVI

It had been years since I had heard the melancholic lilt of the alghozas, the paired flutes, that I did last night—the like of which I used to hear during my childhood. It was doleful and touching. At times it had a tremulous quality as if someone was sobbing. Shifting in my bed, my gaze fixed on the moon, I had heard this sound all of last night. All the other members of the household were fast asleep. I got up from my bed and started strolling around our home. The night looked very bright in the moonlight. Planting my foot on the low wall, I climbed up onto the roof. I looked around. The entire village was gripped by the eerie silence of a graveyard. Not even a dog could be heard wailing. During my childhood, we would always hear dogs crying out, particularly after midnight. Mother considered this canine wailing ominous so she would chase them off. Sometimes she woke my father up and asked him to shoo the dogs away. Bapu would get irritated at his sleep being interrupted and sometimes, he would pretend that he was still asleep. But at times he would pick up a stick and hit the troublemaker, causing it to scamper off, yelping, to join others of its kind. But last night I didn't hear even a single sleep-disturbing wail. Who was this *Homo sapien* who had the audacity to violate the stillness of the night? I saw Bapu lying in the courtyard, fast asleep, perhaps due to fatigue caused by hard toil. I felt my heart sinking. I was irritated with myself for leaving my family in the city and coming alone to see father. The silence of the night was horrible. It was frightening. Anything could happen in such an atmosphere. What was the fun of coming to the village at this time? Particularly after mother's death, this house seems ready to swallow me. I have asked Bapu so many times to come live in the city. But no, he will not even listen to such a proposition. At times, I have even had a bit of a heated exchange with him over the issue. I fail to understand what attraction the village has for him. Many a time I had pledged in his very presence that I would never come back to the village but I don't know what impels me to come here every three or four months. I feel like visiting the streets of this village. Usually, I would come in the morning and return by evening. This time I was staying overnight in the village after many years. I had spent a long time wandering in search of a livelihood. All these years I had been frequenting clubs, cinema houses, taverns, etc. for the gratification of my inner self. My spiritual appetite had died once and for all. It had suddenly been revived last night with that doleful tune of the alghozas. I felt a tug at my heart and tears streamed down my cheeks spontaneously. I felt like waking up Bapu to ask him about this soul-stirring music. But I stopped myself, fearing that he was not going to reply pleasantly to my query. Rather he would say, 'You are a man of strange habits. What a brain you have that spends all its energy on useless things: why have the Persian wheel wells stopped? Why don't we hear the tinkle of bells tied to the bullocks' necks? Why don't people keep sitting at the bhatthis drying grain over the fire and in the shops till late in the night? What kind of education have you gained, I wonder? *Sa-ince* has made wonderful new inventions. When does a person have leisure now to keep sitting at bhatthis and shops? And what makes you pine for nothing and wonder who's playing the alghozas? He must be someone like you, a victim of women's wiles.'

Anticipating such a response, I did not dare ask him anything. Moreover, Bapu considered the pursuits of both vocal and instrumental music a sordid pastime.

'Son, Dev Sihan, are you all right? What's the matter?' Perhaps

Bapu had seen me going upstairs. When I did not come down for a while, he had come onto the roof to enquire about my well-being. I did not reply.

'Thinking about your family? Well, it's natural in these times. Come down and relax for some time. I know you don't find any time to rest during the day.' Bapu's tone was unusually soft.

'This Rala Haripuria is always out to disturb others' sleep with his ragas. To me they sound more like elegies.' Bapu said and climbed downstairs. Hearing Rala Haripuria's name from Bapu's mouth startled me. The music of alghozas was honey to my ears. Suddenly I was surrounded by the memories of my childhood.

Rala Haripuria, Allah Ditta of Dherian Wala, and Peeru—the threesome used to perform together. Peeru was the leader of this trio. He played the sarangi. Haripuria accompanied him on alghozas, and Allah Ditta played the dhadd, the hourglass shaped percussion drum. This trinity was known hundreds of miles around the village for their talent. Whetted by the presence of high calibre maestros, they would never miss out on the well-known festivals of Punjab like the Visakhi of Takhtupura, the Hola Mohalla of Anandpur Sahib, the kabaddi tournaments of Mari, the Roshni fair of Jagraon, the wrestling matches of Shama Nangal, and the Hazrat Pir fair at Jhiri. They would settle down with their musical instruments on one side and prepare for their performance. Peeru would clean his sarangi with his shoulder cloth and tune it. Haripuria and Allah Ditta would also get ready. Peeru would touch the sarangi with his forehead and start touching its chords with the bow. He would bow as if paying obeisance to Mother Earth and, covering his ear with his left hand, he would start singing: *Ho…. O…O…ho….*

With this he would begin to straighten himself gradually and by the time he sat up fully, his voice would be echoing in the surroundings.

Similarly, Haripuria would start playing on his alghozas in the bow-bent position and the music would increase in clarity by the time he straightened up. With the increase in the pitch of Peeru's voice, the tune of the alghozas would change. Soon Peeru and his sarangi, Allah Ditta and his dhadd, Haripuria and his alghozas—all came into sync with each other. A crowd of people in the fair would start gathering around them. Allah Ditta would play his dhadd ecstatically. As the gathering grew in size, Peeru would start his performance with an invocation:

> First of all, I salute the Eternal Almighty who created the Sun, Moon, and Earth.
> Second, I bow my head before the parents who brought me into this world.
> Third, I pay obeisance at the feet of my master who has made the dead familiar with the art of living.
> At last, I bow at the feet of the listeners who confer so much honour on me.

This would trigger a downpour of currency notes upon the trio. The notes would lie scattered all around but the musicians would not touch them during the performance. Money wasn't of paramount importance to them. People would shower praise on them in a rapturous mood. Peeru would bow in acceptance and rise again and again.

'Goddess Saraswati descends on Peeru,' someone in the audience complimented. The audience would listen to him spellbound. Someone holding a stick would come forward to ensure that the listeners stayed in the circle. The dancers, eunuchs, and mimics would pack up their own akharas and gather around Peeru. The chief of eunuchs, white-clad Devi Mahant, would take out currency notes of different denominations from the pocket of her kurta and shower Peeru with them. The wayward children would try to steal the notes but they could not escape the sharp eyes of the man wielding the stick. At times, they succeeded in dodging him. The fair as a whole converged around Peeru. Once they had begun, the performances knew no end. The people would keep requesting their favourites—popular ballads of Punjab like that of Kaulan Shahni, Dhru Bhagat, Jaani Chor, Shamo Naar, Inder Bego, King Dahood, Roop Basant, Sadhu Daya Singh's 'Zindgi Bilas', and so on.

One or two faint voices in favour of Mirza Sahiba were also heard. But these voices were too faint to become part of public favour. Peeru would sing at the request of listeners in general. He would start the folk legend according to the wishes of the people. He would never tire of obliging his listeners. But he would definitely sing Rani Kaulan, which was his personal favourite. Before starting this performance, he would silently make rounds of the akhara with the sarangi hanging from his neck. Haripuria and Allah Ditta would follow him.

Then Peeru would start, saying, 'Pious gathering! Kaulan was the daughter of Bania Pahor Mal, a merchant of Dharmdeep. Her mother's name was Shardi. Through her birth she made up for the lack of a child in her parents' life. Delighted, Pahor Bania pleased the poor and needy by doling out money to them. Everybody in the city was happy at Kaulan's birth. Just listen to how the circumstances of those times has been narrated by Chhajju Singh of Rattoke:

"*Dharmpur was a beautiful city.*
There lived in that city a usurer named Pahor.
His wife, Shardi, was exceptionally beautiful.
She gave birth to a daughter
and the lala was very happy to have a child in his home."

And, so, the saga of Kaulan would continue on. Having reached the sequence of Kaulan drying grains at the bhatthi and carrying fuel wood for the fire place, his sarangi seemed to bewail the plight of Kaulan. Rala Haripuria too would reach the climax; the intensity of the cry emanating from his alghozas would pierce the skies. Sitting on his knees and raising his face he would release a long note that would make the entire universe want to cry. Tears would flow from his eyes, demolishing all dams of restraint. Peeru's voice would become heavy with sorrow:

'Addressing her father Kaulan—the protagonist—says:

"O my father, your darling daughter has been pushed out of her home by her husband.
The one who lived in the royal palace has been thrown to the floor by Fate.
The daughter, who had full control over servants and slave girls, is herself facing a very tough time.
Digging in the grass and gathering fuel for the bhatthi, she lives with the water carrier woman.
The slanderous words of the people stab my heart.
I am running around in tatters.
So, please do come and listen to the woes of your daughter."'

The hands holding the sarangi would start trembling. Wearied and unable to continue singing, Peeru would collapse. Rala Haripuria and Allah Ditta would start gathering the money. Two or three self-styled helpers would join them and with this the akhara would conclude.

Peeru never sang Mirza in his akhara. If at all he was forced to sing it, he would do it briefly at the very end of the session. Peeru sang very clearly and precisely. That is why he always refused to sing Mirza. Mirza, he said, was not a true lover. By transforming sacred love into the profane, the purity of love was stained. According to Peeru, singers of Mirza were mercenaries.

'When I have no craze for making money, why should I sing Mirza? What is the use of money, after all? Even the pimps and prostitutes are people of affluence. Peeru cannot sing for money. Singing is prayer. How can you earn money out of prayer?' he would say.

Peeru was a man of great self-esteem, gutsy and God-fearing

as well. The fair of Hazrat Pir attracted a massive gathering at the shrine which was the site of the fair. One year there was an unprecedented crowd on the eleventh of the month of Sawan. The pir's temporal seat was occupied by Saain Husn Shah at that time. He was known far and wide for his spiritual stature. He was a big patron of singers, dancers, wandering monks, fakirs, eunuchs, and artists. The akhara was set up on an elevated platform. The performing troupe would stand in the centre while the Saain would sit to one side. The listeners sat all around the akhara. The akhara would start at sunset and continue through the night. On one side the singers were busy regaling the audience with their musical talent while on the other, the eunuchs and dancers presented their performances. The youngsters preferred watching the dances. Some fakir could also be seen taking puffs from his chillum and narrating a story to some grey-haired listeners. The singing troupes would perform when it was their turn; the secretary of the fair had allotted every troupe a spot in the programme. Peeru would also visit the fair with his associates. He was given his turn last of all. It was believed that if Peeru performed first, then nobody would listen to any other singer after him. Peeru had come that year as well. When Peeru moved his bow on the strings of his sarangi, its musical twang scattered the gatherings of dancers and eunuchs who themselves joined the audience. Peeru raised his voice and cast a spell on his listeners. He kept singing and the people listened to him in an ecstasy. The Saain fished out a bundle of currency notes from his shoulder bag and showered it on Peeru.

Peeru started with the ballad of Roop Basant. People listened to him with bated breath. Suddenly at a particular point in the story, tears began to roll down his cheeks. Haripuria and Allah Ditta began playing with double enthusiasm. The audience of this performance also included wealthy landlords from the area. They vied with others in raining currency notes down upon the heads of the artists. Unlike average singers, Peeru and his comrades did not shout the praises of such affluent 'admirers'. That year Sardar Baghel Singh sat there among the listeners. He had curled moustaches, a well-oiled beard, and a double-barrel gun slung from his shoulder. The pockets of his waistcoat were stuffed with currency notes. He sat there in such a majestic posture as if he were the king of this area. But Peeru was unconcerned and indifferent towards all this. As he got to the saga of Kaulan Shahni, Baghel Singh lost patience. The influence of home-distilled liquor became manifest as he extended his hands, full of hundred-rupee notes, towards Peeru.

'Oi, leave it, Peeru. Why are you out to narrate the story of a slut? Tell us the love tale of Mirza—the gallant Jat....'

Mirza, the protagonist of the love tale 'Mirza–Sahiban' boasts to his sweetheart that even the angels and God himself dreaded his mare.

The sycophants of Baghel Singh also followed him in this joyful exclamation! Some in the audience also raised their voices, demanding: 'Mirza...Mirza...Mirza....' Peeru kept his cool for some time. He stopped singing and his eyes became red with rage. He picked up the notes fallen on the floor, walked straight up to Baghel Singh, and threw them in his face. Then he disgustedly spat on the ground before him. Baghel Singh felt highly insulted by this. Now it was his turn to rage. He was about to say something when Saain Husn Shah got up and took Peeru in a warm embrace. People shrieked with joy at this. Baghel Singh's rivals showered notes on Peeru even more generously; they had found this rare God-sent opportunity to lay him low. They complimented the singer openly saying, 'Wow! What a dignified singer!'

'Salute to the mother who gave birth to such a gem.'

'Long live Peeru!'

'He may be the sardar in his own home. What have artists to do with this?'

The akhara had become a centre of much noise. There were so many such jibes against Baghel Singh that his supporters became highly irritated. They got ready to take up cudgels. Baghel Singh too wanted to give Peeru a piece of his mind but he swallowed the insult and silenced his followers with a glare. Seething with rage, he left the concert halfway.

Baghel Singh put up with the insult on that day, but he didn't forget his rancour against the 'arrogant' singer. So in connivance with the area police inspector, with whom he was friendly, he got Peeru implicated in a case of selling opium. He made the inspector give the singer a sound thrashing in his presence. The police officials gave Peeru such a severe beating and caned the back of both his hands so mercilessly that he became unable to play the sarangi. Baghel Singh kept sneering at Peeru while he was being beaten. The police officer asked Peeru to apologize to the sardar if he wanted to be released. In response, the stiff-necked Peeru looked at Baghel Singh and spat scornfully.

Baghel Singh's adversaries and Peeru's supporters got him released with the intervention of senior police officials. Peeru returned to his village badly broken. He was in tremendous pain. But he continued walking like a conqueror with a stiff neck.

The police torture had rendered him unable to walk around and give performances for some time. Those who visited him to enquire about his health concluded that he would no longer be able to sing or play the sarangi. People would try to lift his morale and pray for a speedy recovery in his presence but behind his back they would shake their heads in disappointment.

'Peeru will become infirm.'

'A police beating prevents anybody from standing on their own feet.'

'The bastards hit him on his hands. I don't think his hands will be able to hold and play the sarangi any more.'

'What wrong had Peeru done to anyone?'

'Peeru's sarangi has become a thing of the past now—merely a dream,' they would remark with a sense of dismay.

People from the entire village, except Baghel Singh and his

henchmen, had come to enquire about his health. They would talk at length of the injustice he had suffered, his dignity and guts. They would empathize with him. Peeru's accompanists Rala Haripuria and Allah Ditta left no stone unturned in taking care of Peeru and nursing him back to health.

The Visakhi fair was as crowded as usual that year but the earlier life and soul of the event was missing. The singer, dancers, eunuchs and the dhadd–sarangi musicians set up their respective akharas. But they were not comfortably settled in any of the akharas. People missed the lilt of Peeru's sarangi. All of a sudden, the mellifluous tones of a sarangi could be heard. Its cadence reached the heavens and the dhadd seemed to be begging for the attention of the wonderstruck people. Peeru played his instrument in a rapturous mood. Nobody expected Peeru to have his akhara in the fair this time around. Intoxicated with joy at his sudden arrival, some music lovers had shouted joyously in welcome. Peeru's sarangi had become more melodious. He had a brighter glow on his face than before. There was more grace in his gait and better depth and rhythm in his voice. Despite his brute power, Baghel Singh had not succeeded in throttling Peeru's sarangi. From that day on, Peeru's sarangi become the talk of the village.

ᒉ

Then one day people felt that he had grown old. People thought that his age would definitely ring the death knell for his sarangi. The sudden and mysterious death of Peeru's son who was studying in the city had also triggered a wave of sorrow among the people.

'He was so sensible—as gentle as a cow. Such boys are very rare.'

'Really God did a great injustice against such a noble man as Peeru. Perhaps, God too no longer likes men of nobility.'

'But the police say he was killed in some rivalry. Some of his adversaries killed him and threw the dead body into a ditch.

What enmity could such a studious boy have with anybody?'

People had their doubts and suspicions.

'It's only a cooked-up police story. He had been in their custody for the last ten days. The police had tortured him greatly. They cut his flesh and filled the gashes with salt and chillies. They reportedly pulled his nails out. They tortured the boy also by placing him on ice slabs,' Palu said in a hushed tone, as he looked around.

'How do you know?'

'My relative from village Ghania is head constable at the police station. He told me all this.'

'But how can the police book anybody for no fault?'

'These boys are creating a lot of trouble. They are talking of the rule of the poor labour class. They say they will eliminate the landlords. Peeru's son Shaardi too must have become a part of this movement. They had secret meetings in the city. Someone tipped off the police who nabbed them in the middle of a meeting. Most of the boys managed to run away. Only Shaardi and two other boys got caught. Shaardi is also said to have been complicit in the killing of the Kuttiwal sub-inspector.' Palu of Gidrya village seemed to know a lot about Shaardi.

'You are right, Chacha. He used to talk like this—just weird talk.' This was Ginder.

'Weird…meaning…?' Everybody wanted to get to the bottom of this.

'I met him recently.

"How are you?" he asked.

"How can you expect us to be? The situation is not very good. We toil hard all day long but still can't manage two square meals. It's no better than starvation."

And, you know what he said to me with an inflated sense of pride?

"Ginder, the bad days are not going to last forever. The days of these men with paunches are numbered now. Just let them come within our sights." By God, the boy's face had turned red while saying all this to me.

'He again said to me, "Ginder, where is justice here? We earn by toiling hard in the fields and the produce is taken away by these alligators. We spill our perspiration in the construction of buildings only for these people to live in them. And we don't have even a proper roof over our heads. The haves are few in number. If we—the deprived lot—unite, they can be blown away so easily. It's only the poor working class that will rule here." Chacha, for a moment I was also convinced by the boy's arguments.... Do you think I am lying? He was killed by the police.'

'Anyway, whoever killed him, it's very unfortunate.'

'Really it's a great misfortune. Peeru will be confined to bed for life now. He isn't going to recover from this setback.'

'Peeru was the soul of the area as a whole. His sarangi could infuse life into a dead man,' someone immersed in grief would say.

'We shall no longer hear Shahni Kaulan on his sarangi,' an aged person said.

'He will not survive very now. The grief of a son's death is not possible for everybody to bear.'

'The poor man had only two sons and this one alone was wise and intelligent. The other one is a vagabond and does not listen to his father.'

'In a nutshell, Peeru's sarangi has died.'

This would put an end to the conversation. This topic was the main issue of discussion at every crossing, every turn, and every street of the village. Peeru was almost confined to bed. He could not get up from his bed for more than two months. Then, by and by, he started venturing out. People would sigh deeply as they saw him walking about like a sick man.

But these conjectures of the populace fell flat when Peeru's sarangi tugged at the hearts of listeners in the Roshni fair of Jagraon. Peeru performed with redoubled zeal. This time he started with Banda Bahadur's tale. He sang the ballads of Dulla Bhatti and Shaheed Bhagat Singh as well. Peeru's younger son Qaadri too had come with him to the akhara. As Qaadri raised his voice for the first time, the people were astonished to find in it the same texture, the same tonal quality as Peeru's. They just could not believe their ears. Qaadri had dropped out of school in the fifth or sixth standard. He always kept the company of shepherds and had also become addicted to drugs. Peeru felt very sad to think of the future of the boy. In addition, he was not very obedient to his father. So the audience was both happy and amazed to see him accompanying his father. Peeru too felt delighted at the transformation in his son.

Thus Peeru started taking Qaadri with him to the programmes. The young man had started going to akharas even without Peeru and with Rala Haripuria and Allah Ditta. His hands moved with nimbleness on the sarangi, just like his father's.

'Peeru's son is exactly like him with the same voice quality, the same hands.' Peeru was also happy with his son—the inheritor of his talent. When Qaadri sang in the akhara, Peeru would get drunk with glee. People viewed it as the Goddess Saraswati in Peeru. 'That is why his sarangi is getting more and more melodious day by day. The advancement in age was no hindrance.' They were all praise for his fortitude which had helped him bear the untimely death of his son in the prime of youth.

This was the first time that Peeru had not been at the fair of the Hazrat Shah. He had gone to visit his daughter's in-laws' home in Badbar. Peeru's relatives had got into a dispute with someone and Peeru's son-in-law was now in police custody.

Although Peeru was not at the fair, Qaadri had handled the akhara. Like his father he sang the folk tales of Dhru Bhagat, Dahood Badshah, Kundha Daku, and Sucha Soorma, much to the audience's satisfaction. Sardar Baghel Singh's son Gurbir Singh was also a part of the audience. He too had rained a shower of currency notes at his performance. When the akhara was at its climax, he asked to hear the love story of Mirza. Rala Haripuria tried to stop Qaadri but he acquiesced to the request and sang:

> 'When Mirza rode his steed to abduct Sahiba,
> A Jat named Vanjhal told him that women are not at all trustworthy.
> Let their friendship go to the flames!
> A woman's brain (as per a popular misogynist belief) dwells in her feet only.
> They ensnare men with the hook of their broad smiles but then expose it all through tears.
> So ye Mirza, beware! The repute of the wise once lost is never regained.'

Gurbir Singh and his followers whistled as Qaadri continued to sing to their whims. Allah Ditta and Rala Haripuria could not stop him. The younger sardar's sycophants lifted him onto their shoulders. Saain Husn Shah left the program halfway with a heavy heart and retired to his room. Gurbir Singh and his followers shouted exultantly during the performance as the folk tale of the love birds doubled the intoxicating effect of the alcohol they had imbibed.

On his way back home, Peeru came to know about the violation of his professional sanctity at the hands of his own son. Agonized, he found it difficult to reach his destination. By chance, he came across Baghel Singh on the village outskirts. Peeru could not look him in the eye. The mischievous smile in the elder sardar's eyes pierced his heart and soul. Baghel Singh, who used to lower his eyes at the sight of Peeru, was now twirling his moustaches and coughing mockingly in his presence. Peeru felt vanquished by this man for the first time. Even after reaching home, he kept walking up and down in his courtyard out of sheer restlessness and desperation. Qaadri returned home in the evening. He held in his hands the currency notes he had earned from the akhara. Immediately after stepping in, Qaadri went to his father. Touching his father's feet, Qaadri extended the notes towards him. An irate Peeru snatched the notes from him and flung them in his son's face. Picking up a cane lying in the courtyard he began to beat Qaadri without uttering a single word. He kept hitting the young man until he himself collapsed, wearied and panting hard. He commanded Qaadri to get out of his sight and never show his face ever again.

After this Peeru was confined to his bed forever. He stopped going out of the house. On the fifteenth day after this, people heard the lamentations of Rala Haripuria and Allah Ditta from Peeru's home. Peeru's death threw a pall of gloom over the entire village. Soon thereafter, Allah Ditta also followed Peeru out of this world. Now Rala Haripuria was the only survivor from the legendary trio.

'What to say, Peeru took with him the very heart of our village. Not just Peeru, the sarangi too has died with him,' those living with only the memories of the lute would say to each other with a sigh.

⌡

'Putt Dev Sihan, come down! Go to sleep now. You have to leave tomorrow,' Bapu called out again. So, I went downstairs without saying another word.

'Ever since Peeru died, Rala Haripuria sometimes starts playing his alghozas in the stillness of the night. People say he is possessed by Peeru's soul, otherwise how could the sound of the alghozas be so sweet?' Bapu said.

Translated by Parvesh Sharma

THE COLOUR OF BETRAYAL

AJMER SIDHU

Motto 1: 'The sincerity of a friend is tested at the time of eating sugar cane. It has to be observed whether he keeps the root for himself or gives it to his friend.'

This motto lies imprisoned in the wilderness of my diary. The pages of the diary are fluttering in the air, sounding like the wings of a caged bird. My attention is focused on it as well as the slowing down of the air from the ceiling fan. I was about to start writing a short story but was caught as another one unravelled. My grandfather used to tell me that there is no war bigger than life itself and there is a lot to learn every moment, everywhere.

The sugar cane metaphor aligned my consciousness with my grandfather's. He had tamed the jungle of the bar wasteland region with the sweat of his brow and set the family up on a strong economic footing. He used to tell us that sometimes bonds lasting centuries can be snapped in moments if there is spuriousness in the mind. We could never forget a particular story he narrated to us. He told us about two Muslim brothers in the bar region. They were Jats who tilled the land together and lived together like a joint family. But their relationship came to naught because of sugar cane.

The brothers were peeling the sugar canes in the fields when their sons arrived to chew on the sweet stems of the crop. The elder brother picked up a sugar cane, peeled it and cut it in two with a sharp blow of the sickle. While giving it to the boys he crossed his arms so that he gave the juicy root of the plant to his son and the top leafy part to his nephew. The younger brother was watching all this from a distance. Immediately, he protested. 'Bhaijaan, our relationship ends right here. You discriminate between your son and nephew.' And he threw the sickle down in the field then and there.

This anecdote related by my grandfather came to me often. How pure and guileless were the people those days! If there was any point of dissent or bitterness, they had the courage to point it out and deal with it fairly.

A sudden noise from the fan jolted me out of my reminiscences. My eyes opened to the world of reality. The speed of the ceiling fan increased as the voltage increased, and the wind knocked my pen onto the floor. I feared that even today I would not be able to start this new story. When I start to write a new story, my mind does not stay in the present. I cannot concentrate. It slips back into the past.

I had tried writing this story two months ago. The life of Anandjit Singh, the protagonist of the story, was full of ups and downs. I have been living with this character for a long time but I could not present him the way I wished to. I could not express his anguish convincingly. So ultimately, I abandoned the very idea of writing this story.

I can visualize his face clearly. I also know his innermost feelings. I am witness to his stresses and strains. I want to lay bare for the reader Anandjit Singh's thought process. Yet, I find myself unable to present him suitably. I have not been able to decide so far whether I should even attempt to write his story or not. But he will not let me be. I feel as though he is constantly nudging me to write it. He knows that it will be written...written by me and no one else.

I have some blank papers attached to my cardboard clipboard. I have one end of my pen in my mouth. I am trying to define friendship in the context of the sugar cane story. I have a motto lying before me. It has facilitated my writing of the story. This motto was composed by a colleague of Anandjit Singh who had it inscribed on the wall of the school. He still has a deep fascination for these mottos. It was only because of this fascination that he had got himself transferred to the Government Senior Secondary School in Judgepur. Prior to this he taught in the Government Secondary Senior School, Majara Chakk. He used to pass through Judgepur on his way to Majara Chakk. The road ran past three sides of the school building. People passing by would definitely see these mottos. Who can say if everybody read the mottos written on the walls but Anandjit Singh certainly read them carefully since he was fascinated by them.

Motto 2: 'Education is the window through which man can watch himself and the world as a whole. Also, through education, he develops the ability to know right from wrong.'

Now I have placed my pen on the first page of the diary. This was the motto written on the back wall of the school and the first that would have caught Anandjit Singh's attention. Because of this, he became an admirer of the anonymous teacher who had thought up such enlightening mottos. His own school was about ten kilometers away from Judgepur. He would go past this school early in the morning. On his way back, he would find that the entire school staff had left for the day. On some days, he would park his motorcycle against the wall and start noting down in his diary the mottos written on the school wall. His Majara Chakk school had mottos of their own but every school is different. Here the mottos were very thought provoking and quite distinct from the usual ones.

One day there was a function held in the Judgepur school, which Anandjit Singh attended. It used to be a high school during those days. The education minister was the chief guest on that occasion. The staff and students from the surrounding schools also attended this function and sat in orderly rows. It was a big function. The person who most attracted Anandjit Singh's attention was a man in his early fifties. He must have been over six feet tall. Attired in white kurta-pyjama and sporting a Patiala style turban on his head, he looked like an important political leader. He had a flowing milk-white beard. His face glowed red; it shone against his snowy beard. He was trying to sit close to the minister and pushed his way to the front whenever a photograph was being taken.

'The High School of Judgepur is being upgraded from today. The posts of principal and three lecturers in Humanities are also approved for the school,' announced the education minister amidst the thunderous applause that was initiated by him. Slogans like 'Education Minister Sahib Zindabad' arose from the gathering. Someone from the stage raised the jaikara ovation at the same time: 'Bole So Nihal—Sat Sri Akal' (Blessed shall be he who chants: Hail the True and the Timeless One).

This white-clad man with a flowing beard and well-tied turban clapping crazily on the stage is none other than my second character—Harjog Singh. He is a complex but very affable, forthcoming, and helpful sort of man.

Anandjit Singh had mistaken him to be a political associate of the minister as he was hovering around the chief guest. The truth unravelled only during tea after the function. The minister's cavalcade had left. Harjog Singh was serving the guests with great humility as is expected of a good host. Anandjit Singh's colleagues were all praise for his efforts to take the Majara Chakk school to the heights of glory, with the result that he felt greatly flattered. But when he came to know that the credit for the motivational slogans written on the Judgepur school's walls went to Harjog Singh, Anandjit forgot about his colleagues' adoration and spontaneously raised his folded hands with reverence towards Harjog Singh.

So far Harjog Singh had been the de facto headmaster of the high school. This school had never had a regular principal. Two women had joined the school at the start of the new session as lecturers. One of these lecturers occupied the principal's seat but all the office work—updating the attendance registers, attending to phone calls, interacting with the panchayat and parents of students, organizing meetings of various committees and keeping records, managing the mid-day meal, keeping a record of food, getting the audit done, and much else—was all handled by Harjog Singh.

After that function, Anandjit Singh and Harjog Singh became good friends. Anandjit Singh was very impressed with Harjog. That day Anandjit had seen Harjog Singh himself serving tea to the guests and this spirit of service and humility had inspired him. Ever since then, he had started keeping in touch with Harjog. Sometimes they would meet when Anandjit would pass the Judgepur school on his way to work. They realized that they used to pass by each other earlier too but at that time they did not know each other. Harjog Singh would talk to everybody with great warmth and affection. He had cars at home but came to school on a scooter so that he could wave to everyone he met on the way. The radiance of his face had its own magnetic pull. He would stop his scooter when he saw Anandjit Singh and give him a hug. Anandjit Singh had developed a longing to leave Majara Chakk school and get transferred to Judgepur. He had started treating Harjog Singh like an elder brother. Getting transferred to Judgepur would reduce his daily commute but, above all, the company of such a man would make his life more meaningful. He began to harbour a dislike for the Majara Chakk school.

I too am fed up. I find myself unable to trace the contours of the story. I have been sitting in this chair since I came from the village. Clipboard, papers, and diary are all here. I have been grappling with this story all this while! What to say of changing clothes, I have not even removed my turban so far. But now I have an itch on my head. So I have removed my turban and put it on the side table. Untying my bun, I have combed my hair and left it open, letting it trail down my back. I have changed my clothes also. I have washed my beard and combed it too. Now I feel light. The atmosphere of the room also feels pleasant now. My attention has returned to the Majara Chakk school and the pen has started moving again.

The building of the school flashed before my eyes. A magnificent L-shaped building. Anandjit Singh has really turned this temple of learning into an idyllic place with the help of the NRIs of this village. The huge shade trees and fruit trees have given the school a verdant look. The sprawling playground has in it the smaller grounds marked for kabaddi, hockey, football, and kho kho. Immediately on entering the ground one feels…like joining a game. Even if you are not playing, you can at least entertain yourself by sitting on the benches that line the grounds and sweetly singing songs of your choice. The songs can also be in the form of panegyrics to eulogize the contribution of Anandjit Singh who has taken the school to such an elevated level. His diary also has a comment from a peon of the school. But should this be a part of my story? My mind considers the lowly position of the peon and the value of his testimony.

'It was all due to the efforts of Master Anandjit Singh. He used to be the in-charge when this was a high school. Then it was upgraded to the senior secondary level but no principal or lecturer ever joined here. He remained in-charge for about twelve years. Just see the rooms of the school, the furniture and labs. This must be one of the rarest schools in Punjab. It has its own bus to bring students from various villages; he got an NRI to donate the bus.' The peon would narrate the whole story without waiting for any response from the listener.

'He made the NRIs start scholarships for the gifted students. First of all, he himself set up a scholarship in fond memory of his father. These days, the government provides computer labs in all schools but computers had already been introduced here many years back. You will find all amenities here including fans, coolers, fridge, generator, and submersible motor. You won't find an English teacher of Anandjit Singh's calibre anywhere around here. He has never missed a single class and has taught outside of school hours also, both in the morning and evening, at no extra charge. Had he wished, he too could have minted money like others by taking tuitions.'

Harjog Singh is also familiar with these qualities of Anandjit Singh. How can anything remain hidden from friends? He wants his friend's school to touch the dizzying heights of glory.

My hand has shifted to my chest. The pen refuses to move ahead. The protagonist of this story is about to land in a mess. No one will help him. What should he do? I run my fingers through my hair and pick up the pen again.

Due to the consistently good performance of students, Majara Chakk school had a good reputation throughout the area. Consequently, students of this school would get admission easily in quality colleges or go abroad to study. The clubs and associations of the area started conferring honours on Anandjit Singh. Harjog Singh was the first to felicitate him. Once the village panchayat also decided to honour him. One of the relatives of the village sarpanch had his own private school in the adjoining village. Some of his students had also shifted to Majara Chakk school even though the private school was fully equipped to teach up to the tenth grade and had a high standard of education. The owners of the private school had poisoned the ears of the sarpanch against Anandjit Singh.

At that time, an educational tour was taken to Chandigarh under the aegis of Sarv Shiksha Abhiyan. There, a friendly female teacher started taking photos with Anandjit Singh. While boating on Sukhna Lake, she sat with him. Being by nature a happy-go-lucky kind of woman she would break into laughter easily. Moreover, her dupatta would slip off her shoulders time and again. This became a cause for concern the next day in the village—the sarpanch had found his long-awaited excuse to point a finger at Anandjit Singh.

'If you teachers behave like this in public, what effect will it have on your students?' the sarpanch asked sharply.

The sarpanch's associates also started speaking in the same vein. Anandjit was very upset. He couldn't sleep. His blood pressure became abnormally high. He was always well-dressed and properly groomed; he wore a necktie even in the summer. He expected his students to be well-dressed as well. From their clothes nobody could tell whether they were students of a government school or a public school. Then everything changed. All the slanderous commentary had a negative impact on him. He forgot about wearing a necktie, matching his outfits, and trimming his beard. When Harjog Singh came to know about his melancholic mood, he tried to console him by saying,

'Dear young brother! Take it for granted that it's God's will that you join our school for your livelihood. You simply have to submit an application for transfer and the rest will be taken care of by the Almighty. Your coming will fill the post of the social sciences teacher which has been lying vacant for four years in our school. It will lighten my burden as well since right now I am the one who has to teach it. So just remember God now.'

Somewhat reluctantly, Anandjit submitted the application to Harjog Singh for his transfer. Harjog used his influence with the minister to get Anandjit transferred to Judgepur. When the time of his transfer came, Anandjit was still in two minds whether to leave or not. He had prepared his relieving report but his feet refused to step out of the school. He was about to burst into tears. He still hoped that the people of the village would ask him not to go and lash out at the sarpanch. He hoped they would sit in a dharna and protest outside the school. But nothing of the sort happened.

So with a heavy heart he walked out of the Majara Chakk school for the last time. He was not aware when he had started his motorcycle and reached the Judgepur school. He had reached there in time to teach the last class of the day. Harjog Singh was already there with open arms to receive him.

'We are blessed to have even a glimpse of a pious soul like you,' he said.

Harjog Singh's words calmed him. After meeting him, Anandjit felt that the mottos written on the walls had some meaning. They could only have come from someone who held a deep well of wisdom inside himself like Harjog Singh. He hoped that Harjog and his staff would act as a balm for his bruised heart and make him forget Majara Chakk altogether. The staff had gathered in the staff room. A box of sweets was opened. Sipping tea, Harjog said, 'We feel privileged to have Sardar Anandjit Singh with us as our colleague. We hope that he will bring glory to this school as he did in Majara Chakk school. May God continue to bless him.'

Motto 3: 'Schools ignite knowledge and ability in man.'

I closed my diary and got up. Sitting in one place for too long is not good for one's health.

Anandjit Singh was not completely happy, but things had started returning to normalcy. It had been six or seven months since he had come to Judgepur.

After combing my hair properly, I opened the diary once again. It opened on a page that said Motto 3. This motto was inscribed on the wall of the Judgepur school library. One day Anandjit became engrossed in this motto and kept making notes on this topic all night. He had made up his mind to address the students during the morning assembly the next day.

The next morning, Harjog Singh spoke first. 'Sons and daughters! We should be thankful to God who has sent to our school a teacher like Anandjit Singh who gives his all to cultivate moral values in his students. Besides imparting quality education, he inspires children to the path of remembrance of God. He awakens students against social evils....'

Master Harjog Singh's speech went on for longer than usual and there was no time left for Anandjit Singh to address the assembly. As the speech progressed, the drawing teacher passed by him, smiling, but the reason for his smile remained a mystery to Anandjit. Didn't he know that back at Majara Chakk school he often addressed the morning assembly? He used to read good books and make notes from the books to share with his students. Not only Anandjit, but other teachers also addressed the students in the morning. It had been almost a year since he had joined the Judgepur school but only Harjog Singh had addressed the assembly here all this while.

Motto 4: 'A true teacher not only thinks but even dreams about his students.'

I have flipped through the pages of my diary. It's because a sense of monotony has gripped me now. Motto 4 was written on Teachers' Day—it has the date on it. I land on Teachers' Day in the story.

That day too Anandjit wanted to address the students but he did not get the chance even on this occasion; this would be his last attempt. Master Harjog Singh was repeating his old lecture. Neither the students nor the teachers were listening to him. He thought again of his previous school where the students used to listen to him with rapt attention. The memory of that school made him sigh.

Motto 5: 'Students, the classroom, blackboard, and chalk should be the constant companions of a teacher.'

Anandjit never missed any of his classes. This fifth motto had emerged from within him. He had thought it up and given it in writing to Master Harjog Singh to get it written on the wall facing the office. He would always be in the company of his students.

These days Anandjit gets upset very easily. Ever since he started teaching here, he takes even insignificant things to heart. If a teacher misses his period, it irritates him. Master Harjog Singh is a habitual shirker in this regard. He stays in his office. He is the one who has to look after the official business. Then how can he take classes? Then naturally there will be disorderly behaviour in the classrooms. This is what Anandjit Singh cannot tolerate. Harjog is his friend whom he loves. He is very helpful too. That is why he cannot point this out to him. So he just bottles up his resentment.

Motto 6: 'Serve without expectation of the result.'

Just see how wonderful the fan is. The increased voltage has increased its speed. The pages of the diary have started fluttering. I have placed my pen on this particular page. Motto 6 has appeared prominently. Prior to this I was wandering about in my room. I had gone to my children's room and switched on the TV. I had tuned in to the sports channel. A wrestling competition was taking place in Hakimpur. The spectre of Anandjit Singh suddenly surrounded me. I returned to my room and Motto 6 appeared.

Anandjit was also very fond of sports, which is why Majara Chakk school had beautiful playgrounds. He loved being the commentator and performed this duty on holidays. He could be seen holding the mike wherever there was a kabaddi match or a sports festival, cultural or religious program in the area. He loved to collect awards. I cannot forget the Barnala incident where he had gone to see the bouts of some famous wrestlers. The announcer mentioned his name twice or thrice but he was not called to come onto the stage. His name did not figure anywhere even during the distribution of mementos. The next day he did not go to school due to fever. The teachers teased him saying that he had fallen ill because he did not receive a memento.

Motto 7: 'We can talk a big talk but can't walk the walk.'

Understanding Harjog Singh—the other main character in the story—really is an uphill task. This character is rather elusive. It seems impossible to pin him down, or understand what makes him tick. I get hold of one strand and the other slips away. That is why I am using Guru Nanak's bani to describe him in Motto 7. To walk the talk is not easy.

The second period of the ninth class was Social Studies. The drawing teacher noticed a girl exchanging a mobile SIM card with a boy. Harjog Singh should have taken the class but was in the office flirting with a teacher. Ever since then the drawing teacher had been on the warpath.

'All this man does is lecture. He spends twenty-five to thirty minutes on lectures in the morning assembly. The recess period is also reserved for this. The rest of the day he sits with madam. This is what he is paid for.' The drawing teacher kept repeating this to anyone who would listen till school closed that day.

The drawing teacher is foolish. Harjog knows how to run the school. That is why the 'madam' has delegated all powers to him. An ordinary man cannot run a government school. Little does he know that government schemes are like empty envelopes. Harjog Singh is able to handle all this only because he is the village sarpanch also.

For the last twenty-five years the post of sarpanch has been the monopoly of Harjog Singh's family. Before joining the school, he was the village sarpanch but he did not relinquish this position. He merely passed the title onto his wife or to his brother. Once this position was brought under the reserved category for Dalits he manipulated the election so that his stand-in would win. If he was capable enough to be sarpanch, he could run the school with the same efficiency.

Motto 8: 'Education has turned into a market commodity. Only those with resources can purchase it.'

I had read an article in a newspaper about the reality of the education system. Anandjit Singh had noted down this line from that article and preserved it as a motto as well. Before I forget, let me tell you that the day this article was published, a new teacher had asked Harjog Singh, 'Has education really turned into a market commodity?'

'All that depends on God above. The students here are just the children of God. The Almighty has bestowed on us the service of teaching them. Both my sons completed their studies from a convent school. Then they went to Canada to study further and eventually settled there. That is their destiny, and it is predetermined. It's a divine game of where you are destined to take birth, be brought up, receive education, and finally your livelihood. It is all in His hands. Man is helpless.'

Motto 9: 'The pearl of success is hidden in the oyster of hard work.'

I have two bracelets on my arm. As I raise my arm or start writing they strike against each other. The sound breaks my concentration. I am reading Motto 9. I don't know in which direction the story is going. I have removed one of my bracelets. I had started my story with Anandjit Singh but Harjog Singh has started dominating it. Anyway, unlike the bracelets on my arm, they are not so easily separated from each other. Moreover, Harjog is also an admirer of Anandjit and would sometimes mention him in his speeches: 'Students! You won't find such a hardworking teacher anywhere.'

Then he would start enumerating Anandjit's achievements in education, sports, cultural activities, etc. One day, the panchayat had a meeting in the school office. As Anandjit entered the office, Harjog started listing his various achievements.

'Why don't you apply for the state award?' The sarpanch showed him a newspaper clipping about the award; the government had solicited entries for the prize.

On various occasions, Harjog Singh pushed Anandjit Singh to apply, but the latter merely shook his head in response every time. But Harjog was not one to give up easily. He was dexterous in the art of persuasion. Ashok Kumar Vashisht, a teacher from the nearby village, had secured this award last year. Harjog Singh took Anandjit Singh to meet Ashok Vashisht. The state awardee gave them a copy of his application documents. The thickness of Vashisht's case file was really intimidating but Harjog finally succeeded in convincing Anandjit to apply.

Anandjit Singh started gathering certificates, citations, results, sports achievements, and school activities from the last ten years. So far, he had never truly valued citations, newspaper cuttings, photographs, certificates, etc. but now he realized their importance. Harjog helped him create certificates on the computer and get them authenticated by the concerned officers. They both acquired citations from clubs, schools, panchayats, academies, and theatre teams. They gathered articles published in various magazines and newspapers. Photographs were collected from the photographers. These contents were enough to prepare a thick file. Five copies of the file were prepared. They spent a full month on the preparation of the file. They barely slept or rested during this period.

The files were duly signed by the District Education officer. With the hope that he would win the the award, Anandjit Singh, accompanied by Harjog Singh, submitted his file at the DPI office. Now it was time to decorate the school building like it was a bride. The school building was quite new—it had been constructed just a year ago—and Harjog Singh had already spent a lot on its beautification and that of the surroundings. But Anandjit Singh had the entire building painted again at his own expense. Harjog Singh started adorning its walls with specially selected mottos. Landscaping and new flower beds gave the school building a new look. The staff also left no stone unturned in the beautification of the building. All the furniture was replaced. Harjog Singh himself changed. He started taking classes like Anandjit Singh. He would make the students write on the blackboard, set tests for them, and check their homework properly.

The inspection of the school was awaited impatiently. One day there was a call from the District Education Office asking for Anandjit Singh's complete records. Madam principal, Harjog Singh, and the school clerk carried the necessary papers and records to the district office. At the district office, they checked the record and recommended his case for the state award. Harjog lost no time in congratulating Anandjit Singh on his mobile.

It is very hot today. It was very hot and humid that day too when the Deputy Director-led inspection team came to the school. The D. E. O. office had informed the school of the visit in the morning. Everything had been set in order before their arrival. They checked all the records of the school and made a video of the school classrooms, kitchen, and bathrooms. They tested the students' skills. They also tested the performance of teachers like Anandjit Singh and Harjog Singh by observing their classes for some time. They checked the notebooks of all the students. Ever since Anandjit Singh's application had been submitted, inspection teams began visiting the school often. It began with the D. E. O.'s team. Then came the circle education officer's team. As and when any inspection team came, Harjog Singh showed such marvellous hospitality that they lavished praise on the school in the visitors' book.

A couple of weeks later, when the staff members were sitting in the principal's office after marking their attendance, Harjog Singh began distributing parsad.

'Yesterday, we had a discourse of a great saint at Gurdwara Sahib. At the end of the prayer, I requested the priest to pray to Waheguru that the state award come to my own dear friend and your esteemed colleague Anandjit Singh. It will really add lustre to the name of our school.' Saying this he raised his folded hands skywards.

On the tenth or eleventh day thereafter, Anandjit Singh looked very happy and smiled at everybody in the school. During recess, he distributed sweets saying that he had received a call from the Secretariat where a clerk known to him had told him that the state award was going to Judgepur school this time. The announcement of the teacher's name is awaited, he said. The list would be out on 25 August and the awards would be presented by the education minister on 5 September. He invited the entire staff to attend the occasion. He asked the staff to get new clothes made for the function but simultaneously requested them to keep it secret for the time being.

Motto 10: 'Character is the most valuable wealth in life.'

After reading Motto 10 I have closed my diary. It is half-past midnight. This motto is etched indelibly on the slate of my mind. The contribution and achievements of this department flash off and on. There is a wooden niche behind my writing table. It is adorned with mementos. I remove my spectacles and look at them. I think for a while and turn away. I pick up the pen and turn the page of my diary. My hand moves gently on the fresh page.

It is 25 August today, the date the state award list is to be released. The computer teacher always arrives at about 7.45 a.m. and immediately opens the school's mail. There is usually a spate of e-mails to be replied to. Every time an e-mail is received, he takes a print out of it and submits it to the principal.

Eager to see the award list, the staff marked their attendance and quickly went to the computer lab. They congratulated Anandjit Singh who had come attired in his Sunday best. His face was radiant. They merrily discussed potential locations for the party that Anandjit Singh would have to throw to celebrate this achievement. Then, since the list was not out yet, they left for their respective classes. Anandjit visited the computer lab after every period on some pretext and returned to his class after being told that the final list was not up yet. He was floating rather than walking and showering affection on his students. He wondered what gift he would give to the staff who taught the fourth class. For the first time the building of this school looked more beautiful to him than that of Majara Chakk school....

The recess period was in progress. As the teachers ate their lunch, they talked about whether Anandjit should take them to Jalandhar, Ludhiana, or Chandigarh. The list had still not come; Anandjit's heart was thudding in his chest in anticipation.

Finally the list came during the last period. The entire staff gathered in the staffroom. Anandjit Singh ran his hands through his beard. The list included all of Punjab, so each and every name had to be scanned. One of the teachers kept his eyes on the column of teachers' names while another was scanning the names of the schools. Most of the names were from the Malwa region. At last the name of Judgepur appeared, way at the bottom of the list. Everybody stood there with bated breath.... What...! To the consternation of all, it was Harjog Singh's name that appeared against the Judgepur school. Everyone was dumbfounded. There was a stunned silence in the room. The computer teacher moved the cursor up and down to confirm.

The principal madam, Harjog Singh, and the clerk were sitting in their office. The drawing teacher also joined them. Other teachers followed suit. Harjog Singh was showered with congratulations. Only the computer teacher and Anandjit Singh were left sitting in the computer lab. Anandjit looked puzzled. The colour of hope had fled from his face, which now lacked its radiant glow. He looked shattered. He pursed his lips and his eyes reddened with rage. His nostrils flared. A sort of dense smoke seemed to be rising to cloud his brain.

Guffaws of laughter escaped from the principal's office. The teachers were planning to get a treat from Harjog Singh. He didn't say anything. He sat there holding the school's mid-day meal register. The teachers kept congratulating him. Some of them asked questions about the award but he refused to say anything or accept any congratulations. He looked very gloomy. He only repeated, 'I am worthless.'

'I wonder how they chose a worthless man like me for this honour. I never even applied for it. It was Sardar Anandjit Singh who deserved this award. I fail to understand why God did not bestow His grace and bless him. You know how hard I tried to make sure that he got the award. Now…how can I face him…?'

The bell signalling the end of school rang out. Harjog Singh and some others were still sitting in the office. Anandjit Singh was sitting in the computer lab, opposite the office. The puzzled staff, not knowing how to react, marked their attendance one by one and left for their homes.

'Come on, sir!' a clerk said. 'Cheer up…. You are a state awardee now. Do you see now what wonders we can do? We sent your file along with his and not even a single teacher had an inkling of it. We can cook a goat without letting even a wisp of steam escape from the cauldron.' The clerk smiled, looked knowingly at the principal, and walked away.

Harjog is a seasoned card player. He knows how to bluff. In his own village Masandan Di Patti, Deor-Bhabhi, and Sweep were the most popular card games. But he preferred to play the colour game and would always guess the colours of the cards. One day, sitting on a cemented platform under a banyan tree, he had been playing this game when Anandjit Singh approached him.

'Sir, you play cards?'

'Bhai Anandjit, all games are made by God,' Harjog Singh had replied with his hands folded and raised heavenwards.

'Some people take this game of cards very lightly. But this is the game that teaches you how to win and lose in life.' With this sermon he had drawn the relevant card.

Anandjit Singh recalled this two-year-old incident today. The computer teacher started checking the list again but Anandjit didn't wait for further confirmation of his loss. He gathered his courage and went to congratulate Harjog Singh. His hands trembled and legs seemed lifeless. He felt dizzy and was about to collapse when the computer teacher supported him and sat him on the chair.

...But sitting on a chair is not enough to give you support. I am also sitting on a chair and writing. But this is not the same chair. I am feeling dizzy and feel a squall raging before my eyes. I hear the sound of many things cracking within my being. Ever since I came to know about this, I have not been able to sleep. I am not feeling well and the pages I wrote are now jumbled together. I find I am not able to pick up the thread of my story again. I don't know what possesses me now....

I begin tearing the pages one by one.

Translated by Parvesh Sharma

THE ROD

SARGHI

Many news stories that are telecast on TV disturb me. Some are simply forgotten.

Some others hurt me so deeply that they leave me on the verge of tears. An incident that took place a month ago shook me to the core. And what happened yesterday disturbed my very being.

Now both these news stories are so deeply entrenched within my psyche that I cannot get rid of them. Sometimes the news about the first incident crops up in my mind; sometimes the other.

The first news story.

The first news item concerns Mr and Mrs Anand's family. The dead bodies of their thirteen-year-old daughter—Shruti—and their servant were recovered from their home. Every news channel took to exploring and exposing various aspects of the incident. The minutest details about the incident were telecast. Watching the news story, I could not remain unaffected. Looking at my daughter sitting nearby, I was even more frightened. She too is thirteen. I carefully watched my daughter. I could see the approach of youth in her innocent features. I became anxious. My husband sitting next to me was also watching the same story. Maybe he also felt the same apprehensions but he did not share his unease with me. While leaving for his room, he admonished the girl for no reason...and to me he said, 'You should resign from your job.'

He became his usual self after that. But I cannot just forget the news.... Time and again I have to assure myself—what happened there cannot happen in my home.

Even then, I imagine Shruti's face superimposed on my daughter's and my servant appears to me to be similar to their servant. Whenever I am away from my home, I feel something similar might be taking place in my home. Every day I resolve not to hear or read a word about this incident again. Even so, whenever I come across a news item about this incident in the newspaper, I cannot resist reading it.

I share my problem with my friend who teaches psychology in the college. She tries to help me relax. Our conversation calms me. But when I leave for my home, I imagine all the incidents reported in different newspapers taking place in my home. My mind is in turmoil.

I feel depressed all the time. I try to pray...but even while praying, I cannot stop those evil, terrible thoughts from crossing my mind. The prayer book falls from my hand.... I am on the verge of tears.

Even when I am in college, my mind is completely occupied with thoughts of my home. I constantly find myself wondering where the servant and my daughter are. Perhaps because of this reason, I returned home one day well before time, as if I was conducting a raid on my own home. When the door did not open for ten or twelve minutes, the scenes of that news story began parading before my eyes.

No one came out of my house in response to the ringing of the doorbell. But the ruckus I created caused the entire neighbourhood to collect around me. I could not control my tears. Someone from the crowd asked, 'What happened?' All I could say was, 'Where is my daughter?'

Some of the faces in the crowd are worried, others are smiling roguishly. I felt there was no one in the crowd who understood my pain. I heard someone in the crowd saying, 'This is bound to happen to mothers who stay out of their homes all day long.'

The fifteen-minute ruckus offered the public the chance to

say whatever they liked about my daughter. In that confusion, I tried to call the servant on his mobile.... It rang but he didn't take the call.... I became even more scared.

After five minutes or so, I saw my daughter and the servant coming back.

Seeing the crowd gathered there, the servant was alarmed.

'What happened, madam? Is everything all right at home?'

I felt like screaming, 'No. It is not all right!' But I couldn't. I could only ask feebly, 'Where had you gone?'

'Madam, don't you remember, every Saturday Bitiya goes out for lunch.... I took her out for that.'

The crowd outside my home dispersed. I opened the door, went in, and checked all the bed sheets very meticulously... I felt ashamed of the thoughts that crossed my mind.

The servant said, 'Madam, didn't I tell you everything is fine at home. I don't know what has come over you of late.'

I hug my daughter and calm down, and then burst into tears that do not stop.

The servant asked, 'What happened, madam? Don't worry about anything as long as I am here.' I couldn't find the words to respond but my hands spoke for me, as I folded them before him... He put his hand on my head, blessed me, and then went into the kitchen, busying himself with his chores.

How could I tell him then that he was the cause of all my anxiety? I think perhaps I should sack him. I would then be at peace. These days, I feel irritated with myself. I constantly get upset and the whole household gets disturbed because of me. I keep scolding the servant without any apparent reason. I take the medicine prescribed by my psychologist friend Navjot and do deep breathing exercises. This calms me down a bit...then I happen to listen to some horrible news on TV and lose my peace of mind again...and upset the whole household again.

I try to think well of our servant.... I cannot recollect even a single moment when he misbehaved in any way, or had lust in his eyes. But then his wife was alive at that time. Now his wife is dead and gone and he has nowhere else to go. I look back and recall everything. This servant has a twelve-year-old connection with us. My daughter was only one year old when he and his wife came to us. I had never found them odd; nor were they ever treated like servants—they were family.

But now whenever I see the servant, I go mad with rage. Sometimes I think: no, he cannot do something like that. He cares for my daughter more than me. Then I come across some other news story related to that case that shakes me to the core.

I feel disturbed and depressed. I share all my concerns with my friend Navjot. She calls me to her counselling centre. Preparing my case history, she asks, 'Have you experienced feelings like this earlier?

'No.'

Then she probes further, 'Did you ever feel in your youth or childhood that what happened to someone else could happen to you?'

'Yes. I remember…when my friend's father passed away. I felt the loss keenly and wondered what if my own father should die….'

'Anything else like this sorrow?' she asks again.

I think deeply and try to recollect. Then I reveal to her, 'Whenever I go to Pingalwara, that house of the destitute, I have tears in my eyes and fear this fate may befall my children. Navjot, you know very well I wasn't so suspicious and nervous earlier.'

'This is not simple fear, Deepa. You are suffering from "paranoid disorder". But don't worry, the problem is quite mild as yet.'

'Will I ever be normal again?' I ask her, almost pleading piteously.

'Look, Deepa! There are two kinds of patients. There are those who allow their problem to dominate them and there are others who gain control of their sickness. The patients of the second type are able to overcome their disease and recover much faster.'

Coming back from her clinic I take the prescribed dose of the medicine. After so many days of stress, I feel relaxed. I have finally been able to enjoy a sound night's sleep. But when I wake up and open my eyes, the servant moving around in my home appears to me to be clandestinely eyeing my adolescent daughter.

To distract myself, I open up my laptop and navigate to my internet browser. I have not read or heard any news story about that incident for so many days. I try to control myself and resolve not to go to any site dealing with that incident.... But I don't know how I happen to click on a link called 'Shruti murder case'. Every minute detail connected to that incident plays in front of my eyes like a movie. I am behaving in a bizarre manner. I start reading stories that disturb and pain me. Reading the details in one story upsets me no end. I am worried. What will I do if my servant has made a porn video of my daughter? I push the laptop away. A blank screen is in front of me but I cannot avoid imagining those scenes playing on it. Panicking, I start calling for my daughter.

'What happened, Mama?'

I can say nothing. But I hold my daughter tight in my arms.

'Please let me go...I can't breathe, Mama!' She struggles to free herself with all her might and breaks loose from me.

My Rose sits next to me. I place my head on her shoulder.

'Mama, what has come over you all of a sudden?'

'I don't know, Rose. I don't know what is happening to me.... Rose, do you know when you were a little child and you used to play hide and seek with your dad, I used to hide you in my lap to protect you. Even now I wish...to hide and protect you.'

'What is this, Mama...you can't hide me any more.... I'm big now.'

How can I tell her that her growing up day by day was creating such tension for me! Oftentimes, I think that that when we were children our childhood was not so complicated. Whatever fear there was, it was when we were away from home; inside the home, we were completely safe. But these days, children have free access to all kinds of rubbish on the internet in their very homes. Then I happen to see the servant and I feel it is because of him that all these problems exist.

Then one day I dismiss the servant and turn him out of my home. He who had regarded this house as his home for twelve long years! I broke that bond with a single blow.

It was a long time ago that I stopped liking him, yet he didn't want to leave my house. He asks me in a piteous voice, 'Madam, you were not like this earlier. What have I done wrong? Please tell me....'

'Don't ask me anything. I just don't like you staying in this house any more.'

The day he leaves, his eyes look yellowish. I think for a moment that I should tell him to go to a doctor and get his eyes checked. But my heart has hardened towards him.

While leaving he says, 'Madam, I am going now.'

'Okay, you go now...and never come here again.'

'Madam, I am not going to come back.'

After that he goes silent. There are tears in his eyes. His hand rises towards my head to bless me as usual but then he pulls it back. He wishes me Sat Sri Akal with folded, shaking hands. Then he quickly leaves the room. My husband takes him away in his car and drops him off somewhere.

I cry a lot after he goes away.... That day we don't cook anything in our home. My daughter sulks for a bit and withdraws into a shell. But I feel relieved and at peace.

᪣

He doesn't live long after leaving my home. My husband informs me about his death. We make all the arrangements for his cremation. When I see his body for the last time before cremation, I hear his voice again, 'Madam, I am not going to come back.' I perform his last rites according to my religion. I don't know if those ceremonies were for his salvation or for my own peace of mind. The priest in the gurdwara, while offering the final prayer for the dead, says, 'Free him from the cycle of life and death, protect his soul from wandering. Keep the departed soul under your patronage and protection, hey Waheguru!' I think that if the souls of the dead wander after death, then his soul must be sitting in some nook or corner of my home. Suddenly I think: souls don't matter, the problem arises because of the body.

The servant is dead but still I keep thinking of him every now and then. A song is heard on TV: '*O father dear, my anklets cry; I call you as the day goes by*'. Listening to the song, tears begin to flow uncontrollably from my eyes, tears that had been suppressed for so many days. Earlier whenever I heard this song, I remembered my late father...but today, I don't know why I thought about our servant.

When she learnt about his death, my daughter was quite upset. One day sitting beside me, she suddenly said, 'Mama, do you realize that uncle died because of you?' I am left nonplussed for a moment to hear her words. The very next moment, it occurs to me that it is good that he died on his own.... I won't be blamed for his murder, like Mr and Mrs Anand.

The second news story.

Days have passed since the servant's death. I feel normal now. Life is becoming easy and comfortable again. There is peace at home, maybe because I am calm now. All the turmoil in my head is gone. I attend my sessions of yoga, deep breathing, and meditation regularly. Still, I never miss visiting Navjot's counselling centre. She is worried about me. She begins to talk about the servant on one pretext or the other. I feel she is conducting some experiment on me. Laughing, I tell her, 'I am at peace with myself, no special joy, no particular worry. I don't experience any fear either.'

'I want you to stay like that, easy and comfortable.'

I counter, 'What do you mean. Am I not well?' Navjot does not respond; she just keeps smiling.

But the news story about Nirbhay terrified me again. Oh my god! So dreadful...how could this happen....can any man be so cruel and barbaric? All kinds of thoughts keep troubling my mind.

The 'rod' was also a culprit, a partner in the rape of Nirbhay. She was killed by that rod. She was in no way related to me; but her pain became a part of me. I feel as if all my strength has been sapped out of me. I feel as if my body has been completely crushed by that rod.

I am on the verge of tears as I reach Navjot's clinic. Looking at my face, she notices my expression and asks, 'Are you fine?'

'No dear, I am really terrified...because of the rape case in Delhi.... O my God! Can man be so barbaric and brutish? I don't know what all has gone through my mind.'

'O dear...if man is a social animal, his barbarity would also reveal itself sometimes or the other.'

I don't respond to her.

'Try to be normal, Deepa! Ours is such a huge country... some such incident or the other keeps taking place here.'

'But, Navjot, a young girl, alive and kicking, is violated and torn apart with a rod and you call it an ordinary common place incident?'

'Look, Deepa, there are millions of people, you cannot share or carry the pain of all of them.'

I don't say anything. I get up and head home.

My peace of mind is gone.... I feel the same illness is raising its head again. Navjot is also telling me, 'Only your object has changed...the problem is as it was.'

I go to the college, nervous and tense. Wherever I see a few colleagues standing in a group, I feel they are waiting to pick up a rod. Whenever I am given the duty to take a round of the college to enforce discipline, I wish for a female companion to accompany me. If I have to go anywhere alone, I keep looking back over my shoulder time and time again.

What has come over me? I was not that kind of a person. I try to read good literature…wanting that only good and positive thoughts for all come to me. But this news has filled my very being with negativity…. I am simply unable to be positive.

Almost all the members of the college staff alight at one bus stop. I get down at the last turn. During that two-kilometre-long journey, only I know what kind of thoughts pass through my mind.

I happen to look at a corner of the bus and see a hockey stick and rod lying there. I get agitated. I feel as if that rod is moving towards me. I shriek loudly. The driver is shocked and looks at me. I ask him to stop the bus.

'Madam, you get down at the next stop.'

'I know where I should get down!' Irritated, I snap at him as I get down. I am sweating all over even in the month of December.

When I arrive home, my husband is alone. Without saying anything, I go directly into the bedroom…. I stretch out on the bed, I am staring at the roof. I hear the sound of the outer door being closed. I know the meaning of the door being closed.

I am scared of my husband in my own home! I try to relax a bit. But I just cannot do it…. I sit up.

'Please leave me alone,' the words escape my lips.

'What is the matter with you…whenever I try to come near you, you behave as if I am a stranger.'

'I am not stable right now.'

'But I am stable. Look, I am an ordinary human being…and you know what kind of hungers an ordinary human being has.'

Ignoring what he has said, I go and sit in the drawing room. There was a time when these intimate moments used to have a special significance for me. But now all this looks so meaningless… sometimes I feel like going and joining the Brahmchari shivar, the camp of women practising abstinence.

I visit Navjot's counselling centre again. Maybe she will be able to suggest something to quieten my unease. Today she seems more of a friend to me than a psychologist. I mention the desire to join the women practising abstinence. She warns me against this move and advises, 'Deepa, the way you are behaving, you are going to destroy your home, mark my words.'

I burst out crying and she takes care of me.

'Look here, you have to get rid of your fears, anxieties, and you will be all right on your own.' I nod my head in agreement like an obedient child.

'Navjot, I wish to go to that camp of women practising abstinence at least once.'

'Deepa, why don't you understand…if you go there, your family will be irreparably destroyed.'

'I want to get rid of all these burdens, Navjot.'

'As long as you carry the fears and worries of the entire world inside you, you cannot have any kind of freedom. Don't you feel like spending time with your child?'

'No'.

'Don't you have any attachment to your home?'

'None at all.'

'Don't you feel concerned about the situation of your husband?'

I don't respond.

'Deepa, where is the need for you to join the women who practise abstinence? You are already free from every bondage.'

'Navjot, please try to understand my problem. I have weird nightmares. That night as I was sleeping, I felt as if pieces of flesh were coming off my body and falling down…. I wanted to shout as loud as I could….but I felt throttled…burdened…a shriek…and my husband covers my mouth with his hand…. I was drenched in sweat all over.'

She continued, 'How can I tell you, Navjot, I don't see my husband as a man but as a rod only…the rod, that has made my life so miserable.'

Navjot is listening attentively to every word I utter. She simply responds, 'Abstinence is also running away from life. People like you, Deepa, who are ready to be fugitives on their own, try to escape from their responsibilities.'

'I will come back feeling easy and normal, Navjot.' Navjot and my husband dropped me off at the camp. I went into the camp without any hesitation, and didn't look back even once.

↗

Everywhere inside the camp people were clad in white and engrossed in their jobs. Are these people all alone, with no obligation to any relatives or friends? Are they free from every burden? I wondered. A devotional song was being played. Everyone seemed to be dancing in ecstasy. Tears fell from my eyes...are they tears of joy or sadness? I could not decide. Now a religious discourse was going on. 'All human suffering is because of humans only.... For thousands of years, our saints and seers have been teaching us that this world, the relationships, are all illusion, Maya. But we take this illusionary world to be the truth and our troubles go on multiplying. We can be free from pain and suffering only when we reject this illusionary world...and remember that there is nothing here that we can call our own.'

As the discourse ended, I asked myself if there was anyone that I could call my own. The liberation and inner peace that I was looking for was not available here either. The more the preachers talked about renunciation, the breaking free from the bondage to home, the more I remembered my home. Whenever the preachers talked about the hollowness of relationships in their discourses, I thought about the depth and sincerity of my relationships.

And one day all my delusions about the place came crashing down. The women ascetics who appeared to be so enthralled by the discourses about renunciation were cackling and telling lewd jokes. They were rolling in laughter, sharing incidents with vulgar implications. That night was my most horrible night at the camp.

The next day I collected my belongings and went straight to

Navjot's home. I did not go to her clinic. Perhaps she had seen me coming. Smiling, she came and held me in a tight embrace.

'I was sure you would come back, Deepa.'

'Navjot, I am purged of all my delusions. Do you know there is a rod there in the camp also. I have seen it with my own eyes. That night five or six female devotees were with one another. I just can't tell you.'

'Deepa, I am very happy today.'

'Navjot, I know you are happy for me. I won't ask you now if I will get well or not.'

Navjot smiled again.

'Deepa, abstinence is turning your back to the truth of life. Renouncing your home is also nothing other than avoiding facing the truth.'

'Yes, Navjot, if one could get away from everything by simply closing their eyes, life would be much easier.'

'Deepa, everyone says that rapes must stop...but nobody asks why rapes take place after all.'

'Navjot, you tell me why do rapes take place...why is a young girl, so full of life, violated and torn apart with a rod?'

'Deepa, when love and compassion disappear from the human heart, rapes are bound to take place.'

'Navjot, you are right. I know what happens when love disappears from life...one finds one's own face frightening...feels angry all the time...irritated...always full of negativity.'

'Deepa, man, always brimming with anger, full of hatred, can commit murder...can commit rape—but he cannot love.'

'Okay, Navjot, now guess, do I feel affection or anger now?'

'This question you should ask yourself...you'll come to know.' Looking at me she smiled again.

'Okay, Navjot, I want to go home as soon as possible.'

'The weather is so dreadful, why don't you wait for some time?'

'No, Navjot...it has become fine after such a long time.'

I reach my home in a few minutes. I don't pull the main gate outwards as I always used to do, rather I push it in to open. I don't know why I push it in. There is no one at home except me. I carefully observe the room...wipe the dust from the family photo. Every face begins to come to life...not a single word escapes my lips...my eyes well up. I sit on the carpet and practise deep breathing. Take a deep breath...no thoughts, no fears. I slowly breathe out and the present alone comes alive for me.

Something begins to shine bright within me. The entire house begins to echo with Chitra Singh's ghazal: '*Love is here everywhere, have faith in me, O dear.*' I step out. After many days of terrible weather, it is clear today. My gaze turns towards the lawn of my home. Different coloured flowers almost intoxicate me. I feel as if the flowers are dancing for me. But today I don't like the white roses. I am fascinated by the red, yellow, and scarlet flowers. Far in the corner, a touch-me-not shrub has collapsed to the ground under the weight of its flowers. The flowers are fading. I hurriedly go near the shrub. A thick iron rod has crushed it under its weight.... I remember Nirbhay, but I am no longer afraid of the rod. I pick it up and throw it out of my home in a single swing. After a little while, I look at the touch-me-not again. Now it is in full bloom once more. Looking at it, I feel that I too am blooming. Now in my home there are flowers everywhere...no rod at all.

Translated by Paramjit Singh Ramana

ALL ELSE IS AN ILLUSION

JATINDER SINGH HANS

It was midnight when I regained consciousness. Perhaps it was early morning. I was in the police lock-up.

I tried to sit up. My whole body ached from the internal injuries. The effects of last night's drinking had waned. I was feeling uneasy. It was very hot and humid in the lock-up. Mosquitoes were biting me all over.

A sharp pain reverberated through my bones. Remembering the incidents of the previous night, I felt dizzy. What had I done!

I thought I would faint when I remembered the moment the policeman had handcuffed me, abusing and slapping me, because I refused to get into the police van.

Half the village had gathered at our home. One of them had phoned the police. Before the policemen arrived, no one dared to come near me. I was so aggressive and violent. I held the big cow-dung scraper in my hand and was swinging it menacingly. When the crowd managed to get hold of me, they gave me a sound thrashing. Had the police not arrived in time, the irate crowd might have killed me.

When the policemen were arresting me and pushing me into that van, not a single person spoke in my favour. Rather they looked at me with eyes brimming with hatred and revulsion. Someone remarked, full of anger, 'It is better to be childless; what is the use of having an offspring like this!'

If there was anyone who could have stood between me and the police, who could have stopped the policemen beating me, he was lying on the cot, covered in blood.

I had not planned to kill Daddy; I don't know how and when this happened. It was such a huge disaster.

When I realized what a big crime I had committed, my intoxication evaporated. I picked up the bottle of pesticide and opened it, ready to drink it. The crowd got hold of me, snatched the bottle of pesticide from me, and threw it away. They all started thrashing me.

Mummy was wailing uncontrollably, 'We are ruined, see… this family is done….' Then she fainted.

Two vehicles left our house. Daddy was taken away in an ambulance. Perhaps his dead body was taken for post-mortem. The police took me to the police station. I had a feeling that Daddy would be okay. He was just unconscious. I had seen his hand move when he was lifted into the ambulance.

ᔕ

It was only yesterday, so it appears to me, that Daddy had got me admitted to Model Public School. It was the most expensive school in our area. Only English was allowed to be spoken there. I crammed nursery rhymes like 'Twinkle, twinkle, little star' and 'Johnny Johnny, yes Papa' at school. When I recited these poems at home, Daddy's eyes would begin to shine with pride. He felt like the thousands of rupees he was spending on my education were not going to waste. He would say, 'My son, Jagjit, will grow up into an important and big man…. I will enjoy the best in life because of him.'

And there was Daddy, lying on the cot, his body covered in blood! He looked at me one final time with stony cold eyes, as if to say, 'Great, man, great! You have made me enjoy the best in life!'

ᔕ

Perhaps the police will take me to the cremation ground to light the funeral pyre. I am his only son; it is my right as well as my responsibility. But I can't say such things to anyone. The other person would retort, 'Well done, you performed your responsibility as a son very well!'

The residents of the village had such anger and hatred for me in their hearts that it is quite possible that if I went to light the funeral pyre, they would throw me into the fire next to Daddy.

What have I done? I am full of self-loathing. I feel like committing suicide. But now I can do nothing more than hit my head against the walls of the lock-up.... I will have to spend the rest of my life in prison.

꒰

Daddy's dexterity was amazing; whatever task he undertook, he completed it without fail. He had another skill too: he could talk endlessly. People would avoid being near him. It was said about him, 'Hari Singh will start narrating his "epic" and narrate at least half of it.... He will narrate the whole epic, if the listener has time for him.'

If he did not find anyone to narrate his sermon to, he would go on and on narrating his 'epic' to us at home, even though we had heard the same story many times. We would start thinking of some excuse to get away from him. But Daddy was not one to let anyone get away that easily. He would proudly curl his moustache, fondly pat his long beard and start, 'Childhood! ...I never got a chance to enjoy any childhood. I was only ten years old when I lost my father.... At the time of his final prayer meeting, the ceremonial turban was tied on my head. The turban meant that I had to take on the responsibility of paying back the debt incurred for the treatment of Father's cancer. It also meant that I had to bear all the family responsibilities on my shoulders, look after the farm and my three sisters who were growing up fast.

'Everybody wondered—how will this child look after the family?

'The whole family would sit in gloom and cry thinking of Father.

'There was extreme poverty. Often we had to go hungry.

'One day, grieving for my father, I lay on the cot under the mulberry tree and dozed off.

'I saw the "true Master" riding his blue horse, gleaming sword in hand, eagle perched on his shoulder, and his bright, glowing face, a sight too dazzling to bear. He patted my shoulder and said, "My son, never lose heart."

'All of a sudden, I woke up.

'This single event changed my life. The tenth guru was only nine years old when he sent his father, Guru Tegh Bahadur, to Chandni Chowk in Delhi where he became a martyr because he upheld his faith. He had the responsibility of the whole nation on his shoulders... Could I not take care of a single family?

'I did my best.... I paid back the loan, married off my sisters in a befitting manner, got married, and ran the best farm in the whole village. I also managed to buy some of the adjoining land.

'Had I not woken up so soon, maybe the Guru would have conferred kingship on me like he did on the Raja of Patiala. Anyway, I have lived my life like a king only; anyone who has a wife as sagacious as Baljit Kaur, a talented son like Jagjit Singh who would end up in Delhi, who eats two good meals every day, can his life be regarded as anything less than majestic?'

What Daddy found majestic was abhorrent to me. I could not consider a life with 'two good meals' a day majestic in any way. I wanted to do something so extraordinary that the whole world would acknowledge it. The conflict that turned violent was due to the 'talented' son of Daddy. There was a generation gap because of which Daddy could not understand my perspective and I could not relate to what he said. I felt as if I were his worthless son, always making excuses. An educated idler. He behaved as if he alone carried the burden of the whole world on his broad shoulders. Without him, it would come crashing down. I had not been able to get a job. I wanted to change his methods and plan our farming my own way. Whenever I talked about selling the rickety old tractor or about buying a new more powerful one, and purchasing a harvester and a rotavator and to supplement our income by lending them out, he would immediately start his harangue:

'This tractor, my dear Jagjit Singh, is a gift from the Guru. It is my hardworking son...do you know when we got it? That year, the entire village was able to transplant the rice crop on time. I was the only one unable to do it. It was terribly hot in the month of June. Life had become very hard. The irrigated farms would dry up and be parched in minutes in that heat. Even the rain gods had failed that year. The government's policy was harsher than the rain gods. It was not providing any electricity. The rice in the field was wilting.

'That day I got up well before dawn, prayed at the gurdwara, and went to the farm. Sprayed the weedicide in the field that was ready for transplantation. Scattered the fertilizer in the field where the labourers had transplanted the rice the day before. When I was scattering the fertilizer, I felt as if I was celebrating Jagjit's marriage and throwing a handful of coins over the bride's car. Then, it suddenly occurred to me, who would be so stupid to throw coins in the mud. If the gods are kind, all the money will come back. I should yoke the oxen and start ploughing the field for sowing. I could not bear to look at the pair of oxen suffering the scorching sun. I thought how time had become such a significant factor in farming.

'I went and sat on the cot placed in the shadow of the sheesham tree, near the tube well. You never know when the electricity supply would resume. If we had a tractor, we could have used it to operate the tube well. Exhausted, I lay down and dozed off.

'The Guru again appeared in my dream. At that very moment, Namberdar, the lame, shouted, "Hari Singh, power has been restored, switch on the motor."

'I woke up, switched on the tube well, and went home. Looking at my gleaming face, your mother exclaimed, "What happened?"

'I responded, "Dear wife, celebrate.... The Guru appeared in my dream.... We are going to buy a tractor."

'She smiled, as if I had said exactly what she wanted to hear. Covering her head with her dupatta, she said, "I am going to prepare some parshad."

'"Okay. Make some kheer also," I said laughing.

'"Right. I will cook some kheer too," She said cheerfully and went into the kitchen.

'I went to an agency to buy a new tractor. The manager of the agency made his calculations on a piece of paper and began to advise me. "You pay the money that you can; the rest can be taken as a loan from the bank. You bring the record of your land for mortgage."

'I replied, "Manager sahib, I am not going to take any loan. One loses one's dignity by being in debt."

'The manager only smiled in response. Looking at my ordinary rustic dress and the cloth bag in my hand, he thought it prudent not to waste any time on me. He began to ignore me.

'I emptied my bag on his table and said, "Count the money and put back whatever is in excess."

'The manager was shocked beyond words. He laughed, started counting the notes, and muttered, "Sardarji, this has never happened before.... Oh, boy, come here! Go and bring some tea for Sardarji."

'That very day, the tractor arrived home with a garland adorning it. I also bought a packet of laddoos from the sweet shop.

'This hardworking son of mine transformed our lives, really transformed everything.

'Many necessary implements and accessories were added: the trolley, the cultivator, land-leveller, seeding and ridge-making machines, and many other tools.

'This tractor is a member of our family. It is deeply involved in all the joys and sorrows of the household. It feels happy when it sees the crops standing in the fields. If rain, dust, or a hailstorm happen to damage the crops, it feels sad.

'May god bless everyone with one!'

◡

Daddy's daily schedule was simple: from home to farm and from farm to home. Dayal, the sarpanch's son, was a friend of Daddy's. He often remarked, 'Hari Singh, God has blessed you in every way. Jagjit is doing very well as a student and you as a farmer. I have a piece of advice for you: you need not struggle so much all day long. No one is going to give you a prize. This is my personal experience; a man may do anything for his children, he may build as many palaces of gold as he can, but the children are always going to complain in the end: "What have you done for us?"'

Daddy would just laugh it off, 'One's work is one's achievement. Only the Guru's blessings are essential.'

◡

Daddy was very proud that I completed my M. Tech. without dropping a year. He used to tell everyone with great satisfaction, 'With the blessings of the Guru, he will go very far in life.'

He never objected to anything I did. When I left for college every morning riding my Bullet motorcycle, smartly dressed, and wearing my dark Ray-Ban sunglasses, he would look at me with great satisfaction. I wanted us to adopt new agricultural techniques but whenever I brought this up he would say, 'You just focus on your studies. You have to become a big officer. What is so special about farming? One person can do it. Even if the whole village is involved, it will be no different.'

He wanted me to become an officer and sit in a chair. He didn't realize that incompetent corrupt governments cannot provide employment. They can only impose taxes to serve their own interests. They are more rapacious than the British.

One day we were trying to attach the trolley loaded with wheat bags to the tractor. The trolley slipped from its stand and began rolling away. Daddy ran and put his leg out to stop the trolley from moving. The trolley did not fall but his leg was injured. Mummy was furious with him, 'What would we do if your leg was crushed or broken?'

At this, he began his sermon on Guru Maharaj.

'What is this trolley? Our Guru Maharaj was able to stop a huge rock with his hand. How can you forget that? During the annual sports festival held every year in our village, kabaddi, football, tug-of-war, and wrestling matches take place. Every year Harpal and others from Dhamot village would win all the trophies. All the boys in their teams were strong and sturdy like rocks. Too strong to defeat. After winning, they mocked us and laughed at our village all year round.

'The sarpanch of the village came to our home that year along with other elders. He asked me to lead the tug-of-war team for the honour of the village.

'I was well-built. Because of the physical labour I put in and the good diet I had, my body was sinewy and sturdy. I was hesitant because I had never taken part in that sport; I hardly had any time because of my farming routine. But I could not refuse. All the elders of the village had come. Praying to Guru Maharaj, I agreed.

'On the day of the match both the teams stood in line, ready for the big fight. The referee blew the whistle and, thinking of Guru Maharaj, I took my position as the anchor of our team. Wrapping the rope around my body I passed it over my shoulder for the others to hold. Both the teams started pulling with all their might. I stood there like a rock, firmly fixed to the ground.

I had taken my position after praying to Guru Maharaj. Despite all the efforts of the other team, we didn't move an inch. Soon enough, Harpal's team, which won the tug-of-war every year, was defeated as we were able to pull them over the line. The spectators started clapping, the skies resounding with their joyful cries. Everyone was surprised and shocked; we had been able to defeat a state level team!

'The very next day, the elders of the village came to my home with a tin of ghee and a ceremonial turban, saying, "Hari Singh, you have protected the dignity of our village."

'This is the leg of that same man. Once I put it somewhere it stays put. It is not going to break so easily,' he said, twirling his moustache.

His leg had still not fully recovered from the injury when another unexpected mishap took place.

The rice crop had been harvested, the wheat was to be sown. The land was ready but the rice stubble was yet to be cleared; its presence would affect the yield of wheat. I made the labourers pull out the stubble from the outer edges of the field so that the fire would not spread to the adjoining fields which were still to be harvested.

Just as we set the stubble on fire, the wind suddenly picked up. The flames began to rise up to the sky uncontrollably. I ran and switched on the tube well. The labourers started throwing buckets of water to put the flames out. Some others broke branches from the nearby trees and tried to beat the fire out. The tractor had the cultivators attached to it. I jumped onto the tractor and started ploughing the sides of the field as fast as I could. I completed one round but then I was caught in the fire. I became completely confused. It was the first time that I was doing all this without the supervision of Daddy. The people standing around shouted at me to jump down and save myself. My brain went numb. I was simply unable to decide what to do in that moment. The diesel tank of the tractor was full. It could catch fire at any moment and burst like a bomb. Even the tyres could catch fire. In the meantime, my clothes caught fire. I finally jumped down from the tractor and ran to safety. The people standing around managed to put out the fire covering me even as I lost consciousness. I had never experienced such a close brush with death.

Daddy happened to come limping up at that very moment.

'Thank god, he is safe…. Human life is so precious, the tractor doesn't matter, it can be bought again,' someone in the crowd said.

My father, sitting with my head in his lap, placed me down on the ground. Telling those around to take care of me, he ran towards the fire. Many tried to stop him, 'Don't do it, Hari Singh, you will die for sure.'

He came back driving the tractor at full speed and, going near the tube well, he cooled it by throwing water on it.

People were able to put out the fire and save the crops. Those who had called him a fool for jumping into the raging fire were now praising him for his courage.

'Great man, great…Hari Singh, you have done the impossible,' someone said.

At first I was happy that the tractor had been saved. Then I felt a twinge of jealousy. Was it possible that Daddy cared more for the tractor than me…?

Daddy hugged me and held me close to his heart. But somehow I could not get rid of that envious feeling.

ر

Daddy tried his best to find me a job. He approached many people, but his efforts were in vain.

He would tell people, 'He has been able to study so much with the blessings of the Guru Maharaj. Small jobs are available, but he will not take them…he will go very far.'

After that fire, I started to suffer from an inferiority complex. I began to feel I was not good enough for anything. I would get on my motorcycle and go to meet my college friends. We were all unemployed. We would roam about as idlers, making new schemes every day to earn money. I wouldn't return home for days. We would get drunk to overcome our frustration and curse the corrupt leaders and worthless politics.

At home, Mummy was getting worried about me.

Daddy's injured leg was not improving. I was the one who now ploughed the field. Most of the people in the village had bought new tractors. We had the same old one. I developed a new hobby: participating in tractor races and the testing of power of tractors by pulling each other in opposite directions. I could not win against the new tractors. So every day I returned home after suffering defeat.

Daddy would say, 'The pulling competition damages the tractors. You should eat well, grow strong, and play kabaddi or take part in wrestling.'

᷍

Daddy went to the grain market to sell wheat. He didn't return home for three days. Mummy prepared food for him and asked me to take it to him at the grain market. Daddy and other farmers were sitting at the commission agent's shop with their produce. All day he would narrate his sermons about his Guru Maharaj.

It appeared he would have to stay on in the grain market for a few more days. I hatched a secret plan. I'll bring home a new tractor before Daddy comes back after selling the crop! He will be very happy. Even if he became angry with me, it would last only a few days.

After handing over Daddy's food to him in the grain market, I joined my friends and roamed around, having drinks. Then I went to the scrap dealer and struck a deal with him to sell the tractor. He didn't pay much, but I was in a hurry to get rid of it. I talked to the manager of the agency to buy a new Farmtrac tractor. I happened to know the manager. He said, 'Pay an initial deposit and take the tractor. The mortgage formalities can be completed later.'

But I had to get the mortgage papers signed by Daddy! I felt Daddy would not refuse me anything. The sports festival at Khanpur was coming up and I wanted to use the new tractor for the pulling competition there.

To bolster my confidence, I had a few too many drinks. When I came home, I was dead drunk. The scrap dealer came to take the tractor away. I had told them that I'll hand over the tractor to them at their shop. But they had obviously secured a profitable deal and didn't want to miss it.

When Mummy came to know that I had sold the tractor, she got angry with me. 'Why are you bent upon destroying this house? Let your Daddy come home, do whatever you want....' She begged the scrap dealers to return later. 'Please go back, he is drunk....'

I said, 'I have given them my word.... The tractor will go right now.'

'It will go over my dead body.' Mummy lay down in front of the tractor.

I picked up the pesticide bottle, 'If I can't honour my word, what is the purpose of my life?'

Frightened, she got up and started wailing aloud. The scrap dealers too were alarmed. They said they didn't want the tractor and asked me to return their money. I drove the tractor out and handed it to them. They went away.

It so happened that Daddy arrived home just at that moment. Crying bitterly, Mummy told him everything. On hearing that I had sold the tractor, his face turned red with anger. I still had the pesticide bottle in my hand.

'You fool, the scrap dealers are butchers. We don't sell an animal to the butchers if we've had its milk for a year. And you have handed over to them something that gave you everything all your life. They will dismantle it and sell it piece by piece!

Put that bottle down,' he said seething with anger.

It was the first time in his life that he had spoken to me so harshly. I didn't put the bottle down. He picked up a stick and advanced menacingly towards me. People were watching the drama unfold. Some of them came forward to catch hold of me. Frightened, I picked up the dung scraper and swung it menacingly around. People stepped back. Daddy was even more infuriated. 'Do you dare to hit me? Hit me if you have the courage, or throw that bottle away.' Then he started walking towards me with his head bowed. He was very sure that I wouldn't hit him. To frighten him I swung the dung scraper into the air with all my might. It hit him on the head. Blood came rushing out and he was completely covered in blood from head to foot. He staggered back and fell on the cot.

Now I realized what I had done.

'Call the doctor. Hurry up!' someone was shouting.

'Stop the blood. Tie a cloth around his head,' someone else was saying.

Mother and others were asking him to sit in the car. There was confusion and an urgency to shift him to the hospital. Looking at Daddy's condition, I opened the cap of the pesticide bottle, and tried to drink it. Someone snatched the bottle away from me and started thrashing me. Someone informed the police and called the ambulance. Daddy lay lifeless.

⌄

Next morning, Daddy arrived at the police station accompanied by the village elders. Perhaps he came to the police station straight from the hospital. His head was heavily bandaged; the turban had been tied over it. Seeing him there, I thanked his Guru Maharaj.

I don't know what the village elders told the police inspector. I was brought out of the lock-up. While we were leaving, Daddy stood before the inspector with folded hands and said, 'It is my fault...I must have made some mistakes in bringing him up....

But what can be done, we sow wheat but some weeds pop up there on their own.'

We got into the car and left for the village.

I sat there, deeply ashamed of myself. Dayal, from the sarpanch's family, said, 'Your Daddy was given four bottles of blood. Despite the doctor's warnings, he came for you. It is only due to his grit that he is able to move around. Time and again I tell him, there is no need to push yourself so much. Your children are never going to thank you for anything.'

Daddy said, 'Dayal Singh, parents are victorious even in defeat to their children.... We have to do one more thing before going home. We have to take back our industrious son from the scrap dealer. These people don't understand, our homes become frightening in the absence of children.'

I embraced Daddy and started crying.

He laughed. 'Oye, don't worry. Guru Maharaj's blessings are with us. That blood was bad, so I got rid of it.

'Always remember one thing, something that I have learned from Guru Maharaj: this life here is the only reality, all else is an illusion.' He patted my shoulder and said, 'Once it so happened....' And he started narrating another story about his Guru Maharaj.

Translated by Paramjit Singh Ramana

ACKNOWLEDGEMENTS

It would not be an overstatement if I give, first and foremost, sole credit to my editor Pujitha Krishnan at Aleph, for inspiring me to conceive this book in its present form. With, of course, the help and cooperation of Balbir Madhopuri I have been able to put it together. Their contribution to this volume and their painstaking efforts have been invaluable and I cannot thank them enough.

I am grateful to all the translators who took on the difficult task of trans-creating these stories into English: late Khushwant Singh, late Balwant Gargi, Navtej Sarna, Dr Parvesh Sharma, Dr Paramjeet Ramana, Professor Tejwant Gill, Sukirat Anand, and Amaninder Singh Dhindsa, and to all the writers who are a part of this selection.

Another significant contributor, Jasjit Man Singh—a family friend, herself an author and translator—polished and refined most of these stories. I deeply appreciate her linguistic skills, and conscientious intervention. When she felt exhausted and gave up, Amaninder Singh Dhindsa saved this project by re-translating some of the most challenging stories. I am indebted to both of them for lending me a helping hand. I am also obliged to my friends Shashi Joshi, Bhagwan Josh, Ranjit Walia, and Kabir Saxena for their encouragement and critical suggestions.

Had I not reconnected with David Davidar, the story of this book wouldn't have unfolded. I would like to thank him for publishing it as well as Kanika Praharaj at Aleph for her copy-editing. I am indebted to Amandeep Singh at Punjabi Bhavan for assisting me in the preparation of the manuscript, and my ex-student (now a bureaucrat) Sarah Jayal Sawkmie along with her daughter Aayra Dhindsa Sawkmie for their meticulous proofreading.

Without the privilege of having this precious cultural legacy from my family I wouldn't have ventured to take on this project. My father, late Bhapa Pritam Singh, the foundational figure of the Punjabi literary world, introduced me to most of these writers, and my mother, late Diljeet Kaur, with her warmth and open-mindedness made them a part of our household. How can I ever forget my younger sister, late Ashma Singh, for the jacket designs for many of these books in Punjabi! Even their absence became a presence during this journey.

I do hope this book will partially fulfil their dream of disseminating the Punjabi cultural ethos and sensibility. Last but not least, my sister Jyotsna Paul came to my rescue this spring with all her emotional support and help with the corrections. Thank you forever!

While every effort has been made to locate and contact copyright holders and obtain permission, this has not always been possible; any inadvertent omissions brought to our notice will be remedied in future editions. Grateful acknowledgement is made to the following copyright holders for permission to reprint copyrighted material for translation in this volume.

'Bhabhi Myna' by Gurbaksh Singh, included with permission of Sukirat Anand; translation included with permission of Parvesh Sharma.

'Bowl of Milk' by Nanak Singh, included with permission of Kulbir Singh Suri; translation included with permission of Parvesh Sharma.

'Daughter of the Rebel' by Gurmukh Singh Musafir; translation included with permission of Paramjit Singh Ramana.

'Kung Posh: Kashmiri Saffron' by Devendra Satyarthi, included with permission of Alka Soin; translation included with permission of Paramjit Singh Ramana.

'Dance of the Devil' by Sant Singh Sekhon; translation included with permission of Amaninder Singh Dhindsa.

'Sunrise at Last' by Sujaan Singh, included with permission of Amanpreet Singh; translation included with permission of Amaninder Singh Dhindsa.

'The Moscow Girl' by Balwant Gargi; translation included with permission of Parvesh Sharma.

'Majha Is Not Dead' by Kartar Singh Duggal, included with permission of Suhel Duggal; translation included with permission of Parvesh Sharma.

'Stench of Kerosene' by Amrita Pritam; translation included with permission of Mala Dayal.

'The Great Mother' by Jaswant Singh Kanwal; translation included with permission of Paramjit Singh Ramana.

'The Proverbial Bullock' by Kulwant Singh Virk, included with permission of Sarbjit Singh Virk; translation included with permission of Parvesh Sharma.

'Savage Harvest' by Mohinder Singh Sarna, included with permission of Navtej Sarna; translation included with permission of Navtej Sarna.

'The Charity Coat' by Navtej Singh, included with permission of Rati Kant Singh; translation included with permission of Parvesh Sharma.

'In-Between the Books' by Sukhbir, included with permission of Navraj Singh; translation included with permission of Parvesh Sharma.

'That Woman!' by Ram Sarup Ankhi; translation included with permission of Paramjit Singh Ramana.

'Dog and Man' by Gurdial Singh, included with permission of Ravinder Singh; translation included with permission of Parvesh Sharma.

'The Survivors' by Sukhwant Kaur Mann; translation included with permission of Paramjit Singh Ramana.

'Green Sparrows' by Ajeet Cour, included with permission of

author; translation included with permission of author.

'Hopes Shattered' by Gulzar Singh Sandhu, included with permission of author; translation included with permission of Balwant Gargi.

'The Wind' by Gurdev Singh Rupana; translation included with permission of Tejwant Singh Gill.

'I Am Not Ghaznavi' by Gurbachan Singh Bhullar, included with permission of author; translation included with permission of Paramjit Singh Ramana.

'Doe's Eye' by Mohan Bhandari; translation included with permission of Tejwant Singh Gill.

'Eradicator of Suffering' by Bachint Kaur, included with permission of author; translation included with permission of Paramjit Singh Ramana.

'To Everyone, His Share' by Waryam Singh Sandhu; translation included with permission of Paramjit Singh Ramana.

'Home' by Sukirat, included with permission of author; translation included with permission of author.

'Whither My Native Land?' by Kesra Ram, included with permission of author; translation included with permission of Parvesh Sharma.

'Death of the Lute' by Gurmeet Karyalavi, included with permission of author; translation included with permission of Parvesh Sharma.

'The Colour of Betrayal' by Ajmer Sidhu, included with permission of author; translation included with permission of Parvesh Sharma.

'The Rod' by Sarghi, included with permission of author; translation included with permission of Paramjit Singh Ramana.

'All Else Is an Illusion' by Jatinder Singh Hans, included with permission of author; translation included with permission of Paramjit Singh Ramana.

NOTES ON THE AUTHORS

GURBAKSH SINGH (1895–1977) was a novelist and short story writer. With more than fifty books to his credit in Punjabi, he is considered the father of modern Punjabi prose and received the Sahitya Akademi Fellowship in 1971. Armed with an engineering degree from the Thomson Engineering College (present-day IIT Roorkee), he also studied Civil Engineering at the University of Michigan, Ann Arbor.

NANAK SINGH (1897–1971) is widely regarded as the father of the Punjabi novel. With little formal education beyond the fourth grade, he wrote an astounding fifty-nine books, which included thirty-eight novels and an assortment of plays, short stories, poems, essays, and even a set of translations. He received the Sahitya Akademi Award in 1962 for *Ik Myan Do Talwaraan*. His novel *Pavitra Paapi* was made into a film in 1968, while *Chitta Lahu* was translated into Russian by Natasha Tolstoy.

GURMUKH SINGH MUSAFIR (1899–1976) was a politician and writer. He was the chief minister of Punjab from 1 November 1966 to 8 March 1967. He was awarded the Sahitya Akademi Award in Punjabi in 1978 for his short story collection *Urvar Par* and was posthumously decorated with the Padma Vibhushan, the second highest Indian civilian award given by the Government of India.

DEVENDRA SATYARTHI (1908–2003) was an Indian folklorist and writer of Hindi, Urdu, and Punjabi literature. Born in Bhadaur (Barnala), he did not complete his education and in 1927, started travelling around Punjab collecting folk songs, which he published in his first folk song anthology *Giddha* (1935), considered by many as his seminal work. Satyarthi published over fifty books comprising novels, short stories, poems, essays, and folk song anthologies in Urdu, Hindi, and Punjabi. It is reported that, on advice from Rabindranath Tagore, he wrote mostly in the Punjabi language towards the latter part of his life.

SANT SINGH SEKHON (1908–97) began his literary career as a poet writing in English. He soon took to translating European masterpieces into Punjabi. The ancient Greek play *Antigone*, Shakespeare's *Macbeth*, Goethe's *Faust*, and Tolstoy's *Anna Karenina* and *Resurrection* are his most memorable translations. He published five collections of stories, two novels including *Lahu Mitti*, and three collections of one-act plays. His play *Mitter Piara* won the Sahitya Akademi Award in 1972. In the field of literary criticism, he was the founder of critical norms.

SUJAAN SINGH (1909–93) was born to S. Hakim Singh, in Dera Baba Nanak, a town in Gurdaspur, Punjab. He was brought up by his maternal grandparents and spent his early childhood in Calcutta, after which he started working as a bank clerk. He won the 1987 Sahitya Akademi Award for his short story collection *Shehar Te Gran*.

BALWANT GARGI (1916–2003) was a dramatist, theatre director, novelist, short story writer, and academic. He was born in Canal House in Sehna, Barnala. Gargi completed his M.A. (English) and M.A. (Political Science) from FC College in Lahore. He also studied theatre with Norah Richards at her school in Kangra Valley. Gargi wrote several plays, including *Loha Kutt*, *Kesro*, *Kanak Di Balli*, *Sohni Mahiwal*, *Sultan Razia*, *Soukan*, *Mirza Sahiba*, and *Dhooni di Agg*, and short stories such as 'Mircha Wala Sadh', 'Pattan di Berhi', and 'Kuari Disi'. His plays have been translated into twelve languages and performed around the world, including in Moscow, London, New Delhi, and in the United States.

KARTAR SINGH DUGGAL (1917–2012) wrote in Punjabi, Urdu, Hindi, and English. His works include short stories, novels, dramas, and plays. His works have been translated into many Indian and foreign languages. He has served as director of the All India Radio. He was awarded the Padma Bhushan by the Government of India in 1988. In 2007, he was awarded the Sahitya Akademi Fellowship, the highest honour given by the Sahitya Akademi.

AMRITA PRITAM (1919–2005) was a novelist, essayist, and poet, who wrote in Punjabi. A prominent figure in Punjabi literature, she is the recipient of the 1956 Sahitya Akademi Award. Her body of work comprises more than 100 books of poetry, fiction, biographies, essays, a collection of Punjabi folk songs, and an autobiography, all of which have been translated into several Indian and foreign languages. Pritam is best remembered for her poignant poem, 'Ajjaakhaan Waris Shah nu' ('Ode to Waris Shah'), an elegy to the eighteenth-century Punjabi poet. It is an expression of her anguish over the violence she witnessed during the partition of India.

JASWANT SINGH KANWAL (1919–2020) was a novelist, short story writer, and essayist. He was born in the village of Dhudike, Moga District, Punjab. As a young teenager he left school and went to Malaya. It was there that he first became interested in literature. He returned to Dhudike after a few years and lived there till the end of his life. He published several books and was awarded the Punjabi Sahit Shiromani Award in the year 2007. He won the Sahitya Akademi Award for his novel *Toshali Di Hanso* in 1998. His novels usually have a rustic feel and depict the rural life of Punjab very vividly while questioning firmly held social customs and beliefs.

KULWANT SINGH VIRK (1921–87) was an author who wrote mostly in Punjabi but also extensively in English. His short stories have been translated into several languages, including Russian and

Japanese. Virk was born in the village of Phullarwan, Sheikhupura district, Punjab Province, British India. Virk's writings have won several awards. In 1958, he won his first award for his short story collection titled *Dudh Da Chhappar* (*A Pond of Milk*). He won the national Sahitya Akademi Award in 1968 for his short story compilation *Nave Lok* (*New Folks*).

MOHINDER SINGH SARNA (1923–2001) was an Indian civil servant and novelist. He won the 1994 Sahitya Akademi Award for his short story collection *Nawen Yug De Waris*. He served as an officer of the Indian Audit and Accounts Service from the 1950 batch. He has nine collections of short stories to his credit.

NAVTEJ SINGH (1925–81), got his M.A. in Psychology from Foreman Christian College, Lahore. He was the eldest child of Gurbaksh Singh, eminent writer and founding editor of *Preet Lari*. He was a short story writer of great repute and was awarded the prestigious award for literary journalism by the Language Department of Punjab. A person of sweet disposition, he travelled extensively and wrote about his experiences. His short stories and travelogues have been widely published.

SUKHBIR (1925–2012), alias Balbir Singh, was a Punjabi novelist, short story writer, poet, and essayist. Over the course of fifty years, he published seven novels, eleven short story collections, and five poetry collections, and translated world literature and essays. He adopted the pen name Sukhbir after Partition, when he was arrested during the student unrest in Mumbai in 1950.

RAM SARUP ANKHI (1932–2010) was a writer, poet, and novelist. He started as a poet but ended up as a fiction writer. He was awarded the Sahitya Akademi Award in 1987 for his novel *Kothe Kharak Singh* by the Sahitya Akademi. Ankhi, after completing his education, continued with his ancestral profession of farming. Later, he served as an English teacher in a government school, but continued writing in Punjabi.

GURDIAL SINGH (1933–2016) was a novelist. He started his literary career in 1957 with the short story 'Bhaganwale'. He became known as a novelist when he published the novel *Marhi Da Deeva* in 1964. The novel was later adapted into a Punjabi film in 1989. His novel *Anhe Ghore Da Daan* was also made into a film of the same name in 2011. Gurdial Singh won the Sahitya Akademi Award in 1975 for his novel *Adh Chanani Raat* and was awarded the Jnanpith Award along with Nirmal Verma in 1999.

SUKHWANT KAUR MANN (1933–2016) was a short story writer and novelist. She portrayed the stark social reality of post-1947 East Punjab. Her work sums up three phases of post-1947 East Punjabi village society: Sikh Jats and other peasant communities' lives, displacement during Partition and resettlement, and later dissolution after the green revolution and the onslaught of corporate capitalism. Her five books of short stories and two short novels were compiled under the title *Mannmatiān* (*Wayward Writings*), 2002. She has also published children's stories.

AJEET COUR (b. 1934) is a recipient of the Sahitya Akademi Award and the Padma Shri, the fourth-highest civilian award given by the Government of India. Born in Lahore to Sardar Makhan Singh, she completed her early education from there, where she was also taught by Kartar Singh Hitkari (father of Amrita Pritam). After Partition, her family came to Delhi, where she earned an M.A degree. She has written novels and short stories in Punjabi on social realist themes such as the experiences of women in relationships and their position in society. She received the Sahitya Akademi Award in 1985, the Padma Shri in 2006, and the Kuvempu Rashtriya Puraskar award in 2019. Her works include nineteen short story anthologies, novellas, and novels, as well as nine translations. She has also edited over twenty works.

GULZAR SINGH SANDHU (b. 1935) won the prestigious Sahitya Akademi Award, for his short story collection *Amar Katha* in 1982. Among other awards he was also the recipient of an award from the International Association of Authors, Playwrights and Artists of Canada in 1992 and the Shiromoni Punjabi Sahityakar Puruskar from the Education Department of Punjab in 2001. He has a number of short story books and novels to his credit. He was born in the village of Kotla Badla in Samrala division of Ludhiana district. He was a professor in Punjab Agriculture University, Ludhiana and a former editor of the *Punjabi Tribune.*

GURDEV SINGH RUPANA (1936–2021) was a prolific writer, essayist, and translator. While teaching in Delhi schools he came into a circle of many well-known writers and artists like Amrita Pritam, and became a prominent Punjabi literary personality. Rupana's five books of short stories namely *Ik Tota Aurat, Aapani Akh da Jadoo, Defence Line, Sheesha tey Hore Kahanian, Ranjha Waris Hoyia,* and four novels—*Jaldev, Aaso da Tabbar, Gori,* and *Shri Paarva* are valuable contributions to Punjabi literature and language. The story themes range from politics to village life and life in big cities. Many of his short stories have been translated into some Indian languages along with two novels into Hindi. He has been bestowed literary awards by the Punjabi Academy, Delhi and Punjabi Language Department of the state of Punjab. He received the Sahitya Akademi Award in 2020 for his short story collection *Aam Khas.*

GURBACHAN SINGH BHULLAR (b. 1937) was born in Pitho village in Bhatinda. His father, Hazura Singh, was an ex-serviceman, who had a keen interest in literature and had a personal library containing works of Punjabi literature. Bhullar consequently developed a taste for literature during his early childhood. In 2005, he was awarded the Sahitya Akademi Award for his short story collection *Agni-Kalas.* His eight short story books and a novel are part of the mainstream of Punjabi fiction.

MOHAN BHANDARI (1937–2021) was a Punjabi writer who received the Sahitya Akademi Award in 1998, but later returned it in 2015. He was born in 1937 in the Banbhaura village of Sangrur district, Punjab. Bhandari was influenced by Urdu writer Manto alongside Russian authors including Gorky, Dostoevsky, Tolstoy, and Chekhov. He is credited with as many as fifteen short story collections which include the critically acclaimed *Kaath di Latt*, *Til-Chouli*, and *Gora Bashah*. Bhandari received the Sahitya Akademi Award for his collection of short stories *Moon di Akh*.

BACHINT KAUR (b. 1940) is an eminent writer of Punjabi literature. She was born in district Patiala, Punjab. She received her M.A. and M.Phil degree from Delhi University. She has books. Her autobiography *Pagdandian* is extremely popular and has been published in various other languages in India and abroad. For her literary works, she has been conferred with awards by the Punjabi Academy, Delhi, in 2006 and the Languages Department, Punjab, in 2005. She has attended foreign conferences and presented research papers in Canada, Bangkok, USA, and Pakistan.

WARYAM SINGH SANDHU (b. 1945) is an Indian author of short stories. In 2000, he was awarded the Sahitya Akademi Award for his short story collection *Chauthikoot*. Although he writes in Punjabi, his works have been translated into Hindi, Bengali, Urdu, and English. Sandhu published his first story 'Akhan Vich Mar Gayi Khushi' in *Preet Lari*. In 1998, he released *Chauthikoot*. In 2015, two stories from the collection were adapted into the film *The Fourth Direction*. Sandhu, who has a PhD in philosophy, retired as a lecturer from the Lyallpur Khalsa College, Jalandhar. In 2019, he returned his Sahitya Akademi Award.

SUKIRAT (b. 1956) was born in a family of journalists and writers, and started writing as a child. His first adult short story was published in the prestigious literary magazine *Preet Lari*, when before he turned eighteen years old. He has since produced two books of short stories, but is also known as a memoirist, political columnist, and travel writer. He has more than ten books to his credit in various genres, including some translated works. He was educated in Jalandhar and Russia and is fluent in Russian and English.

KESRA RAM (b. 1966) was born in the village of Talwara Khurd, District Sirsa (Haryana). He has five short story collections in Punjabi (*Ram Kishan Banaam Stat Hajir Ho, Pulsiya Kiyon Marda Hai, Bulbulyan Di Kaasht, Thanks a Lot Puttra, Zanani Paud*) and a novel, *Guddo*. He has translated twelve books from Rajasthani, Punjabi, Hindi, and vice-versa. Four of his short story collections have been awarded by the Haryana Punjabi Sahitya Akademi; he received the Dhahan International Prize 2020 Canada for *Zanani Paud*.

GURMEET KARYALAVI (b. 1968) has five plays, seven children's books, three prose books, six short story collections, and one novel to his credit. He is known for *Aatu Khoji*, his fictional masterpiece, that was made into a successful movie. Many of his stories have been enacted very successfully on stage. Gurmeet Karyalavi dwells upon the lives of the suppressed, oppressed, and marginalized folks of Punjab.

AJMER SIDHU (b. 1970) was born in Jaffarpur village, district Shaheed Bhagat Singh Nagar. His collections of short stories are *Nachiketa di Maut, Khooh Girdahai, Khushakaakh Da Khab*, and *Rang Di Bazi*. He has also published a couple of biographies, namely *Turdepaira Di Dastan* (life history of revolutionary Darshan Dusanjh) and *Baba Bujha Singh* (life history of Gadhari baba, available in Punjabi, English, and Bengali).

SARGHI (b. 1976) was born in Talagarh (Talawan), Amritsar. She started her literary career writing poetry but it was her short stories that brought her recognition. 'Raad', 'Holiday Wife', 'Rababi', 'Kurrian', and 'Apne Apne Massiye' are some of her widely acclaimed short stories. Her collection of short stories *Apne Apne Marsiye* was published in 2020 and she received the

Dhahan Prize, Canada, for it in 2022. She has edited three books—
Khilrey Harf (2003), *Chetan Katha* (2005), and *Vida Hon to Pehlaan*
(2005)—and has also written two books of criticism.

JATINDER SINGH HANS (b. 1978), a teacher by profession,
developed an interest in writing after reading master story writer
Prem Parkash's book *Prem Kahaniyaan* and the Punjabi classic folk
tale 'Heer' by Waris Shah. Hans is a skilled storyteller among the
new generation of Punjabi writers. He has published two books
of short stories, *Pavey Naal Baniyaan Kaal* (2005) and *Ishvar Da
Janam* (2009), and one novel, *Bas Ajey Ena Hi* (2015). A few
of his short stories have been turned into short films and of
these 'Takhi' and 'Lutro' deserve special mention. He received the
Dhahan Punjabi Literary Prize for 2020, Canada.

NOTES ON THE TRANSLATORS

KHUSHWANT SINGH (1915–2014) was, arguably, India's best-known and most widely read author, columnist, and journalist in his lifetime. He was the founder-editor of *Yojana*, and editor of the *Illustrated Weekly of India*, *National Herald*, and the *Hindustan Times*. He wrote several books, including the novels *Train to Pakistan*, *I Shall Not Hear the Nightingale*, and *Delhi*; his autobiography, *Truth, Love & a Little Malice*; and the two-volume *A History of the Sikhs*. He also translated from Hindi, Urdu, and Punjabi. Khushwant Singh was a member of the Rajya Sabha from 1980 to 1986. In 2007, he was awarded India's second highest civilian honour, the Padma Vibhushan.

TEJWANT SINGH GILL (b. 1938) was a professor and held the position of Head of English at GNDU Amritsar. As a scholar of both English and Punjabi literature, he has translated ten Punjabi texts, including *Mahan Kosh*, seven of Sant Singh Sekhon's historical plays, Mohan Singh's last book of poems, and Manjit Pal's poetic play *Sundran*. Likewise he has translated into Punjabi Garcia Marquez's *One Hundred Years of Solitude*. He has written eight books of literary criticism in English including those on W. B. Yeats, T. S. Eliot, Sant Singh Sekhon, Pash, with the last two being on Guru Nanak: *Guru Nanak, Our Greatest Progenitor* and *Guru Nanak: A Reader*. His ten books of literary criticism in Punjabi include ones on Walter Benjamin, Antonio Gramsci, and Amrita Sher-Gil. For the second edition of the *Encyclopedia of Indian Literatures*, he has revised entries on Punjabi literature. Likewise, he has written entries on Punjabi Drama for the *Encyclopedia of Indian Drama*. His forthcoming books include *A Layered History of Punjabi Literature*. He was awarded the Grant of Life fellowship by the Bharati Sahitya Akademi, New Delhi.

PARAMJIT SINGH RAMANA (b. 1954) is an accomplished translator and writer. He is a former Professor of English and Head, Punjabi University Regional Centre, Bathinda, and former Professor and Dean, School for Languages, Literature and Culture, Central University of Punjab, Bathinda. He has a doctorate in English from Punjabi University, Patiala and has more than thirty-seven years of teaching and research experience. He has translated into English works of well-known Punjabi writers such as Gurdial Singh, Mohan Bhandari, Waryam Singh Sandhu, Bushra Ejaz, Ajmer Singh Aulakh, Kartar Singh Duggal, Swarajbir, and many others.

PARVESH SHARMA (b. 1956) is a well-known name in the field of translation. Born in Budhlada, Punjab, he holds postgraduate degress in English, Hindi, Urdu, and mass communication. He has to his credit at least twenty books translated from Punjabi into English, about thirty from Punjabi into Hindi, about fifteen from English into Punjabi, and a full length play from Urdu into Punjabi. He is empaneled with the Sahitya Akademi, New Delhi, and National Translation Mission, Mysore. With a flair for creative writing, he has authored a couple of books in Punjabi.

NAVTEJ SARNA (b. 1957) was India's Ambassador to the United States, High Commissioner to the United Kingdom, and Ambassador to Israel. He has also served as Secretary to the Government of India and as the Foreign Office Spokesperson. His earlier diplomatic assignments were in Moscow, Warsaw, Thimphu, Tehran, Geneva, and Washington DC. His literary works include the novels *Crimson Spring*, *The Exile*, and *We Weren't Lovers Like That*, the short story collection *Winter Evenings*, non-fiction works *The Book of Nanak*, *Second Thoughts*, and *Indians at Herod's Gate*, as well as two translations, *Zafarnama* and *Savage Harvest*. He is a prolific columnist and commentator on foreign policy and literary matters, contributing regularly to media platforms in India and abroad.

AMANINDER SINGH DHINDSA (b. 1978) was born and raised in Punjab, and graduated with a B.E. (Hons) in Computer Science and Engineering from Punjab Engineering College, Chandigarh in the year 2000. After working for a few years, he became a civil servant after being inducted into the Indian Revenue Service. Throughout his career, he has worked on projects for leveraging information technology to improve taxpayer services in the country. He was awarded the National e-Governance Gold Award for Government Business Process re-engineering in the year 2015. He was nominated as an expert on Faceless Tax Administration and represented India at the BRICS Tax Experts and Tax Heads Meetings, 2022. Apart from his professional pursuits as a tax administrator, he has a keen interest in Punjabi literature and golf. He sees his contribution in translating the stories in this book as a tribute to the thousands of people from Punjab who suffered the horrors of Partition. At the same time, it is an effort to offer a glimpse of the rich literary heritage of Punjab to those who cannot read Punjabi.